FRANCIS FRITH'S

SOUTH BUCKINGHAMSHIRE

PHOTOGRAPHIC MEMORIES

MARTIN ANDREW is an architectural and landscape historian and writer on outdoor matters, and he is the Conservation Officer for Wycombe District Council in Buckinghamshire. He specialises in the landscape of lowland England, and combines his love of history, landscape and architecture in his writing. Since 1978 he has lived in Haddenham in Buckinghamshire with his wife and children. He is a keen long distance walker, and enjoys riding his classic motor cycle round the country lanes of the Chilterns. He was born in Doncaster, but spent most of his childhood in Ealing and in Carshalton in Surrey. After university he worked for the Greater London Council's Historic Buildings Division, Buckinghamshire County Council and Salisbury District Council before joining Wycombe District Council in 1990.

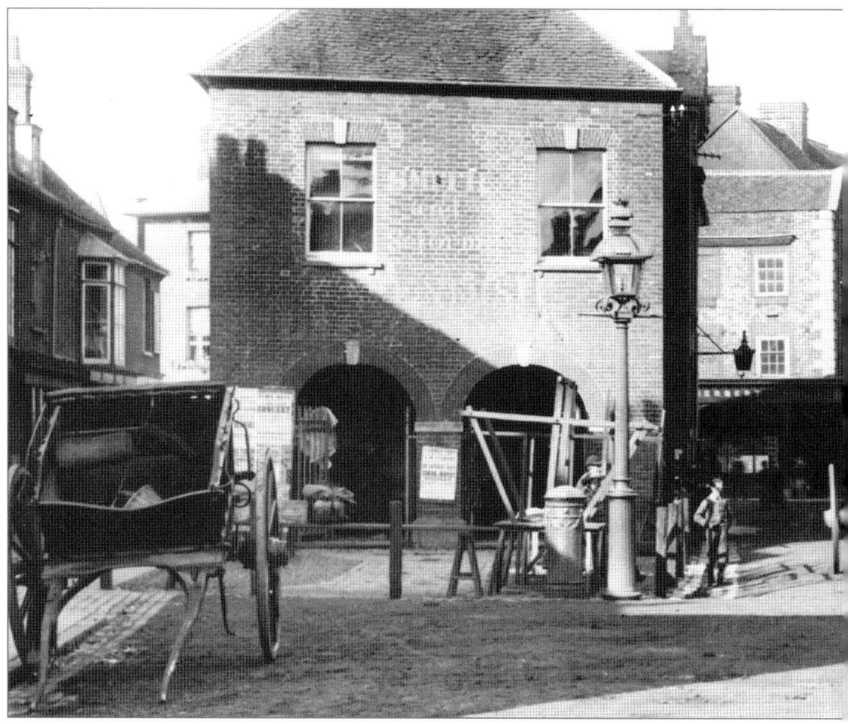

FRANCIS FRITH'S
PHOTOGRAPHIC MEMORIES

SOUTH BUCKINGHAMSHIRE

PHOTOGRAPHIC MEMORIES

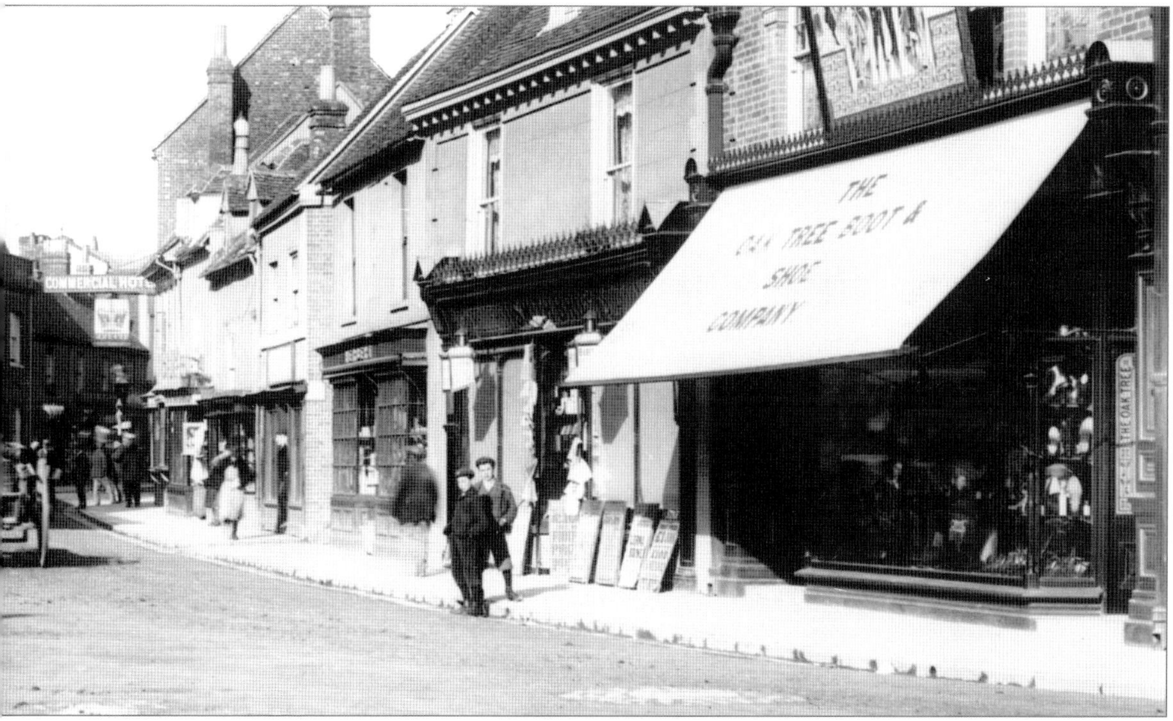

MARTIN ANDREW

THE FRANCIS FRITH COLLECTION

First published in the United Kingdom in 2011 by
The Francis Frith Collection®

Paperback Edition ISBN 978-1-84589-561-7

British Library Cataloguing in Publication Data

Francis Frith's South Buckinghamshire - Photographic Memories
Martin Andrew

The Francis Frith Collection
Unit 6, Oakley Business Park,
Wylye Road, Dinton,
Wiltshire SP3 5EU
Tel: +44 (0) 1722 716 376
Email: info@francisfrith.co.uk
www.francisfrith.com

Printed and bound in England

Front Cover: **MARLOW,** *From the Lock 1901* 47125t
Frontispiece: **CHESHAM,** *Market Square 1897* 40536

The colour-tinting is for illustrative purposes only, and is not intended to be historically accurate

Aerial photographs reproduced under licence from
Simmons Aerofilms Limited.
Historical Ordnance Survey maps reproduced under licence from
Homecheck.co.uk
Every attempt has been made to contact copyright holders of illustrative material. We will be happy to give full acknowledgement in future editions for any items not credited. Any information should be directed to The Francis Frith Collection.

AS WITH ANY HISTORICAL DATABASE THE FRITH ARCHIVE IS CONSTANTLY BEING CORRECTED AND IMPROVED AND THE PUBLISHERS WOULD WELCOME INFORMATION ON OMISSIONS OR INACCURACIES

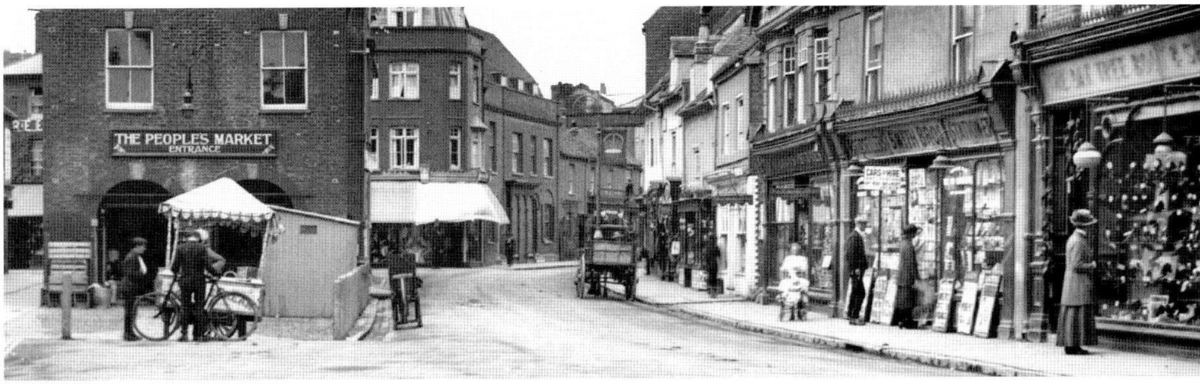

CONTENTS

FRANCIS FRITH

VICTORIAN PIONEER

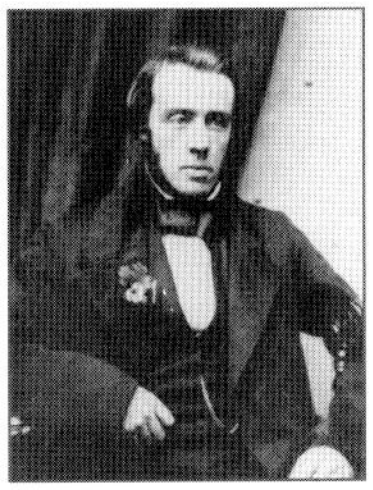

FRANCIS FRITH, founder of the world-famous photographic archive, was a complex and multi-talented man. A devout Quaker and a highly successful Victorian businessman, he was philosophical by nature and pioneering in outlook.

By 1855 he had already established a wholesale grocery business in Liverpool, and sold it for the astonishing sum of £200,000, which is the equivalent today of over £15,000,000. Now a very rich man, he was able to indulge his passion for travel. As a child he had pored over travel books written by early explorers, and his fancy and imagination had been stirred by family holidays to the sublime mountain regions of Wales and Scotland. 'What lands of spirit-stirring and enriching scenes and places!' he had written. He was to return to these scenes of grandeur in later years to 'recapture the thousands of vivid and tender memories', but with a different purpose. Now in his thirties, and captivated by the new science of photography, Frith set out on a series of pioneering journeys up the Nile and to the Near East that occupied him from 1856 until 1860.

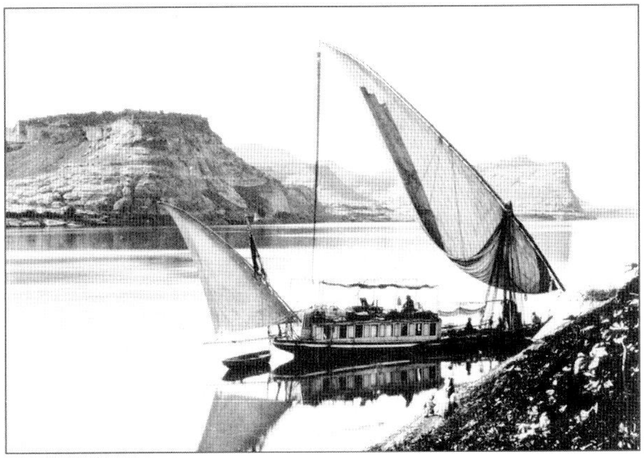

INTRIGUE AND EXPLORATION

These far-flung journeys were packed with intrigue and adventure. In his life story, written when he was sixty-three, Frith tells of being held captive by bandits, and of fighting 'an awful midnight battle to the very point of surrender with a deadly pack of hungry, wild dogs'. Wearing flowing Arab costume, Frith arrived at Akaba by camel sixty years before Lawrence of Arabia, where he encountered 'desert princes and rival sheikhs, blazing with jewel-hilted swords'.

He was the first photographer to venture beyond the sixth cataract of the Nile. Africa was still the mysterious 'Dark Continent', and Stanley and Livingstone's historic meeting was a decade into the future. The conditions for picture taking confound belief. He laboured for hours in his wicker dark-room in the sweltering heat of the desert, while the volatile chemicals fizzed dangerously in their trays. Back in London he exhibited his photographs and was 'rapturously cheered' by members of the Royal Society. His reputation as a photographer was made overnight.

VENTURE OF A LIFE-TIME

Characteristically, Frith quickly spotted the opportunity to create a new business as a specialist publisher of photographs. He lived in an era of immense and sometimes violent change.

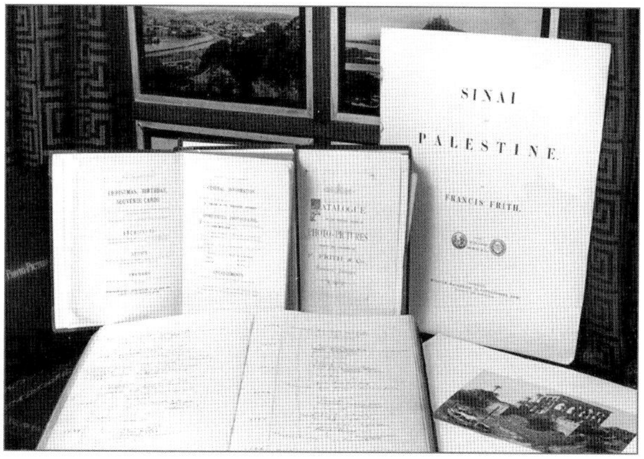

For the poor in the early part of Victoria's reign work was exhausting and the hours long, and people had precious little free time to enjoy themselves. Most had no transport other than a cart or gig at their disposal, and rarely travelled far beyond the boundaries of their own town or village. However, by the 1870s the railways had threaded their way across the country, and Bank Holidays and half-day Saturdays had been made obligatory by Act of Parliament. All of a sudden the working man and his family were able to enjoy days out and see a little more of the world.

With typical business acumen, Francis Frith foresaw that these new tourists would enjoy having souvenirs to commemorate their days out. In 1860 he married Mary Ann Rosling and set out on a new career: his aim was to photograph every city, town and village in Britain. For the next thirty years he travelled the country by train and by pony and trap, producing fine photographs of seaside resorts and beauty spots that were keenly bought by millions of Victorians. These prints were painstakingly pasted into family albums and pored over during the dark nights of winter, rekindling precious memories of summer excursions.

THE RISE OF FRITH & CO

Frith's studio was soon supplying retail shops all over the country. To meet the demand he gathered about him a small team of photographers, and published the work of independent artist-photographers of the calibre of Roger Fenton and Francis Bedford. In order to gain some understanding of the scale of Frith's business one only has to look at the catalogue issued by Frith & Co in 1886: it runs to some 670 pages, listing not only many thousands of views of the British Isles but also many photographs of most European countries, and China, Japan, the USA and Canada - note the sample page shown on page 9 from the hand-written Frith & Co ledgers recording the pictures. By 1890 Frith had created the greatest specialist photographic publishing company in the world, with over 2,000 sales outlets - more than the combined number that Boots and WH Smith have today! The picture on the next page shows the Frith & Co display board at Ingleton in the Yorkshire Dales (left of window). Beautifully constructed with a mahogany frame and gilt inserts, it could display up to a dozen local scenes.

POSTCARD BONANZA

The ever-popular holiday postcard we know today took many years to develop. In 1870 the Post Office issued the first plain cards, with a pre-printed stamp on one face. In 1894 they allowed other publishers' cards to be sent through the mail with an attached adhesive halfpenny stamp. Demand grew rapidly, and in 1895 a new size of postcard was permitted called the court card, but there was little room for illustration. In 1899, a year after Frith's death, a new card measuring 5.5 x 3.5 inches became the standard format, but it was not until 1902 that the divided back came into being, so that the address and message could be on one face and a full-size illustration on the other. Frith & Co were in the vanguard of postcard development: Frith's sons Eustace and Cyril continued their father's monumental task, expanding the number of views offered to the public and recording more and more places

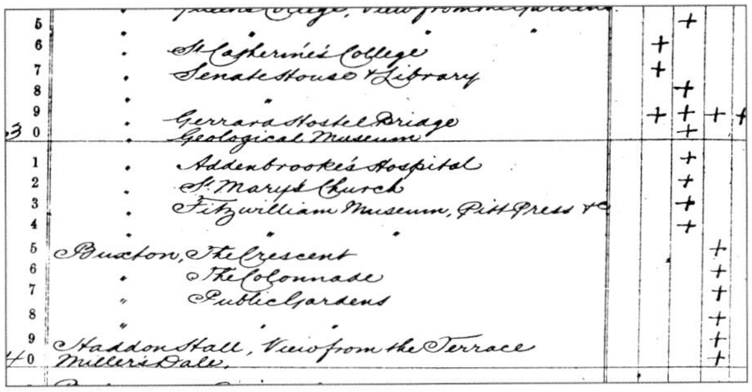

6	St Catherine's College
7	Senate House & Library
8	
9	Gerrard Hostel Bridge
30	Geological Museum
1	Addenbrooke's Hospital
2	St Mary's Church
3	Fitzwilliam Museum, Pitt Press &c
4	
5	Buxton, The Crescent
6	The Colonnade
7	Public Gardens
8	
9	Haddon Hall, View from the Terrace
40	Millers Dale.

in Britain, as the coasts and countryside were opened up to mass travel.

Francis Frith had died in 1898 at his villa in Cannes, his great project still growing. The archive he created continued in business for another seventy years. By 1970 it contained over a third of a million pictures showing 7,000 British towns and villages.

FRANCIS FRITH'S LEGACY

Frith's legacy to us today is of immense significance and value, for the magnificent archive of evocative photographs he created provides a unique record of change in the cities, towns and villages throughout Britain over a century and more. Frith and his fellow studio photographers revisited locations many times down the years to update their views, compiling for us an enthralling and colourful pageant of British life and character.

We are fortunate that Frith was dedicated to recording the minutiae of everyday life, for it is this sheer wealth of visual data, the painstaking chronicle of changes in dress, transport, street layouts, buildings, housing, engineering and landscape that captivates us so much today. His remarkable images offer us a powerful link with the past and with the lives of our ancestors.

THE VALUE OF THE ARCHIVE TODAY

Computers have now made it possible for Frith's many thousands of images to be accessed almost instantly. Frith's images are increasingly used as visual resources, by social historians, by researchers into genealogy and ancestry, by architects and town planners, and by teachers involved in local history projects.

In addition, the archive offers every one of us an opportunity to examine the places where we and our families have lived and worked down the years. Highly successful in Frith's own era, the archive is now, a century and more on, entering a new phase of popularity. Historians consider the Francis Frith Collection to be of prime national importance. It is the only archive of its kind remaining in private ownership. Francis Frith's archive is now housed in an historic timber barn in the beautiful village of Teffont in Wiltshire. Its founder would not recognize the archive office as it is today. In place of the many thousands of dusty boxes containing glass plate negatives and an all-pervading odour of photographic chemicals, there are now ranks of computer screens. He would be amazed to watch his images travelling round the world at unimaginable speeds through internet lines.

The archive's future is both bright and exciting. Francis Frith, with his unshakeable belief in making photographs available to the greatest number of people, would undoubtedly approve of what is being done today with his lifetime's work. His photographs depicting our shared past are now bringing pleasure and enlightenment to millions around the world a century and more after his death.

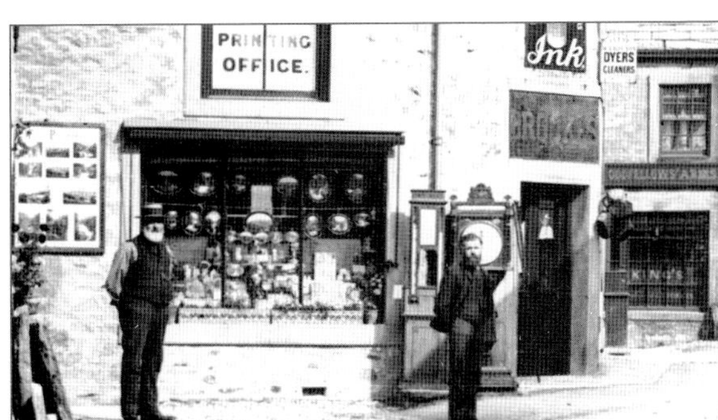

SOUTH BUCKINGHAMSHIRE
AN INTRODUCTION

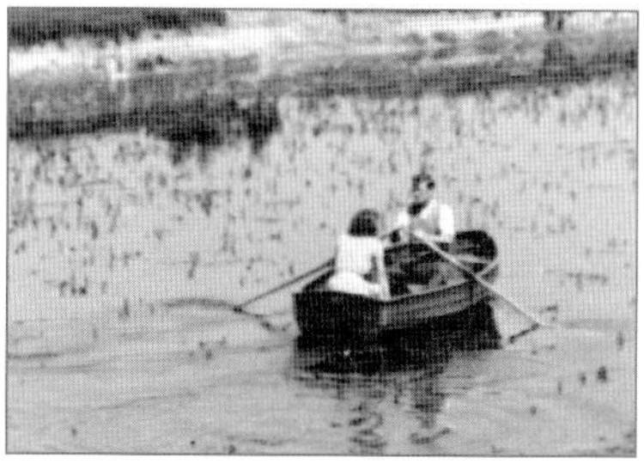

BUCKINGHAMSHIRE is a county that falls easily into two parts, with the chalk Chiltern Hills defining the north edge of the southern parts. As soon as you drop northwards off the Chiltern scarp, you are in the Midlands, where the open field farming of the Middle Ages dominates all the way from Wendover to the Northamptonshire border; this area is covered in the companion volume in this series, 'North Buckinghamshire Photographic Memories'.

The landscape to the south is radically different, and completely dominated by the range of chalk hills that march across the south of the county on a south-west to north-east axis. These are the Chiltern Hills. They start where the chalk ranges cross the River Thames near Goring in Oxfordshire, and cross Buckinghamshire into Hertfordshire and Bedfordshire, where they peter out. The western parts of the Chilterns in Oxfordshire and Buckinghamshire differ from the east, and are more intricate. The escarpment, valley sides and plateau are clad in beech woods, and narrow winding high-hedged lanes link small hamlets. In places there are large hedgeless arable fields.

South of the chalk lie the valley gravels of the Thames Valley, in large part the southern boundary of the county, and at the south-east is the Burnham Plateau, geologically consisting of the Reading Beds and London clays. These are topped by thin acid soils, and the area is heavily wooded. This is the 'leafy Bucks' beloved of London day-trippers, and the best known part of the county; here we find the famous Burnham Beeches, where ancient pollarded woodland occupies soils of little use for anything else, but no less attractive for that. The Chilterns are equally well known, and some of its beautiful scenery, such as in the Hambleden Valley towards the Oxfordshire border, is very popular with visitors and walkers.

Along the north escarpment the Countryside Commission's Ridgeway Long Distance Footpath passes through the county on its route from near Avebury in Wiltshire to Ivinghoe Beacon, and in marked contrast to the north of the county, the Chilterns are criss-crossed by well maintained and signed footpaths, thanks largely to the energetic Chiltern Society.

Amid this intimate landscape are some fine

market towns in the valleys of several sparkling chalk rivers and winterbournes, including the Chess, the Misbourne, the Wye and the Hughenden Stream. Some of the towns are superbly preserved, and have survived the wholesale destruction of the 1960s well. These include Amersham, Beaconsfield and Great Missenden, although towns like High Wycombe and Chesham have been less fortunate. Being so close to London, commuter railway lines arrived in the later 19th century and led to very considerable growth, a growth only constrained by the adoption of the Metropolitan Green Belt in 1959. Much of the area covered in this book was also included in the designated Chilterns Area of Outstanding Natural Beauty in 1965. These two measures have done an enormous amount to safeguard the character of south Buckinghamshire and its countryside, for which we should be immensely grateful. High Wycombe and Slough suffered most: at High Wycombe, modern development covers almost all of its surrounding hills, with only the grounds of Wycombe Abbey preventing total erosion of the town's setting. Amersham and Beaconsfield, and to a certain extent Great Missenden, kept post-railway development separate, Amersham with Amersham-on-the-Hill and Beaconsfield with its New Town, to the considerable benefit of these fine historic towns. Nowadays the M40 crosses the Chilterns and the M25 skirts the Colne valley, and certainly traffic has increased greatly on the main roads, many of which are choked twice a day by commuter traffic into the towns. However, it is still possible to drive or cycle around Chiltern lanes meeting little traffic outside rush hours - when, to the county's shame, many of these lanes are used as 'rat runs' by commuters.

Archaeology in the Thames valley gravels has yielded rich returns from the Neolithic and Bronze Ages, but for more spectacular visible remains we have to ascend the Chilterns. Here we can find burial mounds or long barrows,

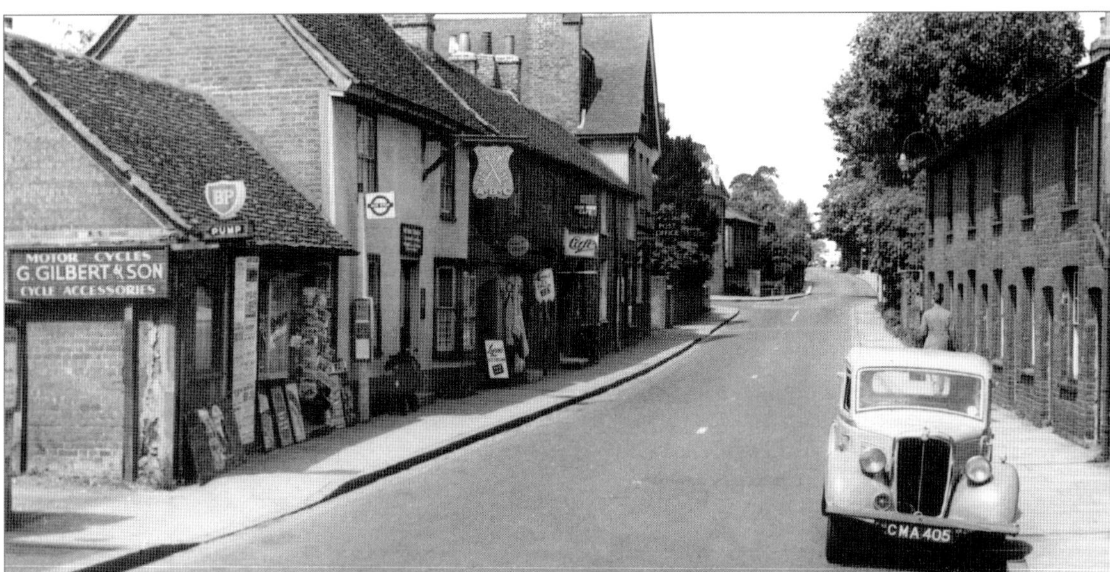

GREAT MISSENDEN, *High Street 1952* G241026

including the Neolithic one on Whiteleaf Hill, and Bronze Age round barrows are numerous hereabouts and elsewhere. Of more immediate impact are the causewayed camps and hill-forts that guard the Chiltern escarpment and valleys. These include Desborough Castle in High Wycombe overlooking the Wye valley, now surrounded by modern housing. Of Iron Age origin, it has 12th- and 13th-century earthworks, so it might have been the meeting place for the Hundred of Desborough, an ancient sub-division of counties. On the other side of the valley, West Wycombe church and the Dashwood Mausoleum are within the earthworks of an Iron Age hill-fort dominating the Wye valley and the strategic Princes Risborough gap through the Chilterns.

Down by the River Thames, the ridge north of Medmenham village is occupied by an Iron Age hillfort which commands the Thames gap, while only a mile east, at Danesfield, there is another hillfort, the steep river cliff of the Thames forming its southern defences. Further north along the Chilterns, the archaeologically rich area east of Princes Risborough has an Iron Age hill-fort on the summit of Pulpit Hill, its ditches and ramparts amidst the beech woods. Others include Boddington Hill above Wendover in the highest part of the Chilterns at over 250 metres (820 feet), and another fort on the plateau above Chesham at Cholesbury. Besides these, there is the Icknield Way, of course; it crosses the county mainly along the Chiltern escarpment or on its lower levels. This is regarded as a Neolithic trackway from the flint mines of Norfolk to the Thames; then it continues west and south-west as the Ridgeway. It also seems likely that there was extensive flint mining in the Chilterns: the earthwork depressions of flint mines can be seen on the slopes of Pulpit Hill, for example.

Quite the most impressive pre-Roman earthworks are the enigmatic linear earthworks often in the centre of the Chiltern plateau known collectively as Grim's Ditch. These have a ditch on both sides of a central rampart or bank, and seem to be boundary markers rather than defences – the current theory is that these earthworks are Iron Age boundaries between tribal groups or estates. The Anglo-Saxons thought these sorts of things the work of gods rather than man, and called them Grim's Ditches; Grim was one of their gods, who was also known as Wan, a name commemorated in Wiltshire's similar Wansdyke. One of the best stretches of these awesome linear earthworks runs north-west from Downley above High Wycombe; they become clearer earthworks from east of Bradenham to Lacey Green, a distance of 4 miles, before turning sharply north-east for two miles. Here, a mile west of Hampden House, Grim's Ditch turns at right angles south-east, and is visible for a further two miles, thus enclosing on three sides an area of about 8 square miles. Across the upper Misbourne and Chess valleys, Grim's Ditches re-appear for a further three or four miles, here surviving in less complete stretches, to cross the county boundary into Hertfordshire.

The Roman occupation of Britain has left excavated evidence in south Buckinghamshire, often in the form of villas in the river valleys, usually associated with agricultural estates – there is nothing above ground level to compare with St Albans' Roman predecessor, Verulamium. Two villas are known in Hambleden, and others in High Wycombe and Latimer, and on the northern foothills of the Chilterns along the spring line at Saunderton, Great and Little Kimble and Bledlow. The most important villa was the one at Hambleden, which seems to have exported its grain along the Thames for the use of the Roman garrisons and army camps.

After the Romans left, Anglo-Saxon invaders arrived, and Buckinghamshire emerged into written history. Buckingham is mentioned in the Anglo-Saxon Chronicle when King Edward the Elder fortified the town in 917 AD, during the Anglo-Danish Wars. By 1014 Buckinghamshire was certainly in existence, but it had probably only incorporated the south and the Chiltern Hills into its boundaries some time during the 10th century. This made Buckingham somewhat off-centre, to put it mildly, and the county town eventually migrated south to a more central location, Aylesbury, to the long-lasting chagrin of Buckingham.

One of the most interesting documents from the Anglo-Saxon period is a land charter of 903 AD which describes the boundaries of Monks Risborough parish. This was written out from memory in 903 after the original had been lost in a fire, so the boundaries presumably long predate the charter. Many features are recognisable, including the famous Black Hedge, which climbs into the Chilterns and is over a thousand years old. Indeed, it is still possible to follow the whole boundary of this typical Chiltern strip parish: it is long and narrow, five and a half miles long by less than a mile wide, and giving the parish a good mix of land from the clay farmland of the valley to the commons and woodland pasture on the Chiltern plateau, with the village on the spring-line where streams emerge from the chalk.

After the Norman Conquest of 1066, several abbeys and priories were founded in the south of the county, but again there are none to match St Alban's Abbey further east. This book visits two of them: Medmenham and Great

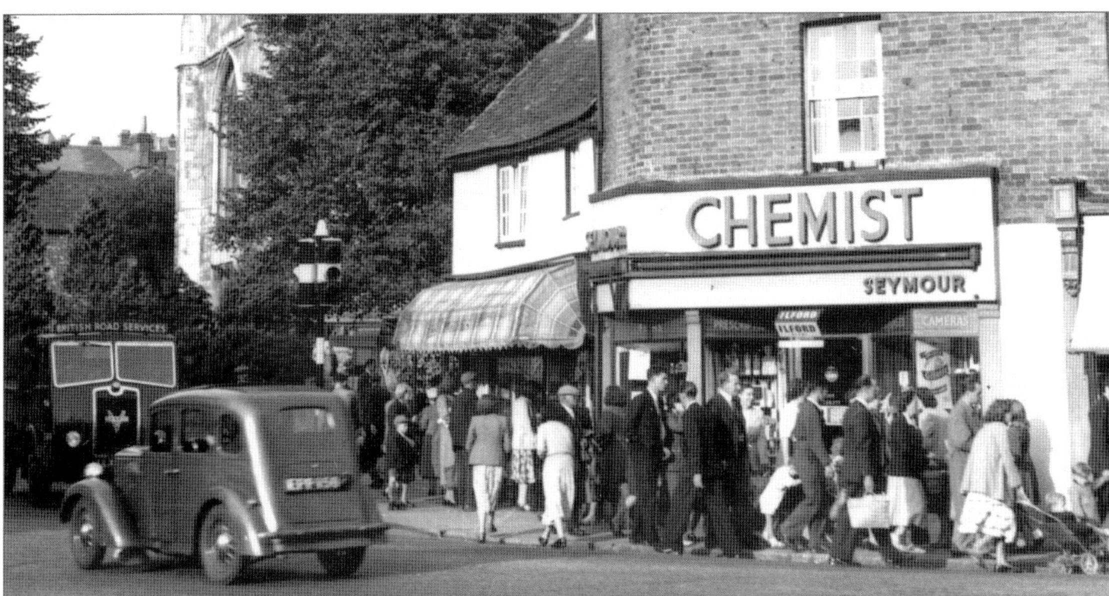

HIGH WYCOMBE, *The Parish Church c1955* H84071

Missenden, both with walling of various quantities surviving above ground, and we also go near a couple of others, Little Marlow and Burnham, but Buckinghamshire did not attract major religious houses. In High Wycombe there is a more impressive medieval building, the Hospital of St John. Here two roofless bays of the infirmary hall of about 1190 survive, mainly because they were incorporated in the 1549 Grammar School and were re-exposed when the later buildings were demolished around them in 1883.

Medieval parish churches survive in greater numbers, and there is often a striking contrast between town and village churches. High Wycombe's All Saints is the largest medieval church in the county, as befits an important medieval market town, and Amersham and Beaconsfield have substantial town churches. Great Missenden, Chesham and Princes Risborough's are medium sized, and so are a few village churches, such as the ones at Hambleden, Medmenham, Monks Risborough and Great Kimble. However, many of the Chiltern villages were little more than hamlets, and so there are some delightful, tiny churches to be found nestling in south Buckinghamshire, such as Ibstone, Fingest or Cholesbury.

The character of south Buckinghamshire architecturally is of red brick and flint with mellow clay-tiled roofs, interspersed with earlier timber-framed buildings. There is relatively little thatch, and slate appears in the mid 19th century. Many regard flint with brick dressings as the building material of the Chilterns, but this only arrived at cottage level when 19th-century deeper ploughing again covered the fields in flints. Locally-made red-orange brick and roof tiles are characteristic of south Buckinghamshire, often encasing or replacing medieval or 17th-century timber-framing, particularly in the towns, where Georgian prosperity saw older buildings modernised or replaced.

The population increased slowly in this mainly agricultural county until the 19th century, when the railways arrived - Slough was the first major beneficiary. While the Railway Age brought immense benefits to vast areas of England, south Buckinghamshire had a love-hate relationship with it. The Drake family of Shardeloes, near Amersham, managed to prevent any lines being built anywhere near until the 1890s, when they permitted a line to pass north of the valley and out of sight of their Palladian mansion. Fortuitously, this resistance helped preserve Amersham as one of the county's finest and most complete historic towns.

When the railways did arrive, they were most successful as commuter lines, ferrying the middle classes and workers into London from stations such as Amersham-on-the-Hill or Gerrards Cross. Local freight never rivalled passenger traffic as an income generator for the railway companies, and Metroland and suburbs spread from the stations in the south and east of the county. Some of the development is formless and regrettable, but other areas are of more interesting quality, such as most of Gerrards Cross and Beaconsfield.

An exception to this passenger-dominated railway story is High Wycombe, where as well as using laden road wagons, the furniture industry used the railway to distribute its products. Nowadays industrial estates such as Cressex in High Wycombe or the Slough Trading Estate and other local industry and commerce is almost entirely road-serviced, with materials, goods and workers coming and going by cars or lorries. The M40, the M4 and the M25 and various by-passes have relieved some of the pressure on south Buckinghamshire's roads, giving them back to some extent to the inhabitants of the county.

The views in this book start in the 1890s and cease in the mid 1960s, before the real explosion of road traffic. I hope they capture the essence of the hilly south of the county, a complete contrast to the area shown in the companion collection of north Buckinghamshire views. There is much more I could mention, including the important historic landscaped parks, such as West Wycombe, Wycombe Abbey, Hughenden, Chequers and Great Hampden, that dot the Chilterns, or Dropmore and Stoke Park on the Burnham Plateau. Buckinghamshire is a richly rewarding county, to some extent a secret known only to us Buckinghamshire residents – it is more often driven through on the way to somewhere else. The south of the county is very much dominated by the picturesque Chilterns, and becomes progressively more rural as we head further away from London. Little can beat the Hambleden valley or the beech woods around Risborough and the Hampdens for scenery within an hour or so's drive from London.

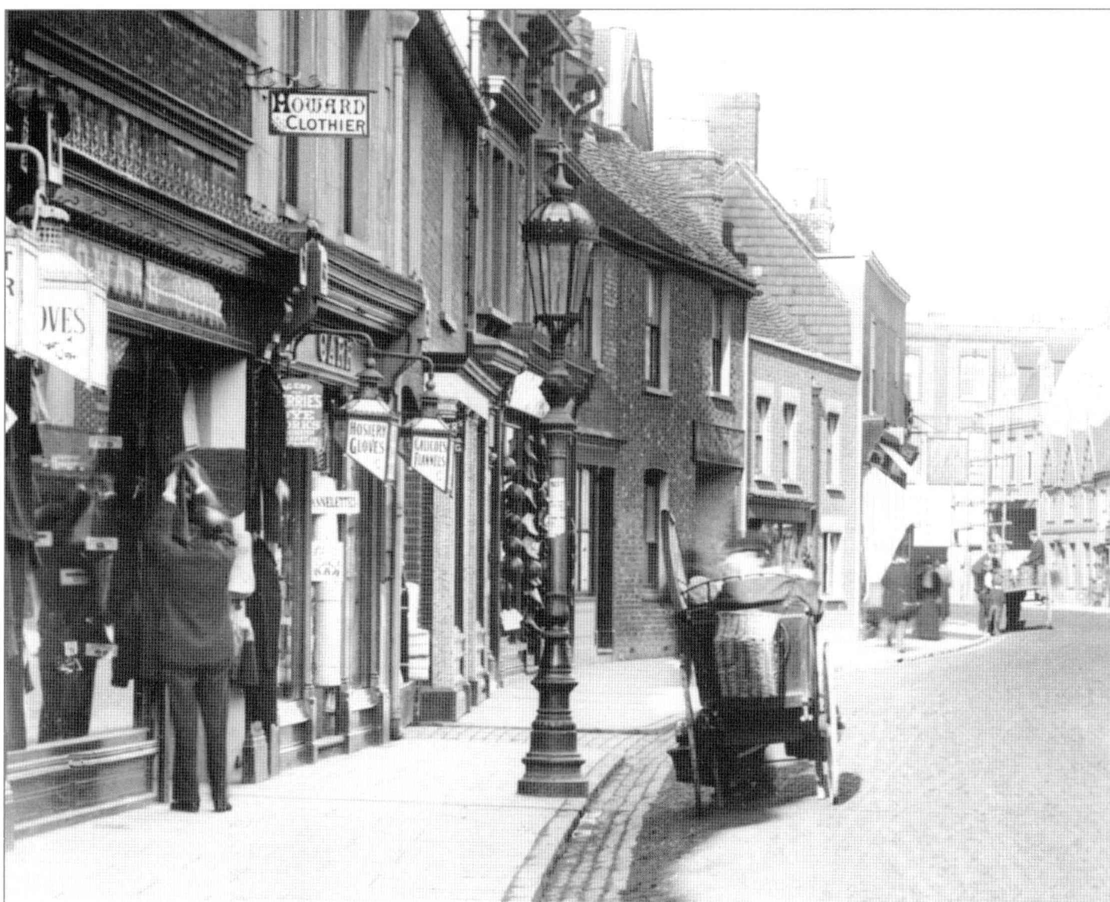

CHESHAM, *High Street 1897* 40538

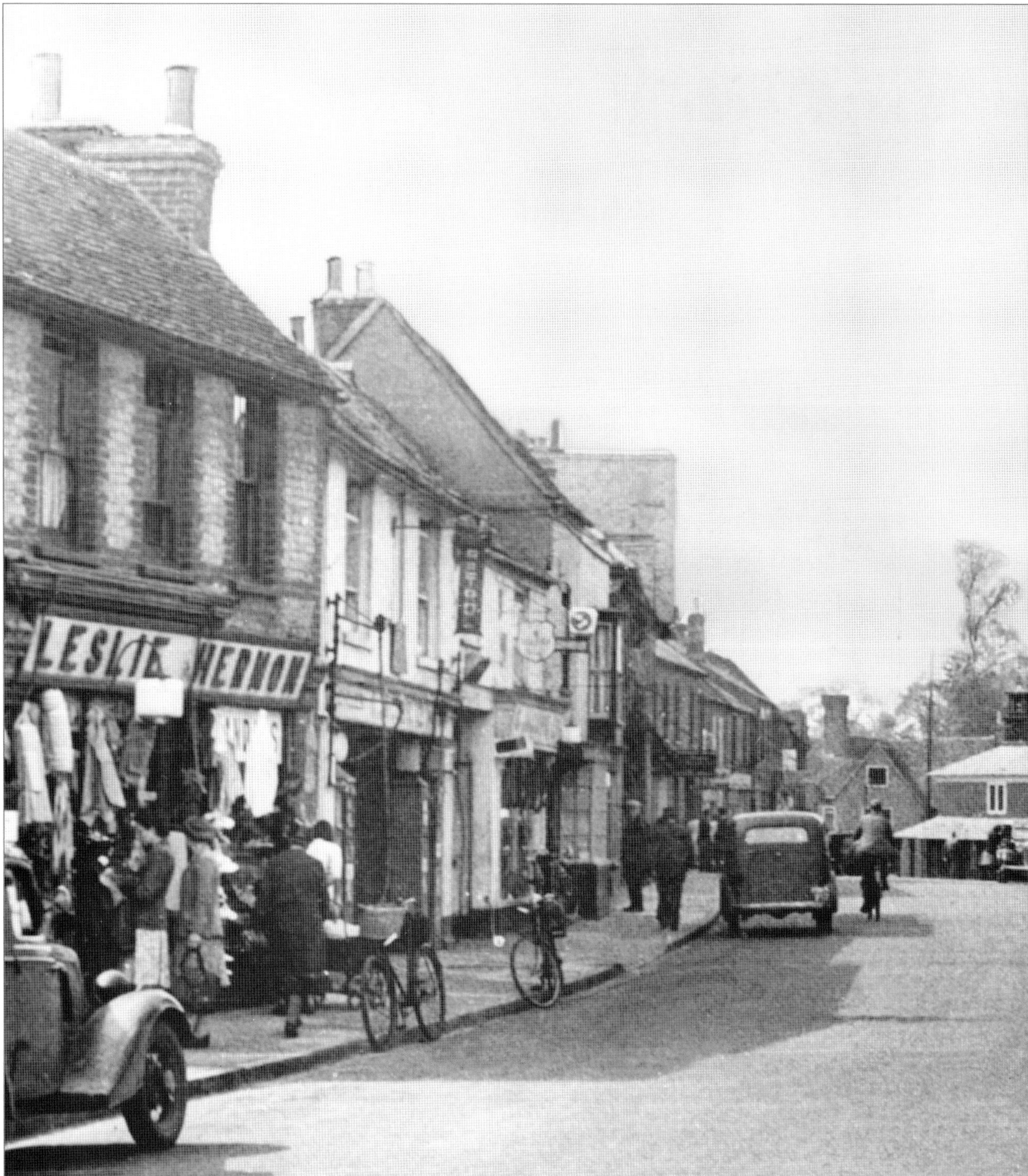
LESLIE VERNON

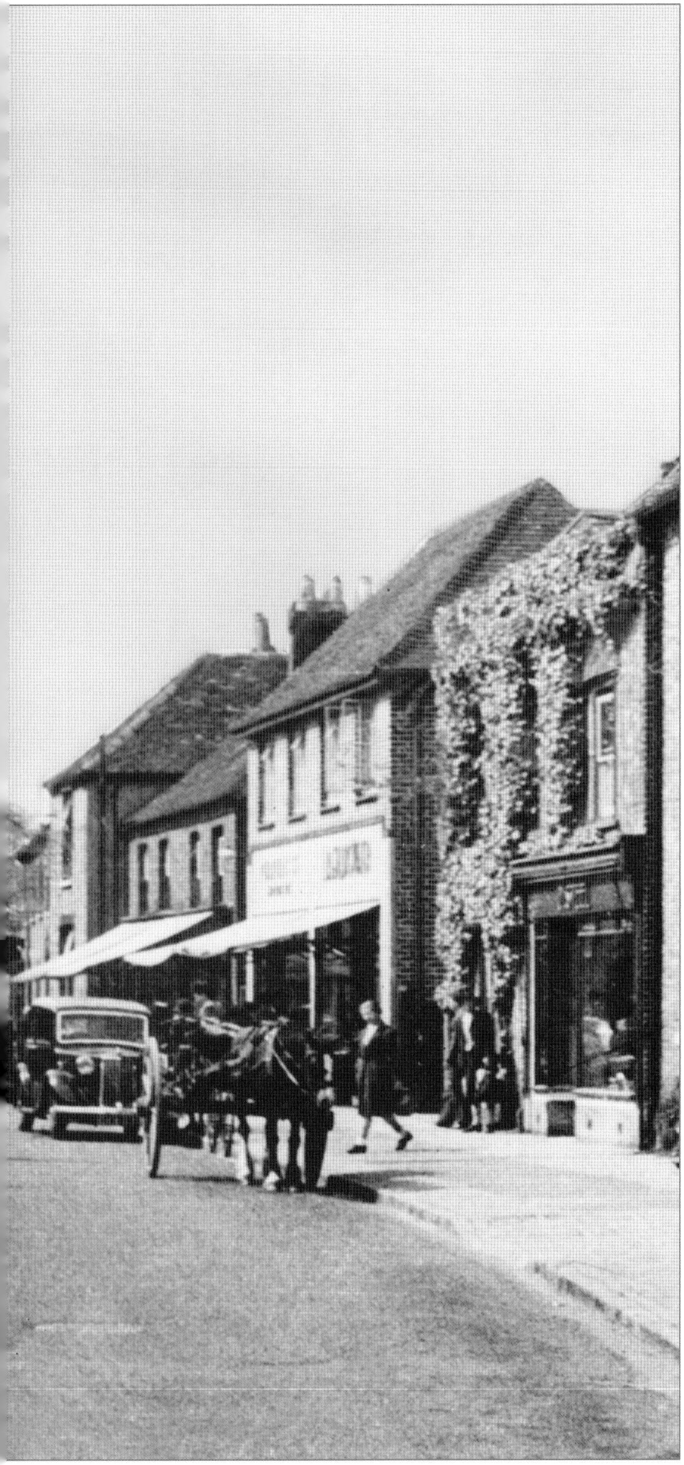

PRINCES RISBOROUGH AND THE NORTH-WEST CHILTERN HILLS

PRINCES RISBOROUGH, *High Street c1955*
P282010

The first tour in this book starts in the small market town of Princes Risborough, which grew up at the foot of the north escarpment of the Chilterns. It was granted a weekly market by Henry VIII in 1523 and two annual fairs, nowadays mere funfairs, and although it has greatly expanded in the 20th century, the town preserves its character well. Apart from the cars and the horse and cart, little has changed in this view up the High Street. Some of the Georgian and later facades conceal Tudor and earlier timber-framed houses.

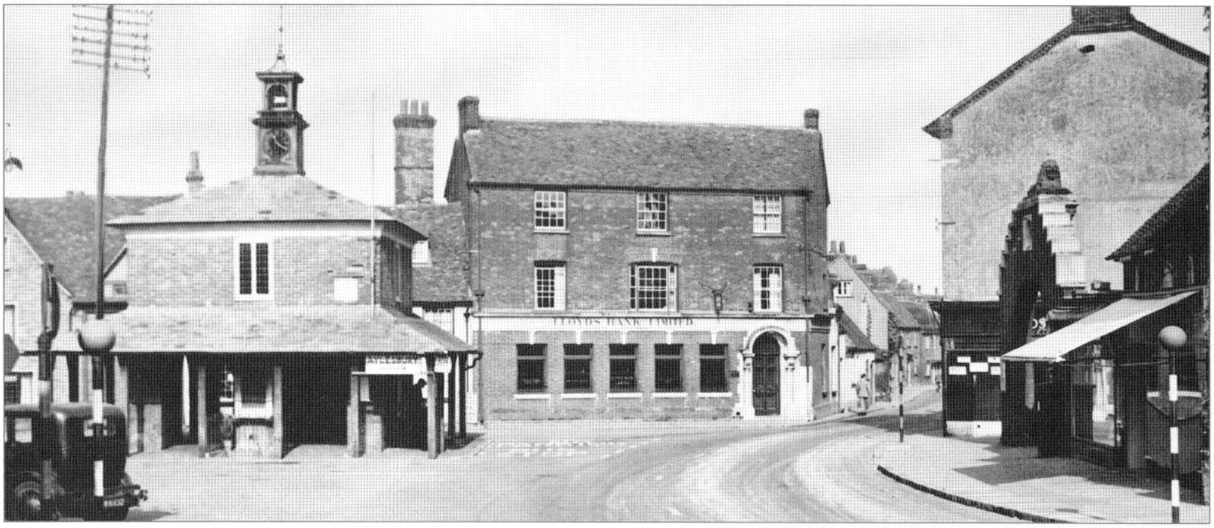

▲ **PRINCES RISBOROUGH,** *The Market House c1955* P282017

Further north along the High Street, Market Square is dominated by the clock-towered Market House, partly 18th-century and partly 1824, which was restored in the 1920s as a war memorial which funded the restoration (the actual memorial tablet is between the posts below the window). On the right is the now demolished gateway with its lion statue; this led into the Lion Brewery, founded by Thomas Parsons in the 1840s. Brewing ceased around 1900, but the buildings survived longer - the archway finally went in the 1960s.

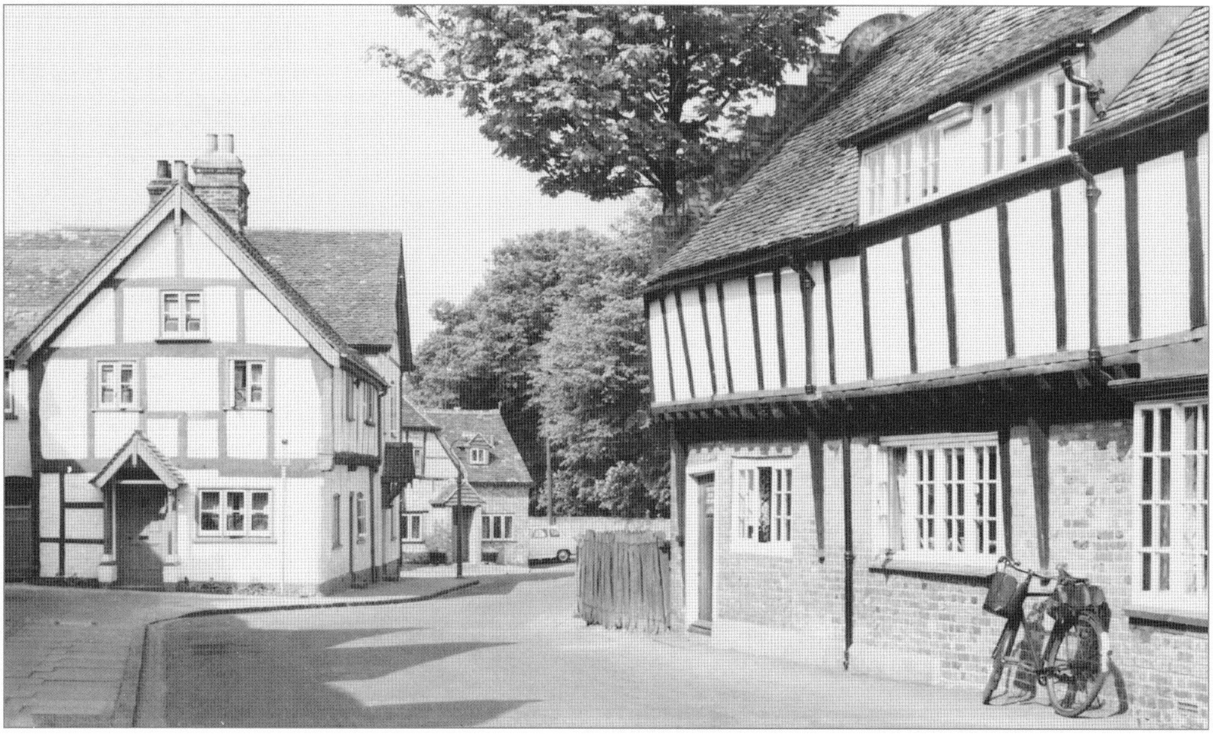

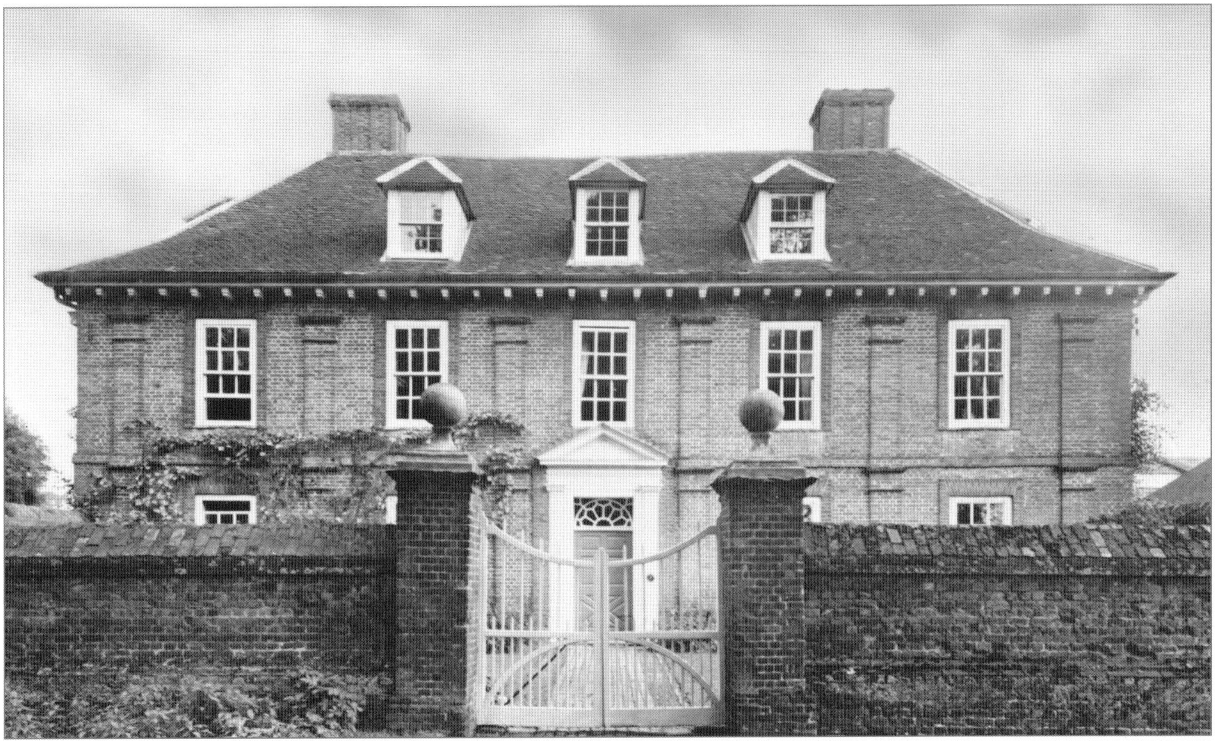

PRINCES RISBOROUGH ▲
The Manor House c1955 P282021

Near the parish church along Church Lane stands the Manor House, an architecturally puzzling house - it might date from the 1630s or the 1670s. Certainly it is a good example of the 17th-century style known as 'Artisan Mannerism'. Decayed by Victorian times, it was bought and restored by Lord Rothschild in the 1880s: it is the extent of this restoration that gives rise to confusion about its original date. It was presented to the National Trust in 1925, and is now tenanted.

PRINCES RISBOROUGH
◄ *Church Street c1960* P282027

Church Street leads west from the Market Square past some of the oldest timber-framed buildings in the town. That on the right was a row of cottages condemned in the 1930s for slum clearance. Saved by a local solicitor, they eventually served as the local branch library from the 1950s until 1986. The trees in the distance belong to St Mary's churchyard.

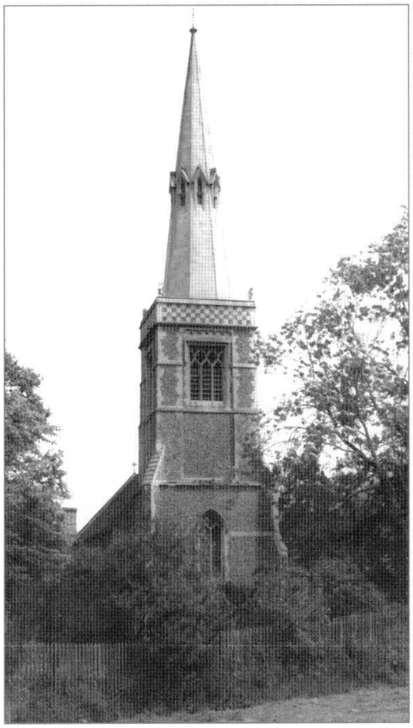

PRINCES RISBOROUGH
St Mary's Parish Church ◄ *c1955* P282042

St Mary's church has some fine 13th-century work, but it was much restored and rebuilt in the 1860s. Its west tower and spire, which we see in this view, were rebuilt in 1907-1908 by John Oldrid Scott. About time too, for the medieval tower and spire had collapsed in 1804 and had been cheaply and unsatisfactorily rebuilt: the new spire was clad in zinc sheets, which had corroded spectacularly by the time Scott arrived. Behind the photographer was the site of the Black Prince's moated 14th-century manor house and stud farm, excavated in the 1950s. The site is now a car park and a Scheduled Ancient Monument.

▼ **PRINCES RISBOROUGH,** *St Teresa's Roman Catholic Church c1955* P282020

At the junction of Duke Street with the main Aylesbury Road stood a Baptist 'tin tabernacle' church – it was later a social club for the Lion Brewery, and is now a church hall for the Roman Catholic church. The 'tin tabernacle' is on the left in this view, with the most unusual church of St Theresa of the Child Jesus in the centre. In a sort of Byzantine style, it was designed by Giuseppe Rinvolucri and built in 1937. By contrast, the white-rendered presbytery or priest's house to its right was in International Modern flat-roofed style. In the 1960s it was clad in a more cosy brick skin.

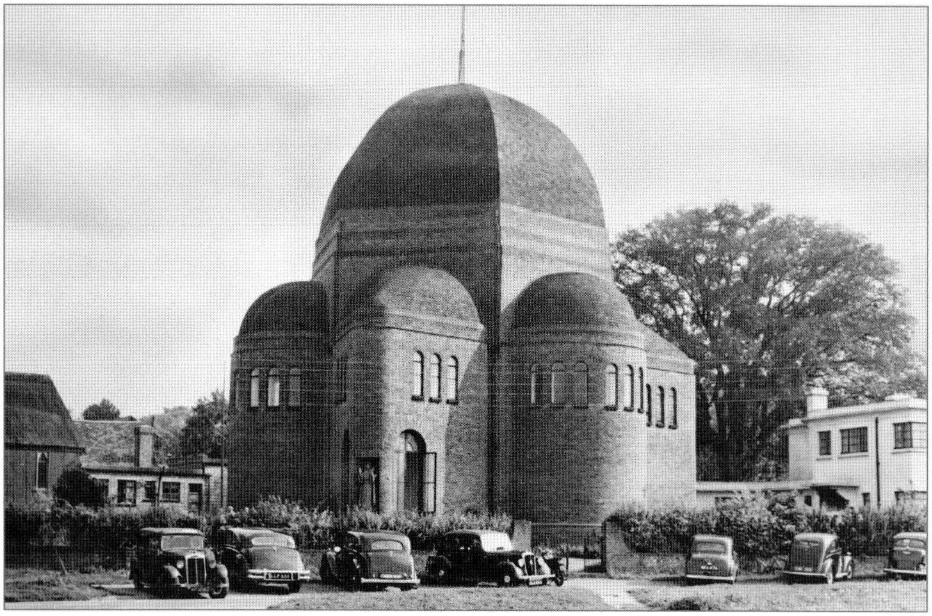

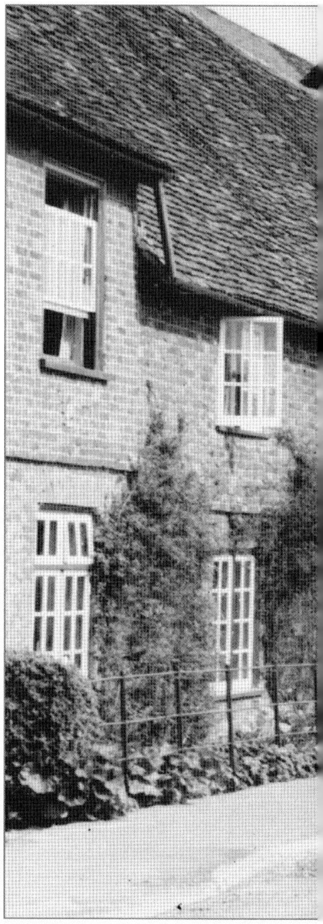

► **MONKS RISBOROUGH**
Aylesbury Road c1955 M390004

Princes Risborough had roughly stayed within its medieval boundaries until after World War I, and indeed it developed relatively slowly until after the Second World War. By the mid 1950s the town had advanced north-east along the Aylesbury Road as far as the delightful village of Monks Risborough, which lies in the distance on the far left, beyond the tall horse chestnut trees. Remnants of old field hedgerows and hedgerow trees were retained by the developers, and the design quality of the 1950s houses was high, certainly higher than in the decade that followed.

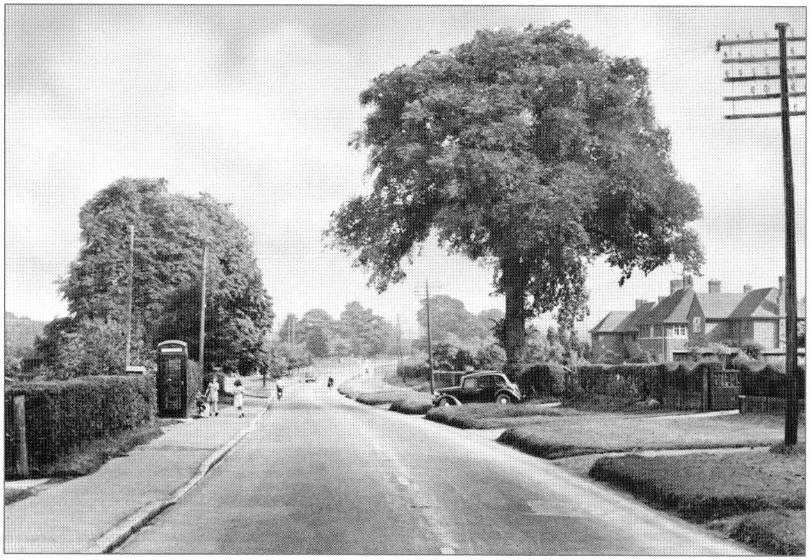

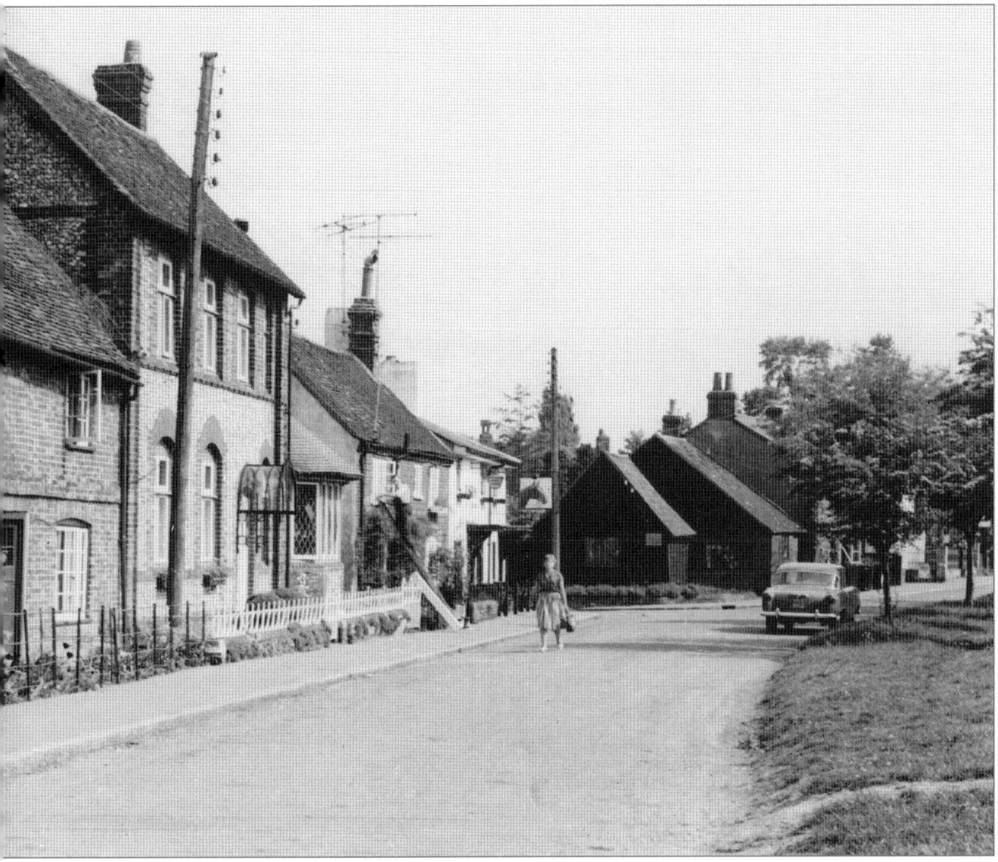

◄ **MONKS RISBOROUGH**
The Village c1960
M390031

We have now reached Monks Risborough; the trees on its small green are the ones we can see beyond the cyclist in view M390004. In fact, the Aylesbury Road had been straightened in the 1920s to produce this fortuitous village green. At the left is Chestnut Farm, no longer a working farm, and one of its 18th-century barns converted into a house. The Nag's Head in the middle distance is no longer a pub, and the village smithy beyond with its two dark weatherboarded gables has long ceased work, having for some years diversified into a petrol station in the 1930s.

► **MONKS RISBOROUGH**
Burton Lane c1955 M390010

Parallel with the main road, Burton Lane is one of the most photographed in the county with its collection of 16th-, 17th- and 18th-century cottages, many of them thatched. The old tile-roofed one on the left has the datestone '1590 AD' to inform passers-by of its vintage. In the distance on the left are the grounds of The Old Rectory, a good brick house of 1670 enlarged in 1863, while behind the cottages is the churchyard of St Dunstan's church, one of the best parish churches in the county. Beyond this is a park with a fine 16th-century chalkstone dovecote with 216 nest boxes.

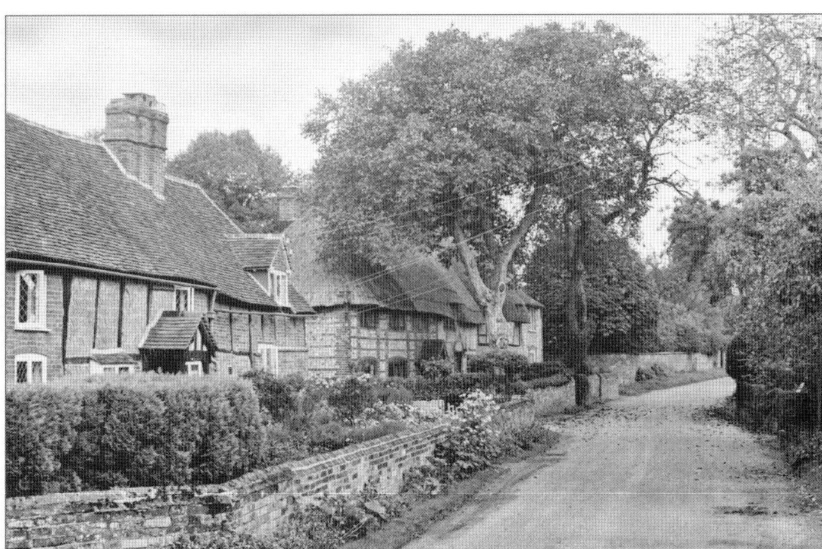

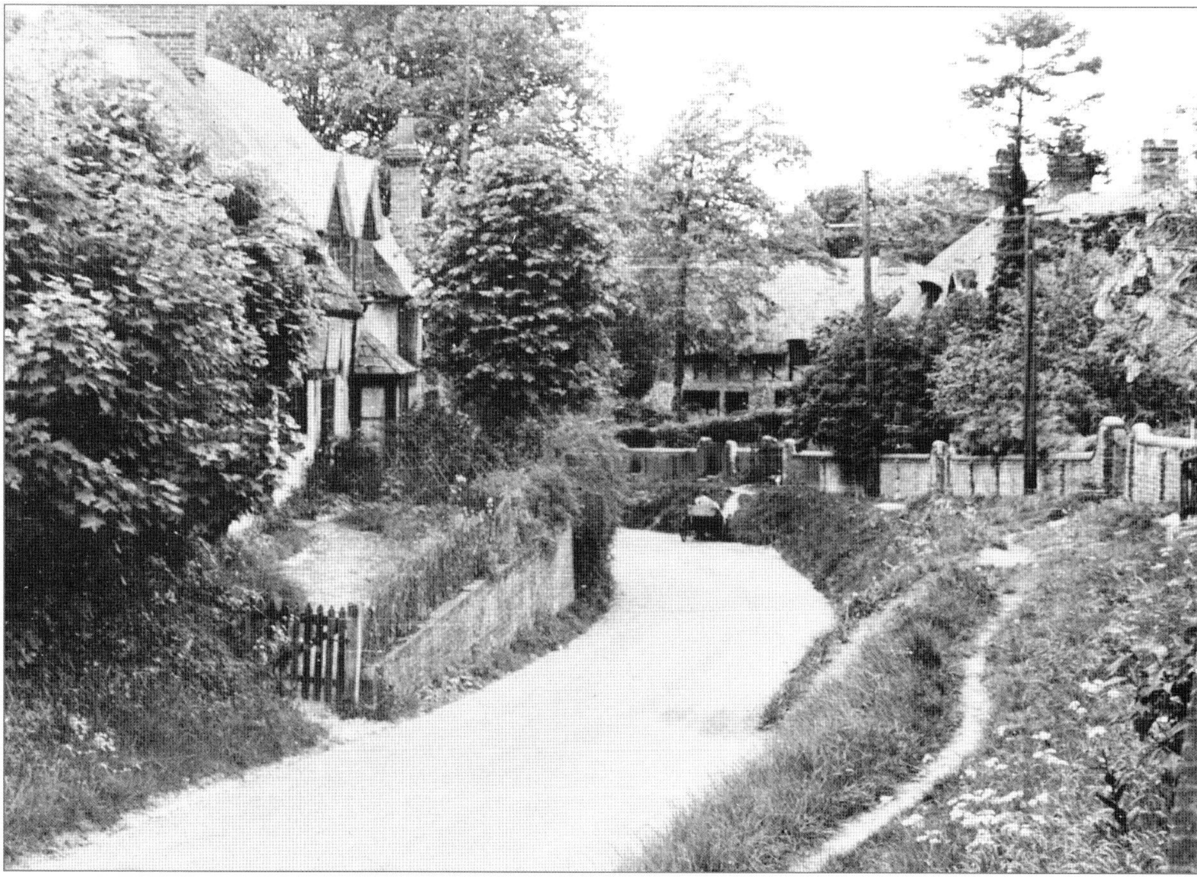

WHITELEAF, *The Village c1955* W632013

To the south of the main Aylesbury-Risborough Road, Whiteleaf, formerly a hamlet within Monks Risborough parish, sits on the lower slopes of the Chiltern Escarpment along the course of the ancient Icknield Way, a route over 3,000 years old that ran from East Anglia to Goring. The lane is lined by old cottages, many of them 16th- and 17th-century timber-framed ones with thatched roofs. This view, in the north part of the hamlet, is little changed today, apart from the nearer thatched cottages on the right, Cavall and High Rood, which burned down around 1960 and were rebuilt in brick with tiled roofs.

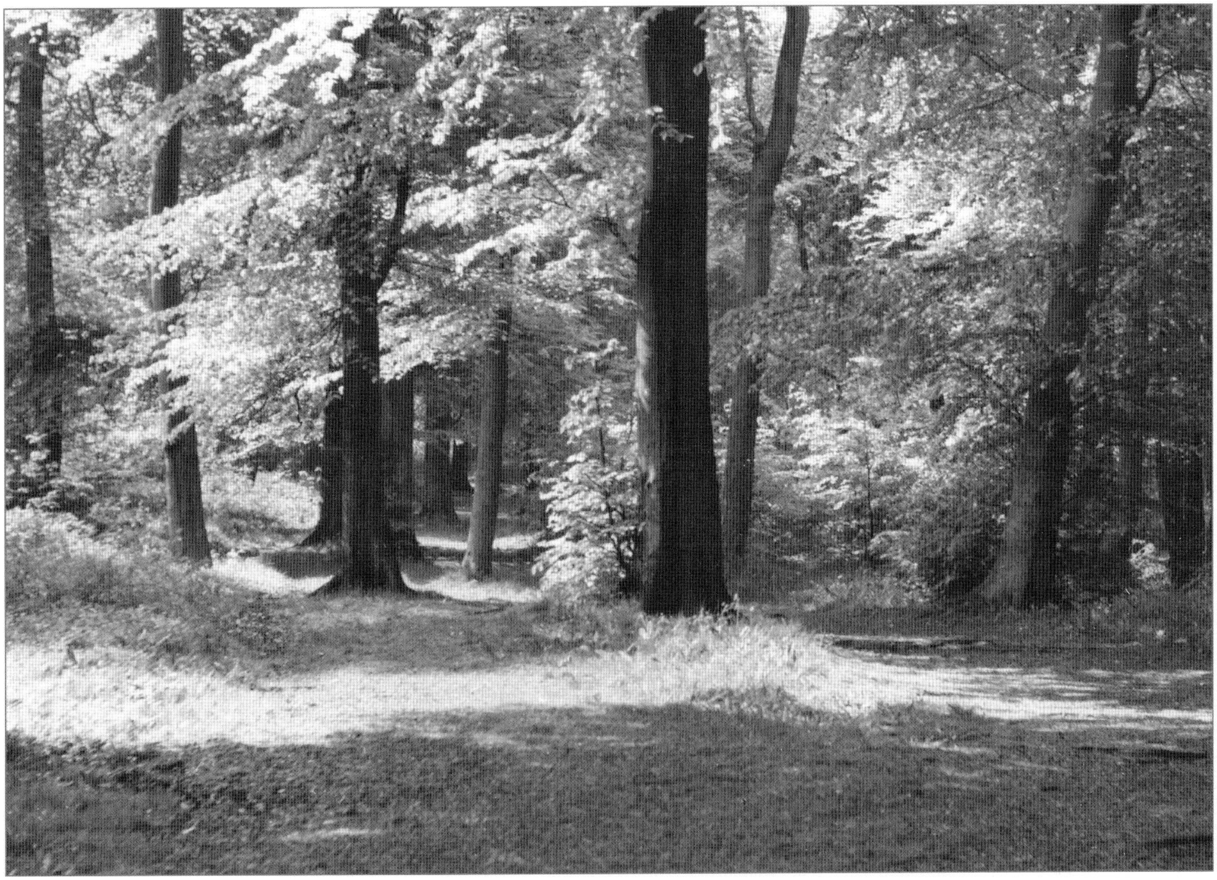

WHITELEAF, *The Woods near Whiteleaf Cross c1960* W632036

Above Whiteleaf there are extensive beech woods, with the Ridgeway long distance national footpath winding through. In Whiteleaf Woods the most noted feature is the Whiteleaf Cross, a chalk-cut cross with a large triangular base that can be seen from miles away. It is currently being restored. Its origins are uncertain, the theories legion. There is another one further along the escarpment at Bledlow, but the earliest known reference to the Whiteleaf Cross is as late as 1742. From near the Cross, there are long views across Princes Risborough far below and across the clay vales.

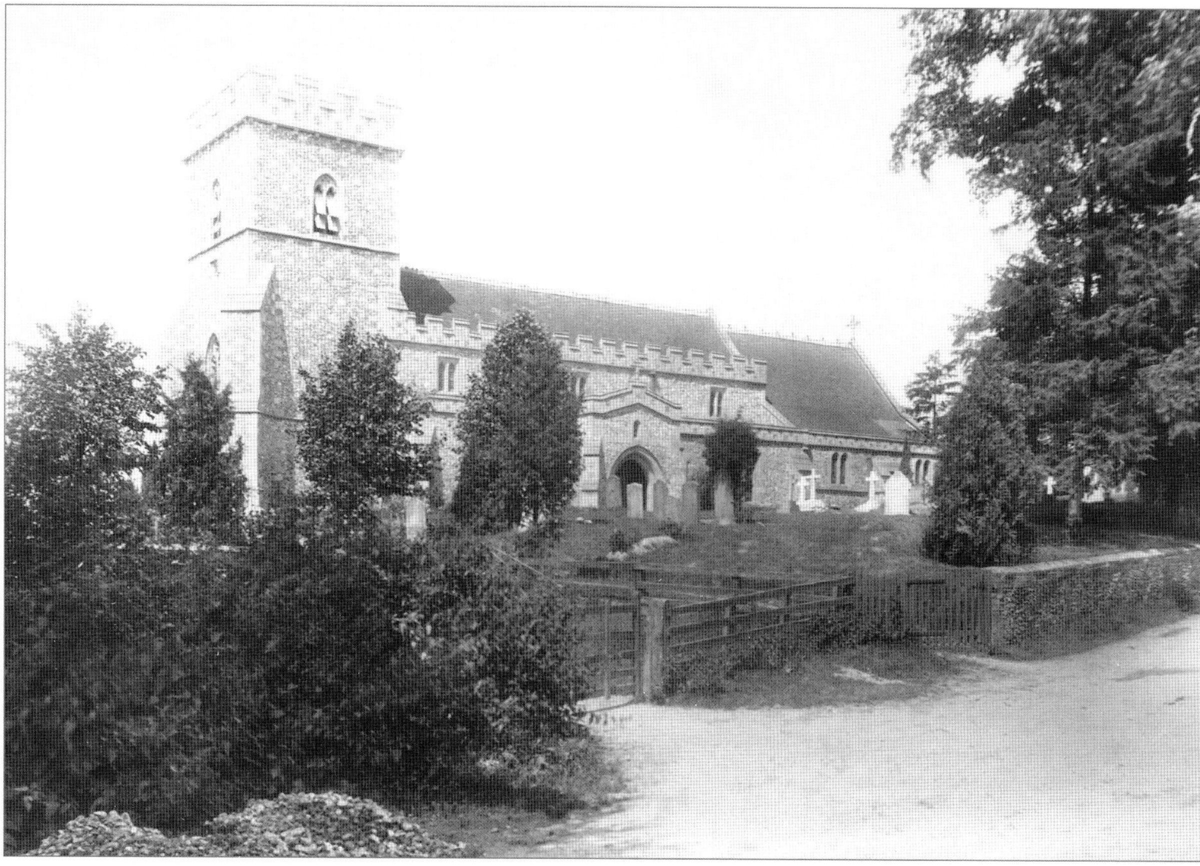

GREAT KIMBLE, *The Church 1897* 39646

Great Kimble, like Whiteleaf, is on the lower slopes of the Chilterns where springs emerge from the chalk. Its medieval open fields in the valley were enclosed by Act of Parliament as late as 1805. To the west of the church, sheep graze the turf-covered earthworks of a moated medieval manor house with its fishponds and trackways. The road edge is now more manicured than in 1897,and has a pavement, but the church is little changed. It is noted for its fine 12th-century Norman stone font of the 'Aylesbury' type: these resemble gold chalices with fluted sides set on ornate carved bases.

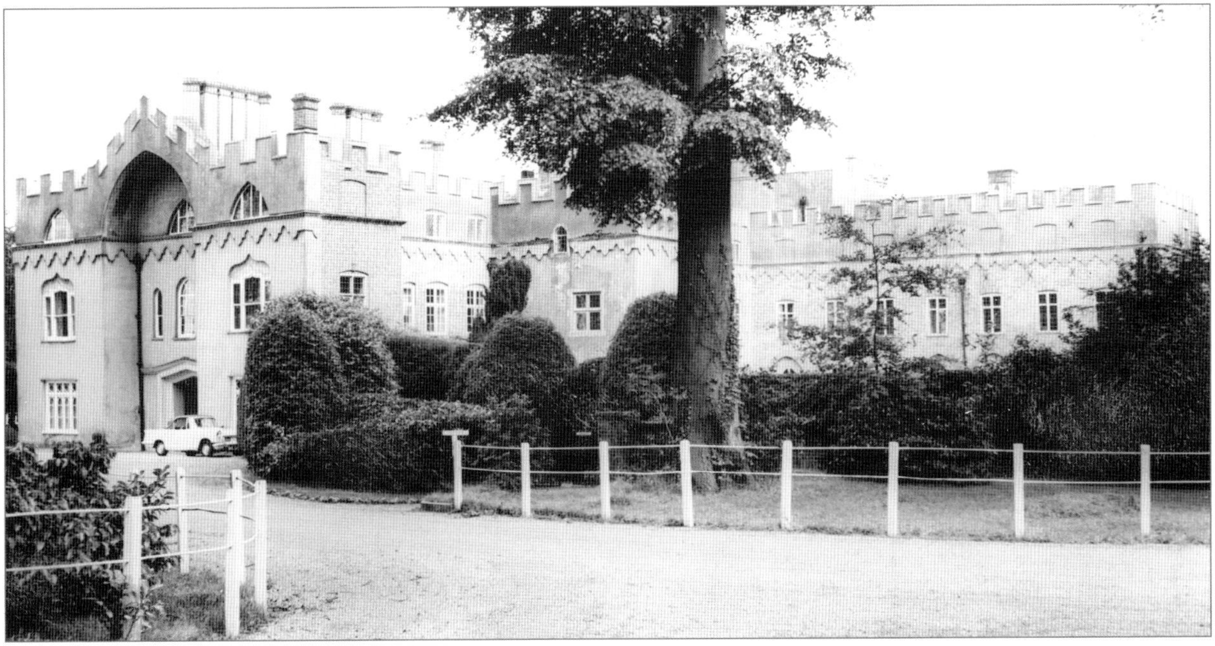

▲ **GREAT HAMPDEN,** *Hampden House c1965* G336006

This fascinating, rambling 18th-century Gothic-style mansion has a medieval and Tudor core. It was the home of John Hampden 'the Patriot', a leader of the parliamentary opposition to Charles I and one of the MPs who refused to pay the Ship Money tax. He was arrested in this mansion in 1637, and was later mortally wounded at Chalgrove Field in 1642 when the Civil War started. The house was rented by Hammer House of Horror in more recent times, and is now offices. It can be seen from the Ridgeway Path, which passes here along the course of the great Iron Age earthworks of Grim's Ditch.

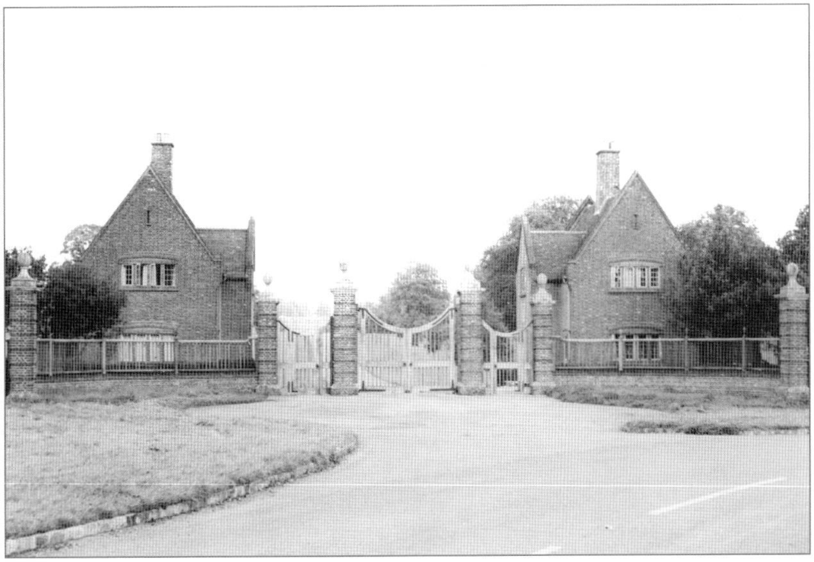

◄ **ELLESBOROUGH,** *The Lodges to Chequers c1965* E210003

Although the original house, dated 1565, was built for William Hawtrey, Chequers is now much more famous as the country house of British prime ministers. Given to the nation in 1917 by Sir Arthur Lee, later Lord Lee of Fareham, premiers have weekended and holidayed here from the time of Lloyd George. From the now little used South Lodge gates we can just see the south front of the house in the distance, restored by 1901, and the walled terraces dating from the 1890s to 1910. The Ridgeway long distance path passes through the grounds, admittedly nowadays supervised by security cameras.

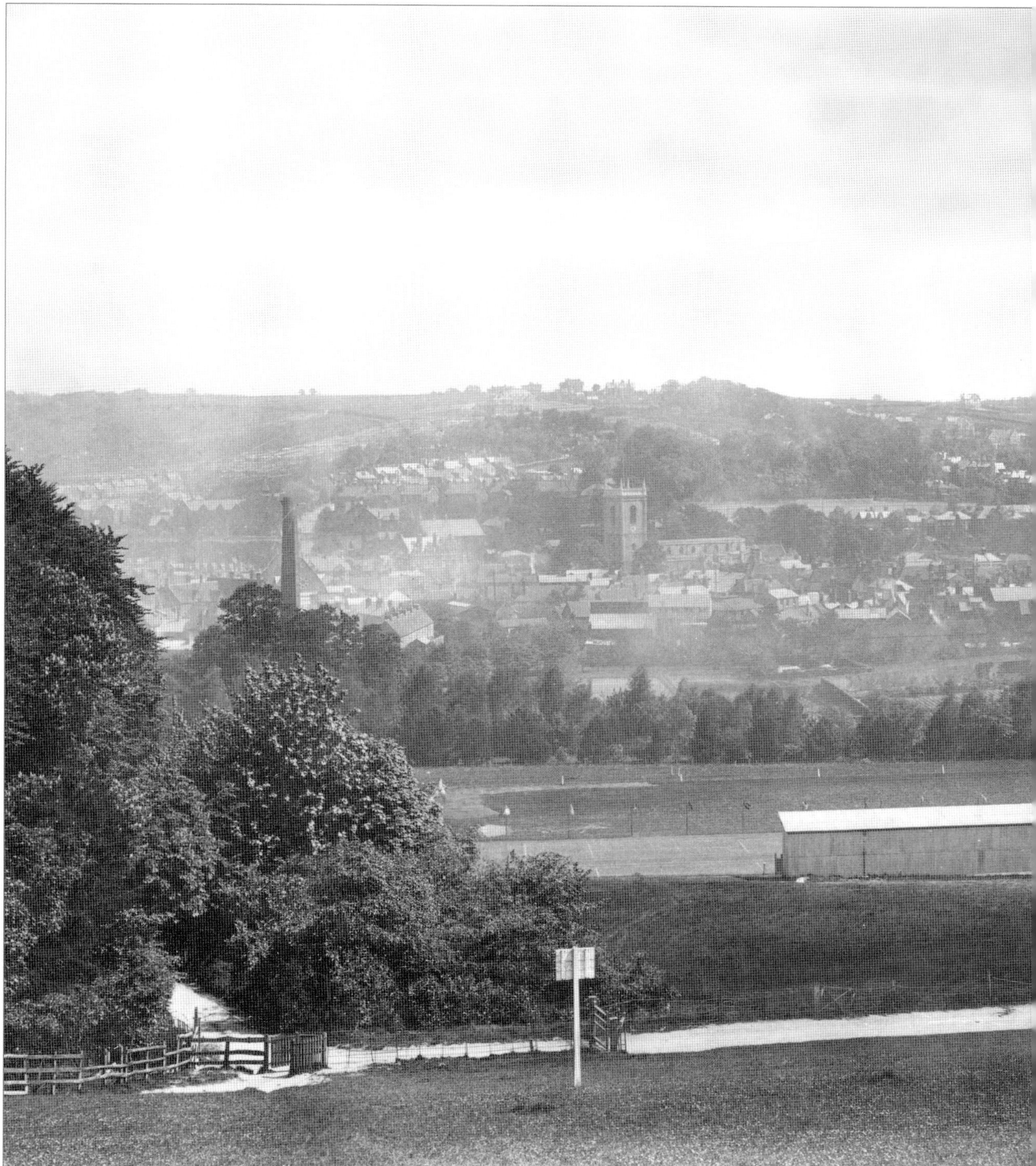

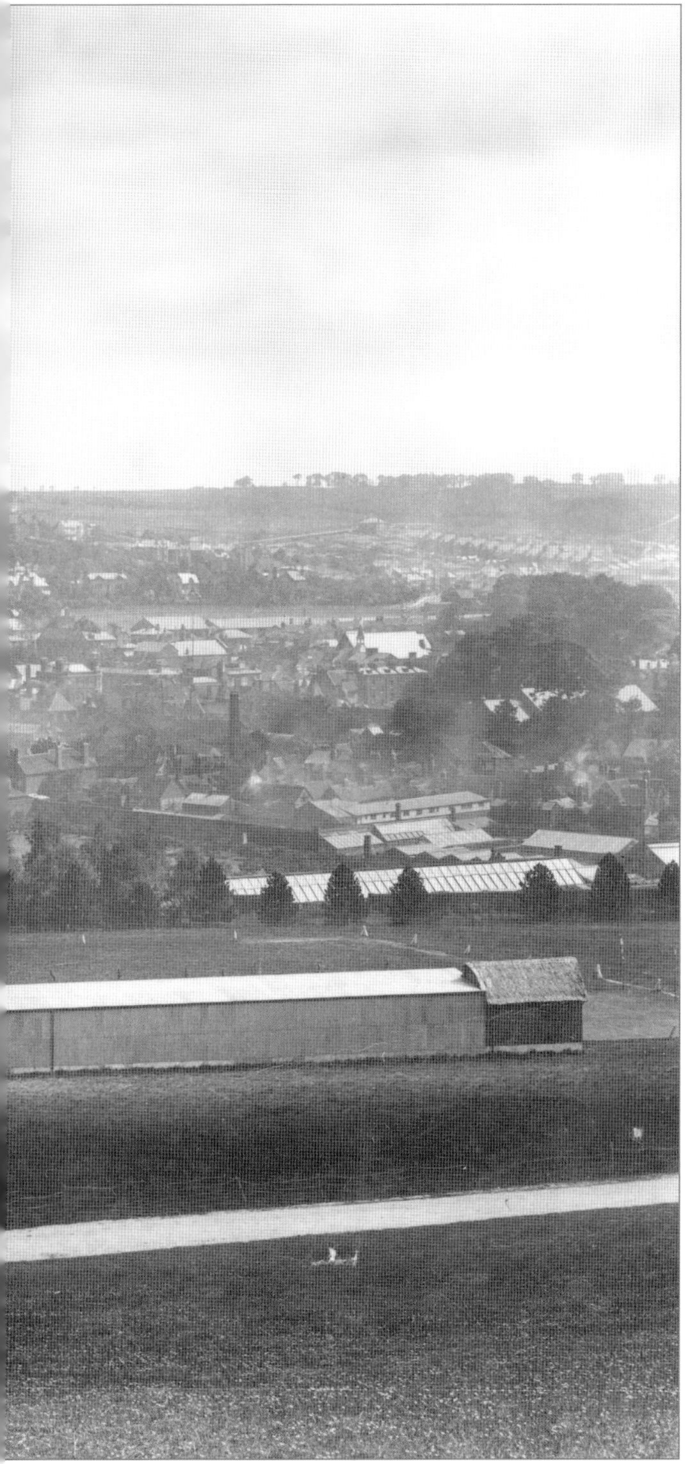

HIGH WYCOMBE AND THE CENTRAL CHILTERNS PLATEAU

HIGH WYCOMBE, *From the South 1906* 53659

The second tour starts in High Wycombe, a medieval borough set in the steep-sided valley of the River Wye. Its earlier growth was based on the corn trade, but from the 18th century furniture-making came to dominate the town's economy, utilising Chiltern beech wood plantations to produce Windsor chairs and other furniture. This view shows the town centre and the parish church in the midst of Edwardian expansion along the valley and up the hillsides. In the foreground is the old Adams Park ground of Wycombe Wanderers football club, now occupied by flats and the hospital car park. The lane to the right of the signboard was Barracks Road, now part of the hospital.

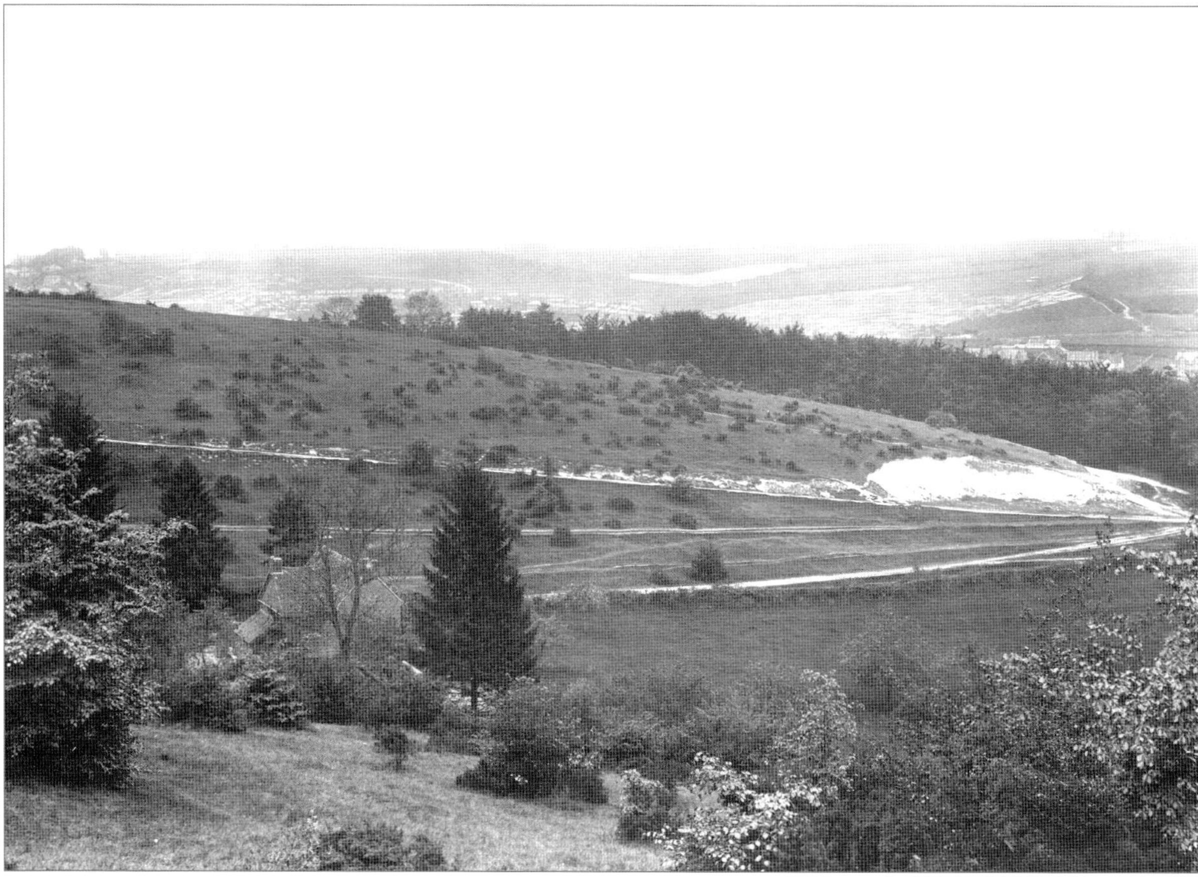

HIGH WYCOMBE, *Keep Hill 1906* 53680

Frith's photographer has moved eastwards from view 53659, beyond the grounds of Wycombe Abbey to its eastern boundary on Keep Hill; the town is mostly hidden beyond the ridge in the middle ground. The view is much changed today: the early 19th-century cottage in front of the camera is now numbered 5 at the end of modern Lowdon Close, an extension of Keep Hill Drive's 1930s semi-detached houses. The bare hill beyond is now covered with a sycamore and ash wood towering over the yew bushes that were here in 1906. The opposite hills have been developed for housing since 1906, although the centre, including the light coloured-field, survives intact.

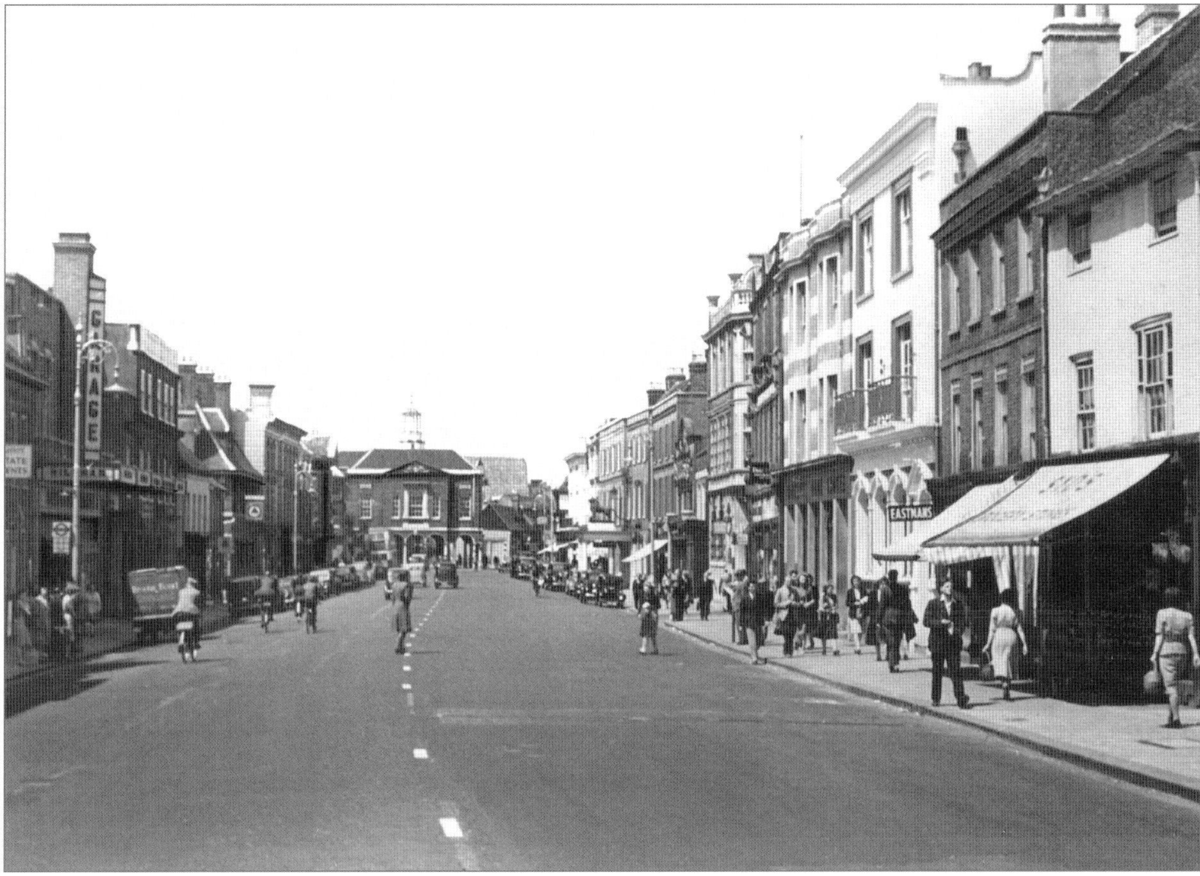

HIGH WYCOMBE, *High Street c1955* H84052

Down in the valley, Frith's photographer took the next few views in the 1950s when the main London to Oxford Road still came through the centre of the town - the through traffic now goes along the M40, and the High Street was partly pedestrianised in the late 1990s. This view looks west along the High Street, a fine wide one laid out in the 13th century and still lined with market stalls three days a week. At the end is the pedimented and cupola-topped Georgian Guildhall, which was designed by Henry Keene in 1757 and given to the town by the Earl of Shelburne who owned Loakes Manor, now Wycombe Abbey.

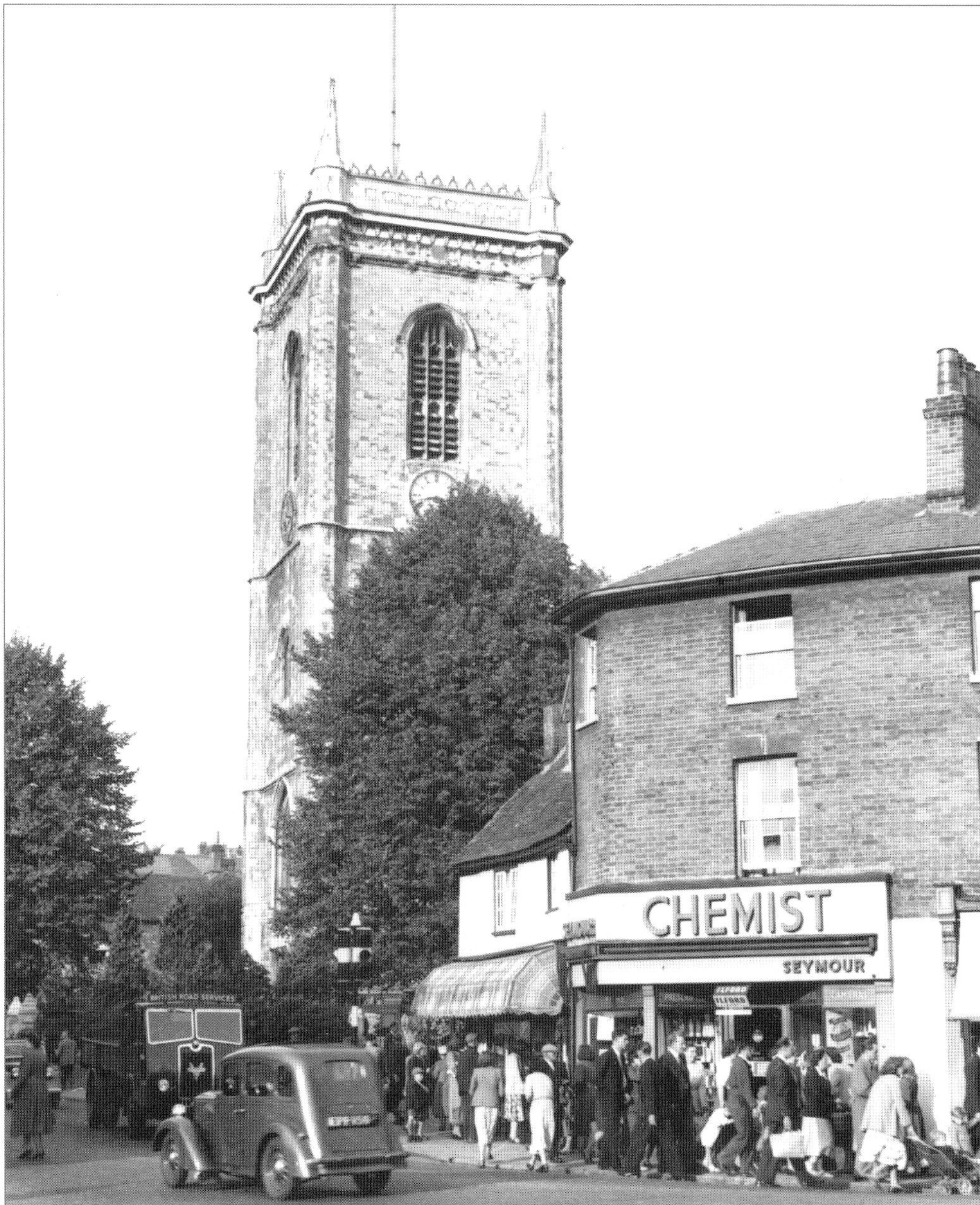

HIGH WYCOMBE, *The Parish Church c1955* H84071

Opposite the Guildhall and in the older part of the town is Cornmarket, a name reflecting the key trade of medieval to Georgian High Wycombe. Here the photographer looks north from beside the Guildhall into Church Street, a view dominated by the superb All Saints' parish church tower. This church, the largest parish church in the county, originally had a central tower, which was demolished in 1510; this noble west tower was built between 1521 and 1535 by Sir Rowland Messenger. The parapets and pinnacles are of 1755 by Henry Keene, the architect of the Guildhall.

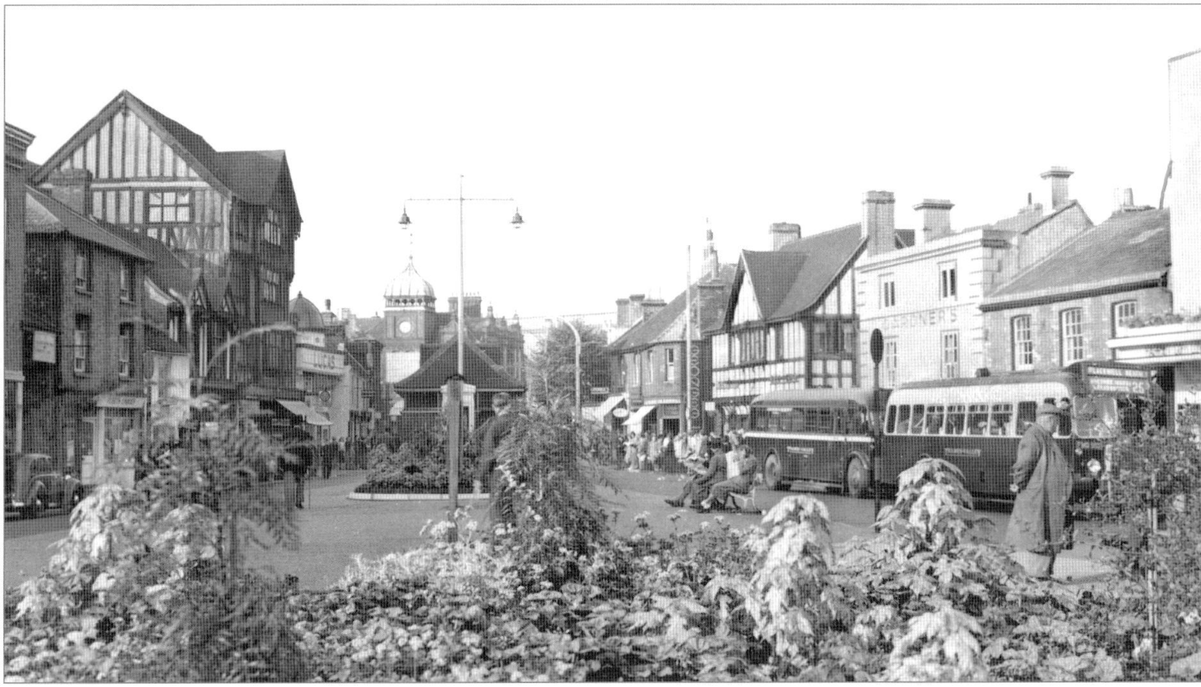

HIGH WYCOMBE, *Frogmoor c1955* H84070

At the end of Church Street lies Frogmoor, a large triangular space, part of the original market place; by the 19th century it was a private garden, but in 1877 it was opened as a public square. This view shows Frogmoor before the present bus station was built south of the 1960s inner relief road. Most of the buildings on the right were replaced by the dominating Chilterns Shopping Centre in 1985. At the far right is the old Palace Cinema. The ogee-roofed clock tower in the distance is the old Science and Arts School opened in 1893; it later became swimming baths, then a theatre, and is now offices.

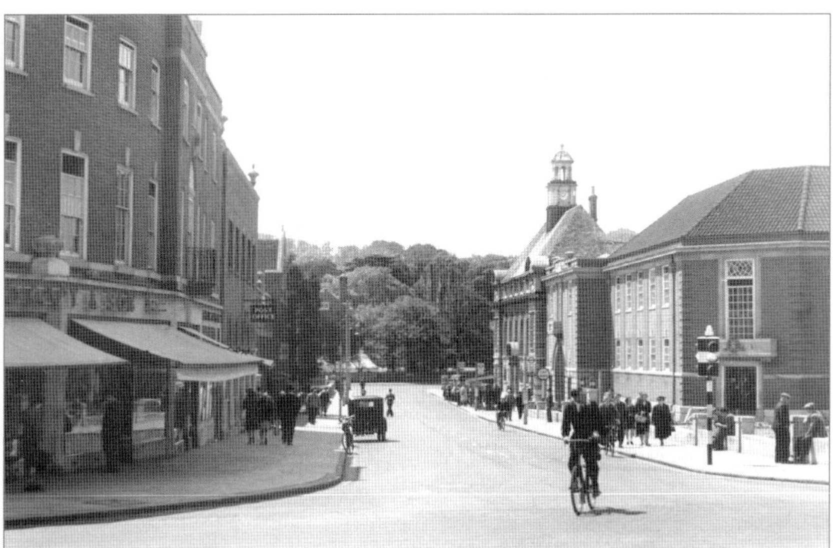

HIGH WYCOMBE, *Queen Victoria Road c1955* H84045

The last view in the town centre looks south from the junction with the High Street on the right from Crendon Street into Queen Victoria Road, a road laid out along the former drive to Wycombe Abbey (we can see its park and some buildings in the distance), and sold in 1901 to the town to form a civic avenue. The clock-towered Queen Anne-style Town Hall opened in 1904, and the library to the right in 1921. The shops and flats on the left date from 1933, and replaced Wheeler's Brewery. Beyond is the now demolished Christchurch Sunday School screening the 1932 Council Offices.

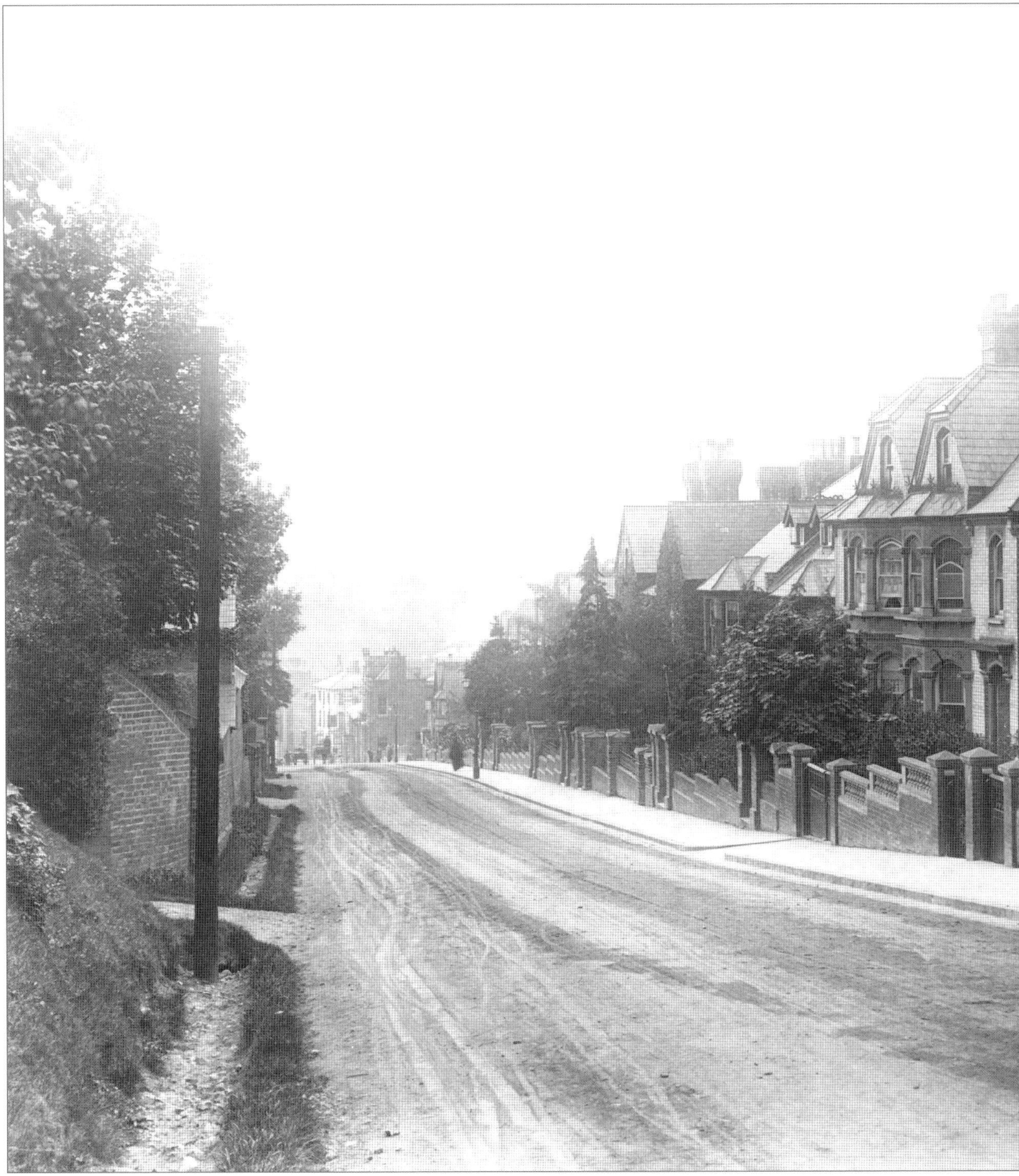

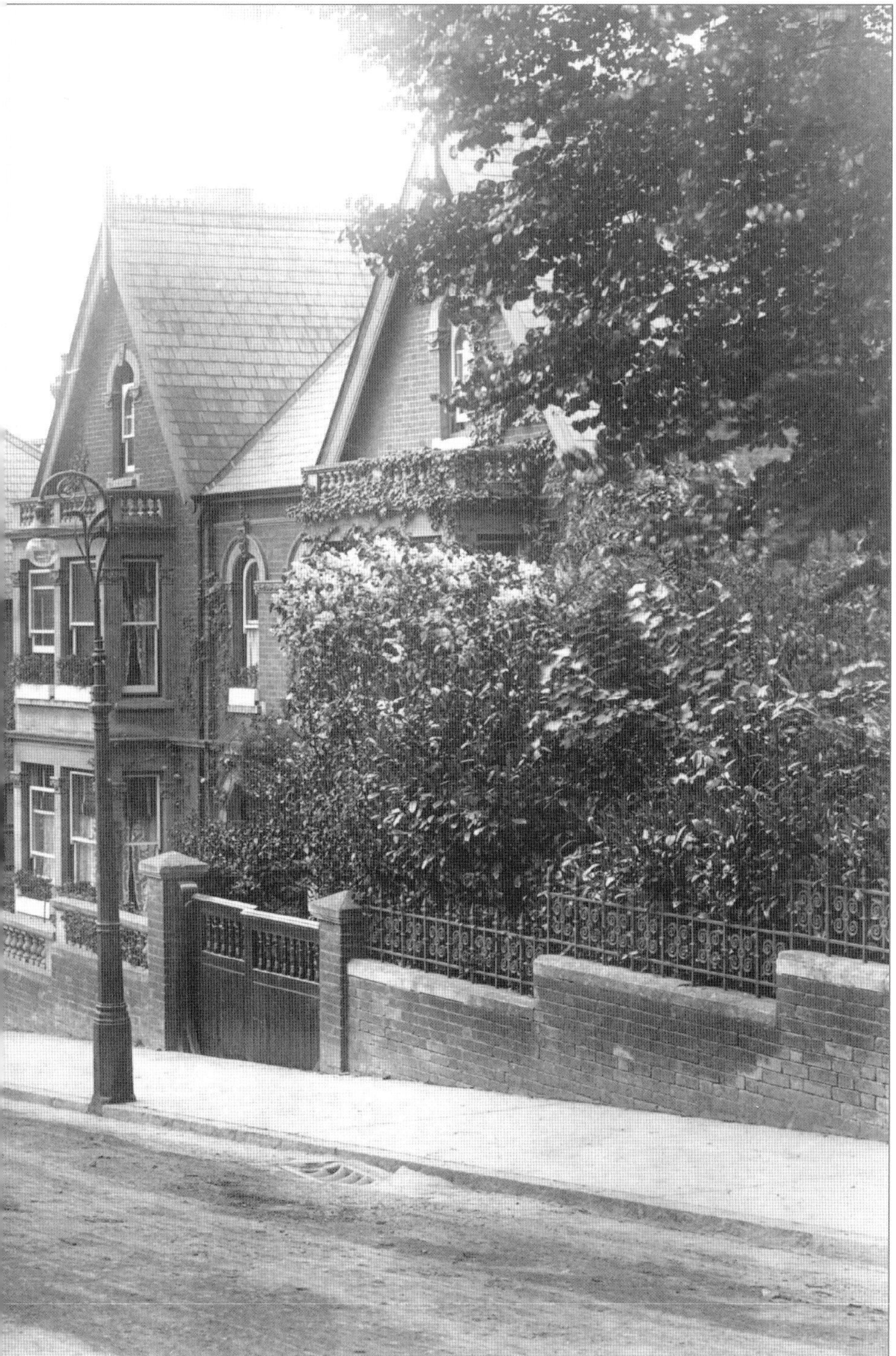

HIGH WYCOMBE
Amersham Hill 1906
53669

Continuing northwards up Crendon Street, we pass the railway station; the line first opened as a branch from Maidenhead in 1854, then continued to Oxford, Thame and Aylesbury. In 1906 the station was rebuilt as part of the Great Central, re-opening in 1906. Further uphill was the first major late Victorian and Edwardian suburb, along Amersham Hill. This view looks downhill past Victorian semi-detached villas on the right. All survive, although the right-hand pair, Nos 35 and 37, were rebuilt in rough replica in the 1980s. The road has since been widened, and the left-hand walls have gone.

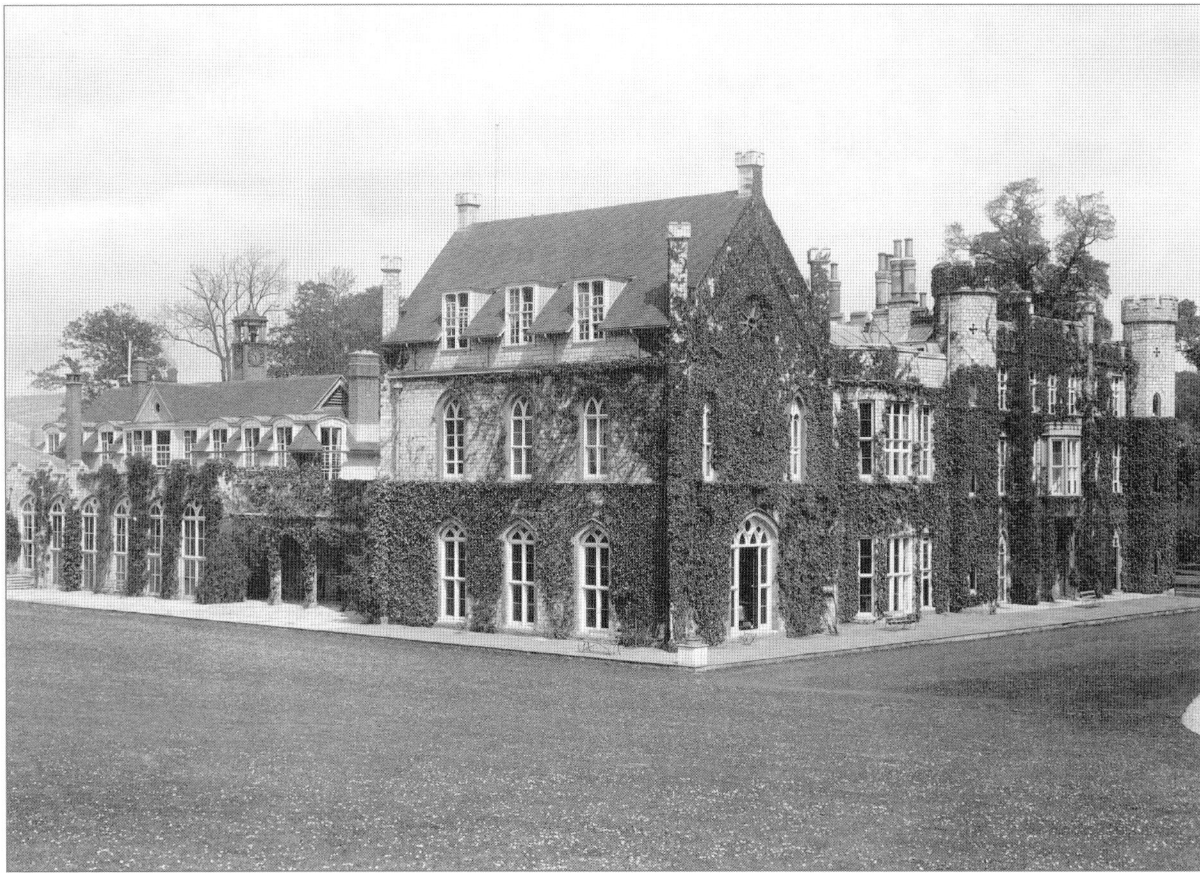

HIGH WYCOMBE, *Wycombe Abbey 1906* 53687

Originally Loakes Manor, and owned by the Earl of Shelburne, it was bought by the Carringtons in 1798. The Georgian and 17th-century house was transformed and enlarged by James Wyatt soon after 1800 into this Romantic Gothic castellated building clad in local Denner Hill stone from the hills north of High Wycombe, and renamed Wycombe Abbey. In 1896 the Abbey was sold and became Wycombe Abbey School under a charismatic headmistress, Dame Frances Dove, also Wycombe Borough's first lady councillor. Here we see the Abbey after the first phase of conversion and extension for what is now a leading girls' public school.

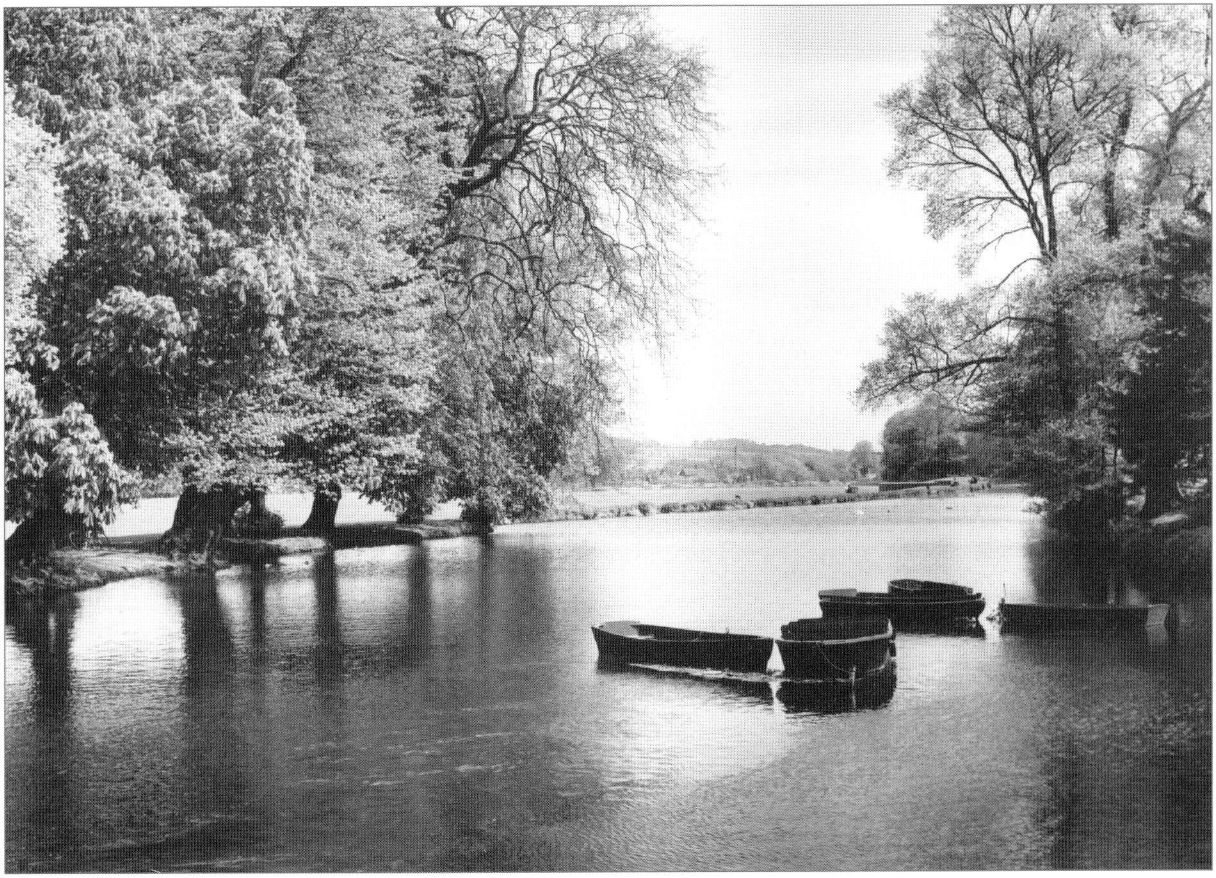

HIGH WYCOMBE, *The Dyke c1960* H84073

The last two Wycombe views are of The Dyke, a fine lake formed by damming the Back Stream, a divergence of the River Wye, which it rejoins further downstream. This was done in the early 1760s for Lord Shelburne as part of the landscaping of the grounds of his Loakes Manor (now Wycombe Abbey), taking advice from the great landscape gardener Capability Brown. This view looks east along The Dyke; the trees mostly survive today. Out of view on the left is the green-painted corrugated-iron boat hire and café building, some of whose boats are moored to the right.

▼ **HIGH WYCOMBE,** *The Dyke c1955* H84034

Originally within the grounds of Wycombe Abbey, The Dyke and its south bank were given by Lord Carrington to the town in 1924 as a memorial to his son, Viscount Wendover, who had been killed near Ypres in 1915 during World War I. The northern fence was removed, and the south bank path, behind the camera, was renamed Wendover Way. The open space beyond is The Rye, bounded in the distance by the River Wye and London Road. Behind the two tall trees is Rye Mill, one of 37 watermills along the Wye and now demolished.

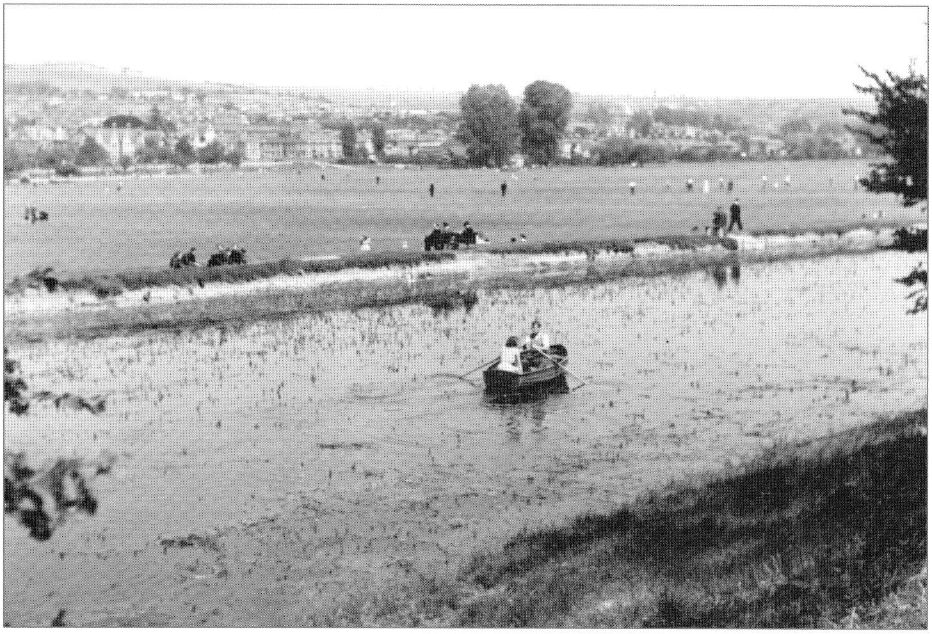

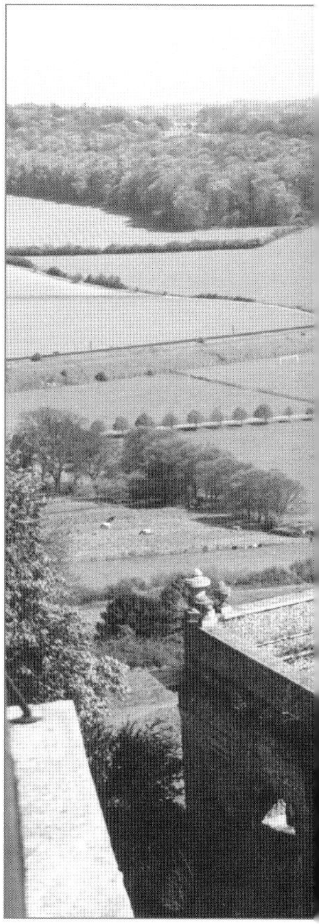

WEST WYCOMBE ▶
The Pedestal 1906 53691

Going westward from High Wycombe along the Oxford road, now the A40, we leave the suburbs behind and reach the junction with the Bradenham Road that leads towards Princes Risborough and Aylesbury. The straight road behind the photographer was constructed by Francis Dashwood, using chalk from the hill - the excavations became the famous Hellfire Caves. This took the road out of his park and provided work for the locals; it was completed in 1752. The Pedestal, or signpost, directing the traveller to the City, the University and the County Town was relocated a little further away when the junction became a roundabout in the 1980s. On the hill beyond are the Dashwood Mausoleum and the tower of the parish church.

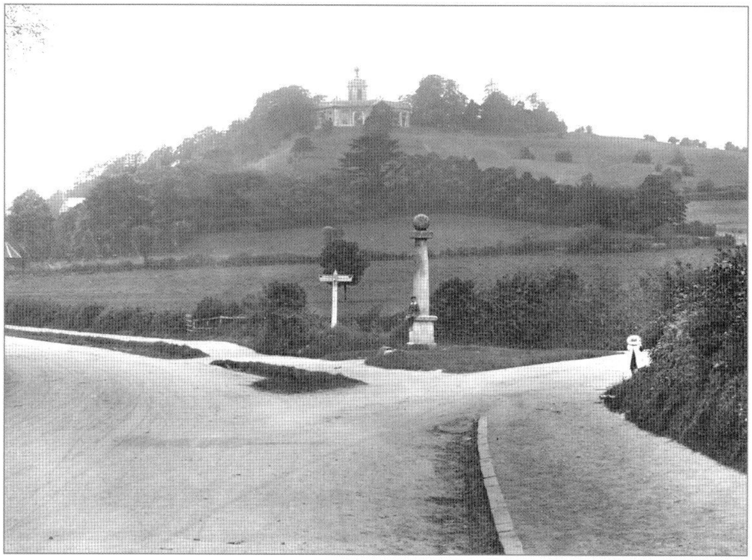

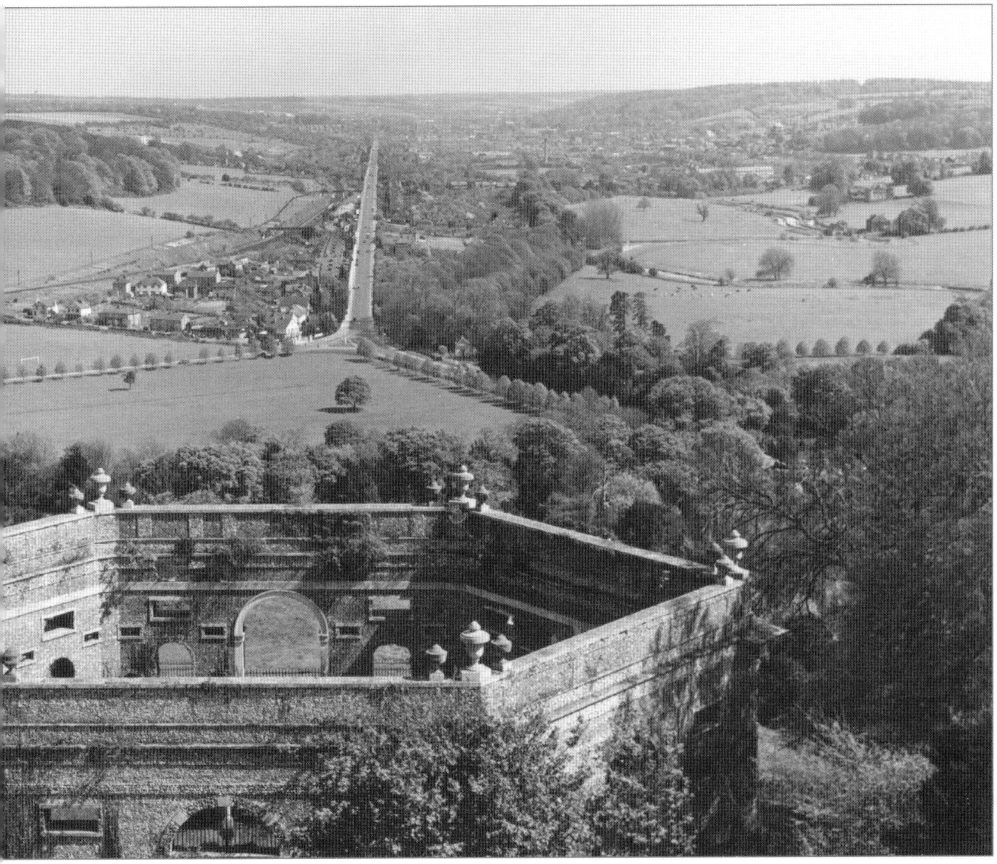

WEST WYCOMBE
The View from the Church Tower c1955 W340026

Now atop the hill, the photographer looks eastwards towards High Wycombe along the line of Dashwood's 1750s road. To its right are the grounds of West Wycombe Park. The hill and woods on the left still survive, and so do the recently planted lime trees at the foot of the hill. This view is taken from St Lawrence's parish church tower - the medieval church was remodelled by Francis Dashwood as a Georgian Classical one in the 1760s. He also built the remarkable open-topped hexagonal mausoleum beyond the church, which was designed by John Bastard in the 1760s.

WEST WYCOMBE
High Street 1954 W340016

West Wycombe is a complete contrast to its big sister, High Wycombe. The centuries have been kinder, and it escaped 1960s transformation. This is partly owing to the Dashwoods, who conserved it until 1929. Then the Royal Society of Arts bought the village, selling it on to the National Trust in 1934. Sandwiched between the hill with the parish church and the Mausoleum on the north and the parkland of West Wycombe House to the south, the village is preserved as one of the finest in the county with its mix of timber-framed, brick, and flint houses and cottages.

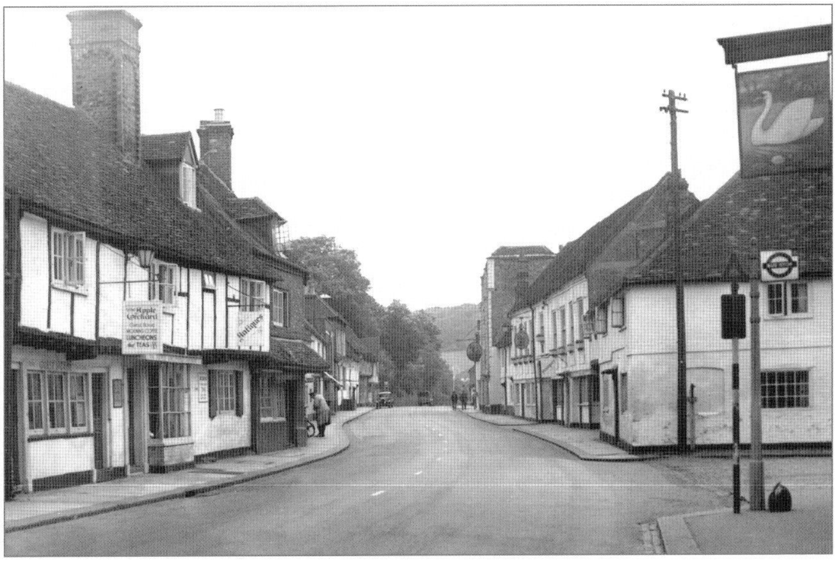

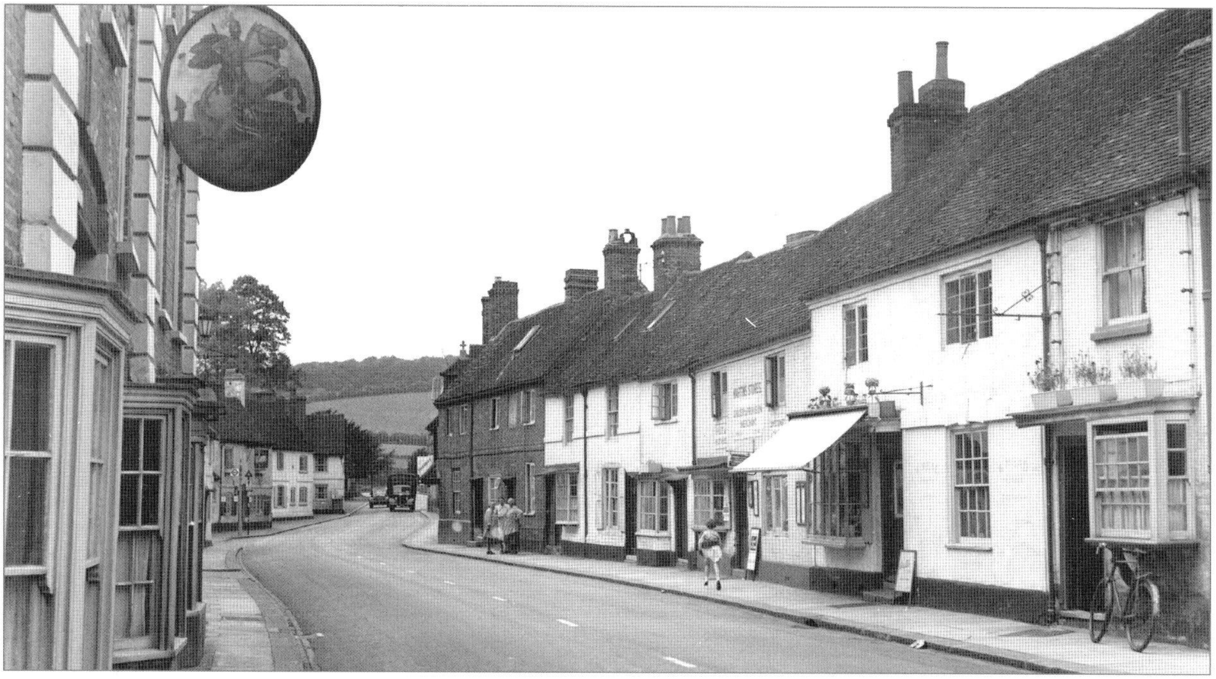

WEST WYCOMBE, *High Street 1954* W340005

Here the photographer looks west past the George and Dragon, a former 18th-century coaching inn on the Oxford road and still a pub (other pubs are now houses). The bicycle leans against the Old Plough pub, nowadays empty, and the Swan is in the middle distance on the left. The grocers and fruiterers, W Mead (right), is now a card shop, with Martin's Stores next door now the post office, but otherwise the High Street is little changed, apart from the heavy traffic which still pours through despite the M40, which in effect is the Wycombe by-pass.

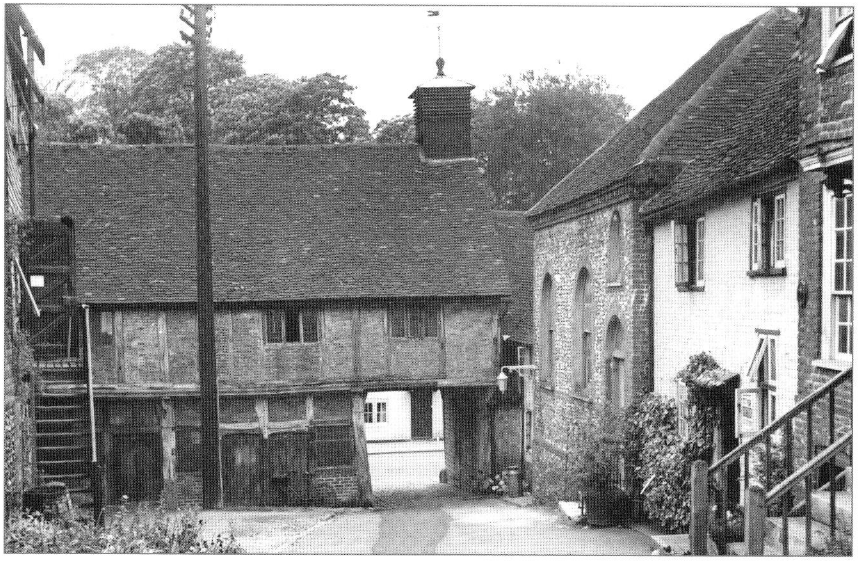

◄ **WEST WYCOMBE**

Church Lane c1955 W340009

Off the High Street, and climbing steeply out of the village towards the church, Church Lane cannot be seen from the High Street, for access is under the Church Loft, a fine 15th-century timber-framed building. This was built with back-to-back shops on the ground floor (we can see two former shop doorway arches to the right of the telegraph pole), with an open hall for the full length of the upper floor. To the left is Brown's of West Wycombe, a still-functioning carpentry and furniture workshop, a reminder of the chair-making past of this part of the Chilterns.

WEST WYCOMBE ►
Church Lane c1955
W340017

The photographer is now looking uphill along the delightful but precipitous Church Lane through the archway from the High Street and under Church Loft. On the left is the brick and flint Christadelphian Ecclesia, dated 1815 and originally built as a Methodist Chapel - a brick is inscribed 'I Bigg, Mason'. From the 1890s it had been used as one of the village's many furniture workshops. There are Georgian-fronted cottages up the hill, one dated 1722 and others older ones re-fronted, while on the right are the grounds of the old vicarage and the Dower House.

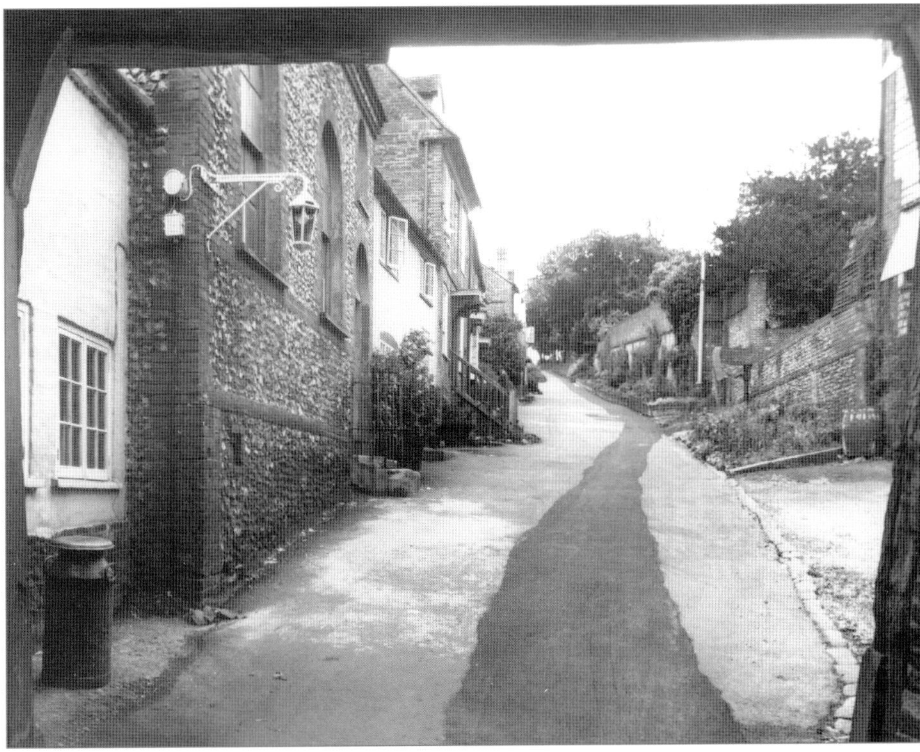

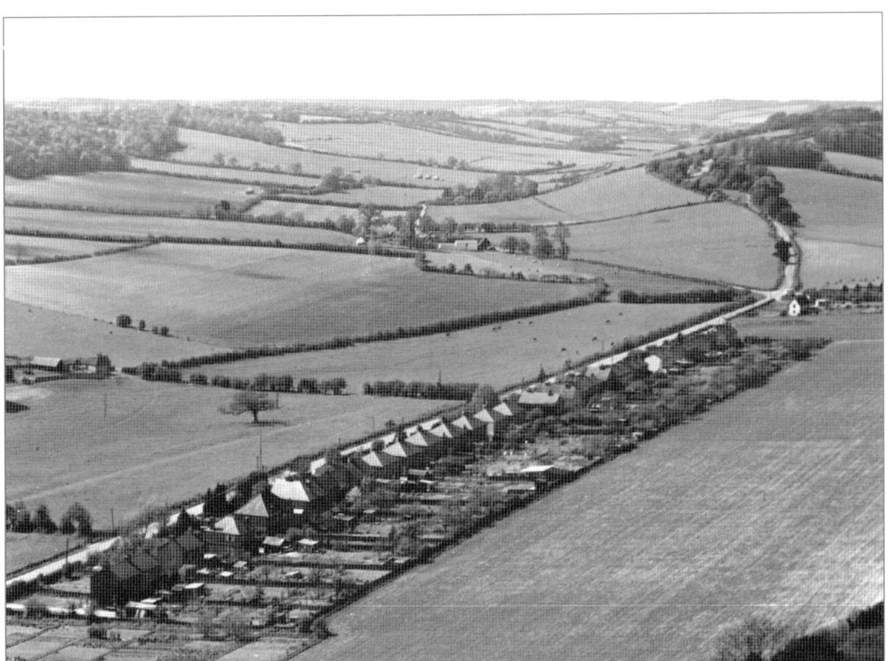

◄ **WEST WYCOMBE**
Chorley Road c1955
W340023

This view from West Wycombe Hill looking north-west along Chorley Road shows the sort of early 20th-century ribbon development that resulted in the first Town and Country Planning Acts of the 1930s. Pairs of suburban 1930s semis advance into the countryside, spoiling one side of the valley where previously there had only been farmsteads. Unchecked, this sort of thing could have linked every town and village, so we have something to thank the planners for. There is a similar ribbon along the Bradenham Road in the same parish on either side of the railway bridge.

STOKENCHURCH
The Village Green c1955 S685008

Further west, the village of Stokenchurch is a typical plateau village. It grew up around a series of commons, and its chief buildings are the medieval church and the partly 18th-century coaching inn, the King's Arms (left). Until 1895 the village and its fields were within Oxfordshire, its church a chapelry of Aston Rowant at the foot of the Chilterns to the north-west. The remains of the much-encroached commons were enclosed in 1861, and for years the village was noted for its July horse fair.

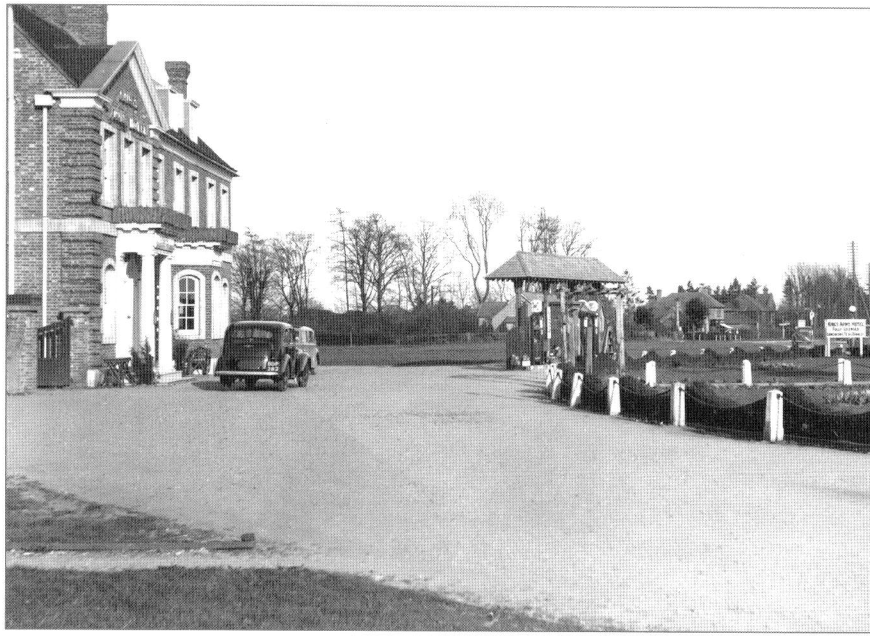

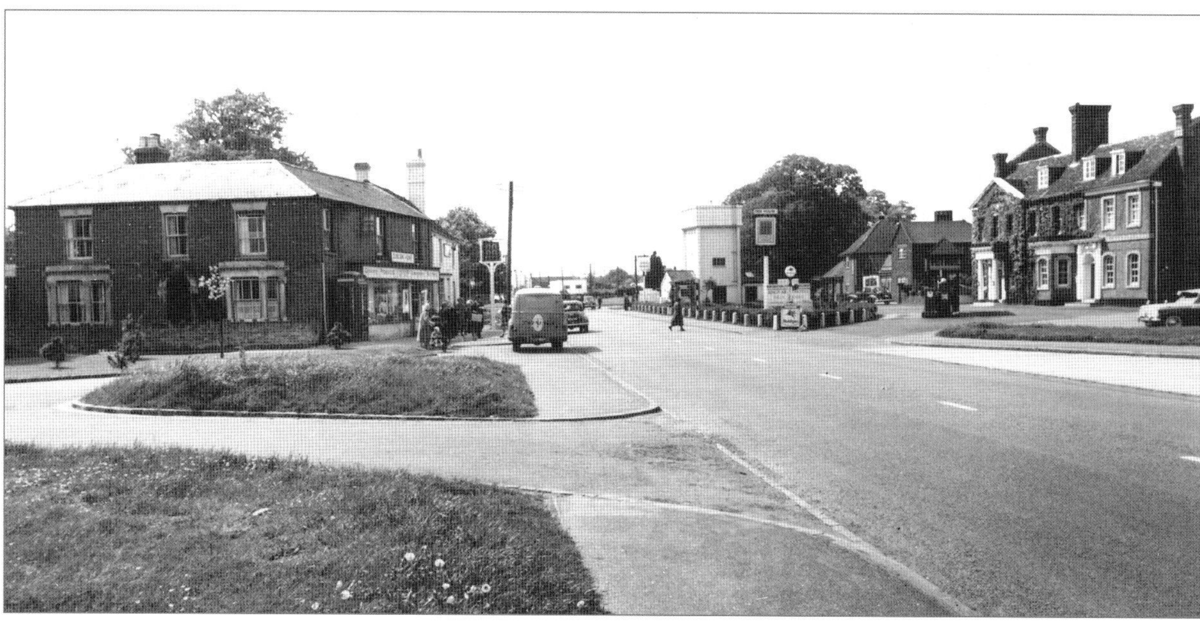

STOKENCHURCH, *The Post Office and the King's Arms c1955* S685022

This view looks north-west along the Oxford Road towards the King's Arms Hotel, extended, refurbished and flourishing in the 1990s. Water had always been a problem for Stokenchurch up on the dry plateau, and until the 1960s the concrete water tower, built in the 1930s (centre right), supplied much of the village's needs. This ugly structure has long gone, as have the petrol pumps below their tiled roof in front of the King's Arms. The great trees on the commons mostly still survive.

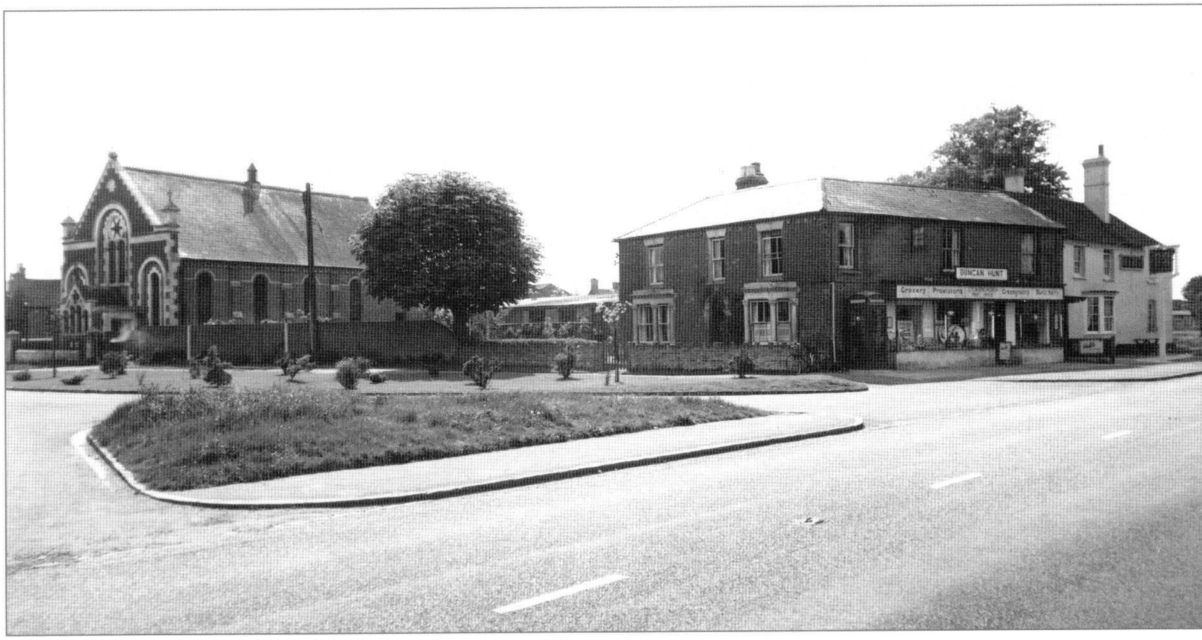

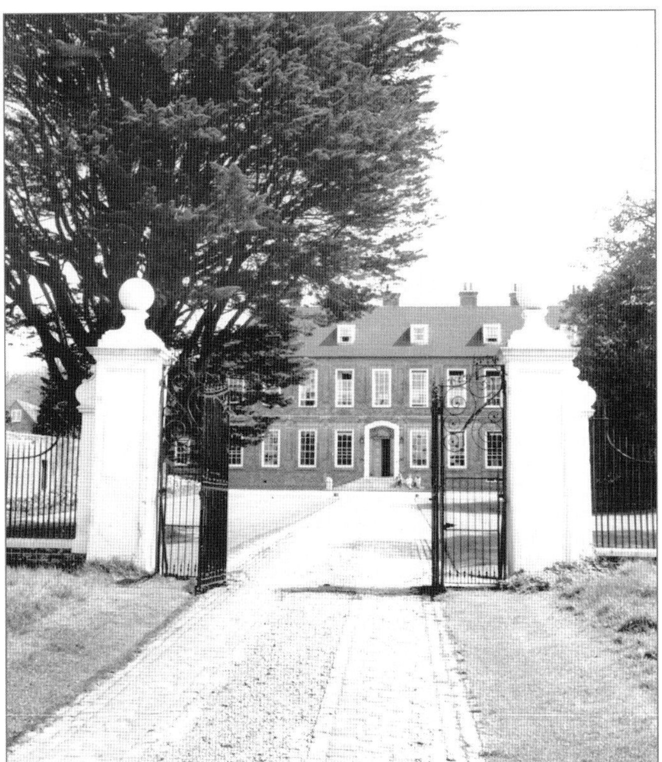

▲ **STOKENCHURCH**
The Post Office and the Methodist Church c1955 S685025

The Four Horseshoes pub on the right remains, but Duncan Hunt's building was rebuilt in the 1970s - part is now Delboy's superstore, and part a dental surgery. The Methodist Church of 1896 on the left survives in all its curious and unlovely Italianate Gothic detail. Can anyone have thought it beautiful even in 1896? It is similar to another chapel in Stewkley in the centre of the county, and the architect may have come from Swindon.

◄ **BRADENHAM,** *The Manor c1955* B738006

From the rather amorphous Stokenchurch, we move on to Bradenham, a village scattered around a long green, and, like West Wycombe, owned by the National Trust. Isaac D'Israeli was a tenant during the 1830s and 1840s, and his son Benjamin, the great Tory Prime Minister and novelist, bought nearby Hughenden Manor in 1847. Passing to the National Trust in 1956, this very attractive brick-built manor house was built in the mid 17th century, and retains remnants of its formal garden. Here we look from the village green through the later 17th-century wrought-iron gates and piers to the west front; the churchyard wall is on the left.

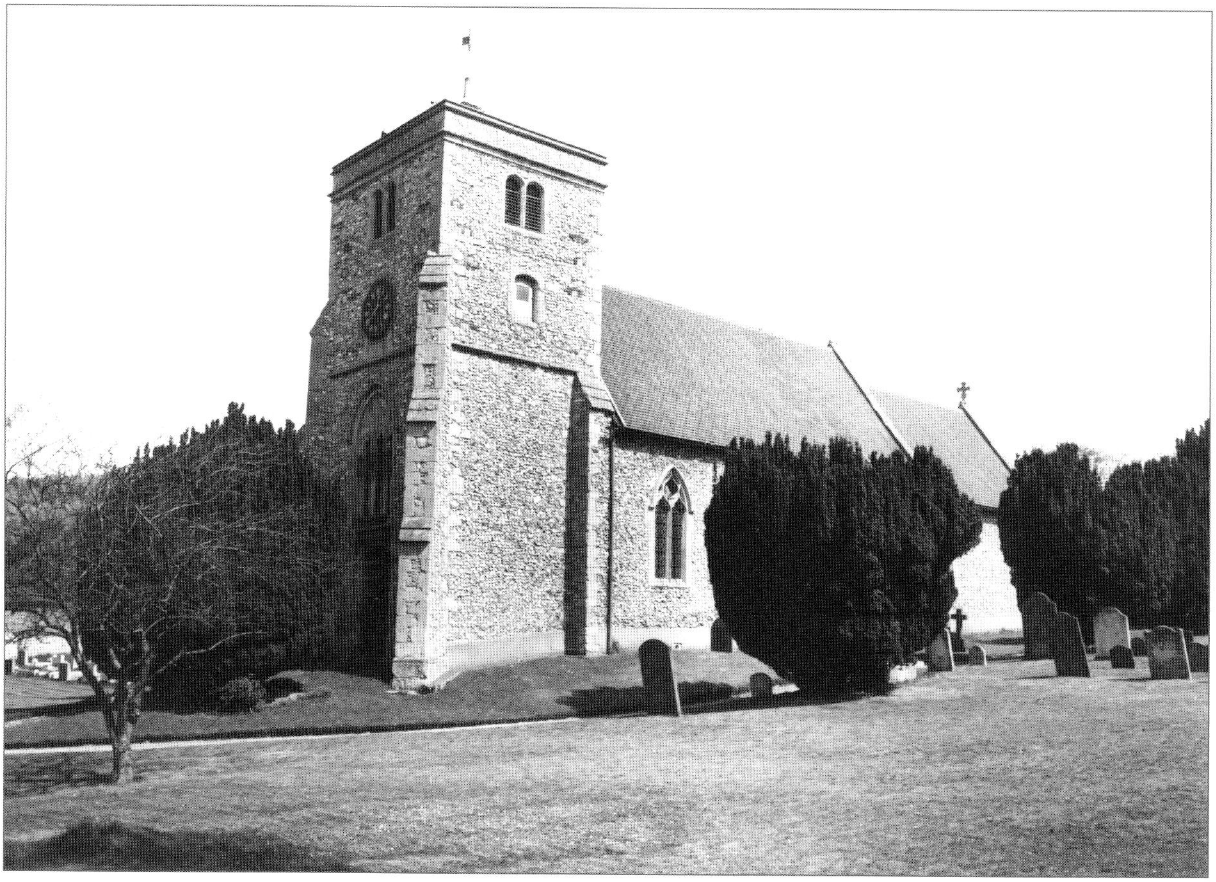

BRADENHAM, *The Church c1955* B738005

The church of St Botolph, a relatively rare Anglo-Saxon dedication, closes the east end of the village green; it has high 17th-century brick garden walls separating it from the grounds of the Manor around three sides of the churchyard. It is a simple aisleless church set in a pretty churchyard, its late 14th-century west tower a key feature in the village scene. The chancel was rebuilt in 1863, while the north chapel was built in 1542 for William, Lord Windsor. Nowadays the yews are trimmed to be smaller and neater, and the flagpole has gone from the tower, but otherwise the scene is unchanged.

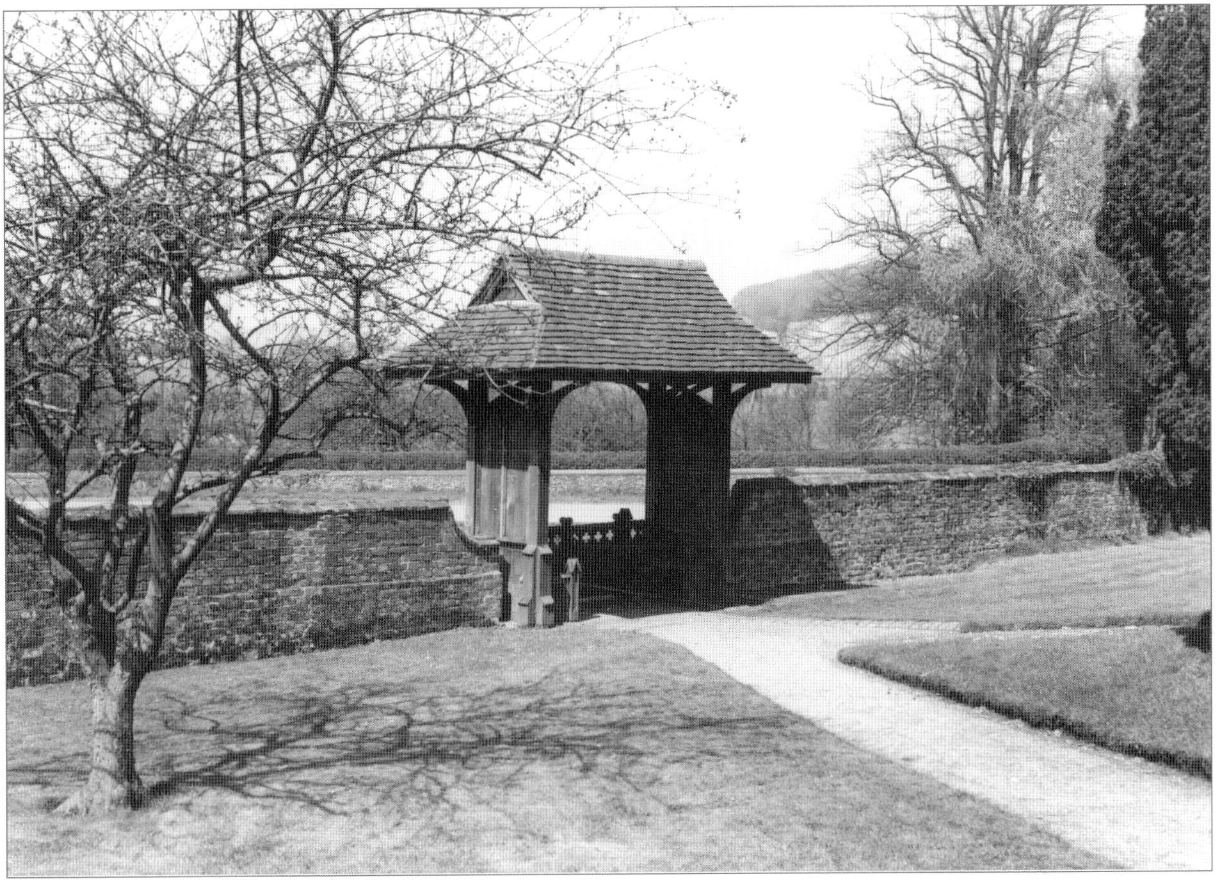

BRADENHAM, *The Lychgate c1960* B738008

The lychgate which leads out onto the charming village green dates only from 1920, and was built as a memorial to those of the village who died in the First World War: two army captains and four privates. The oak gates to the centre have been replaced by less attractive iron ones, and the left side of the porch is partly obscured by a large viburnum. The flint wall on the far side of the green belongs to the White House, a picturesque Gothick stucco fronted house of 1800, complete with battlements, the façade concealing an older house.

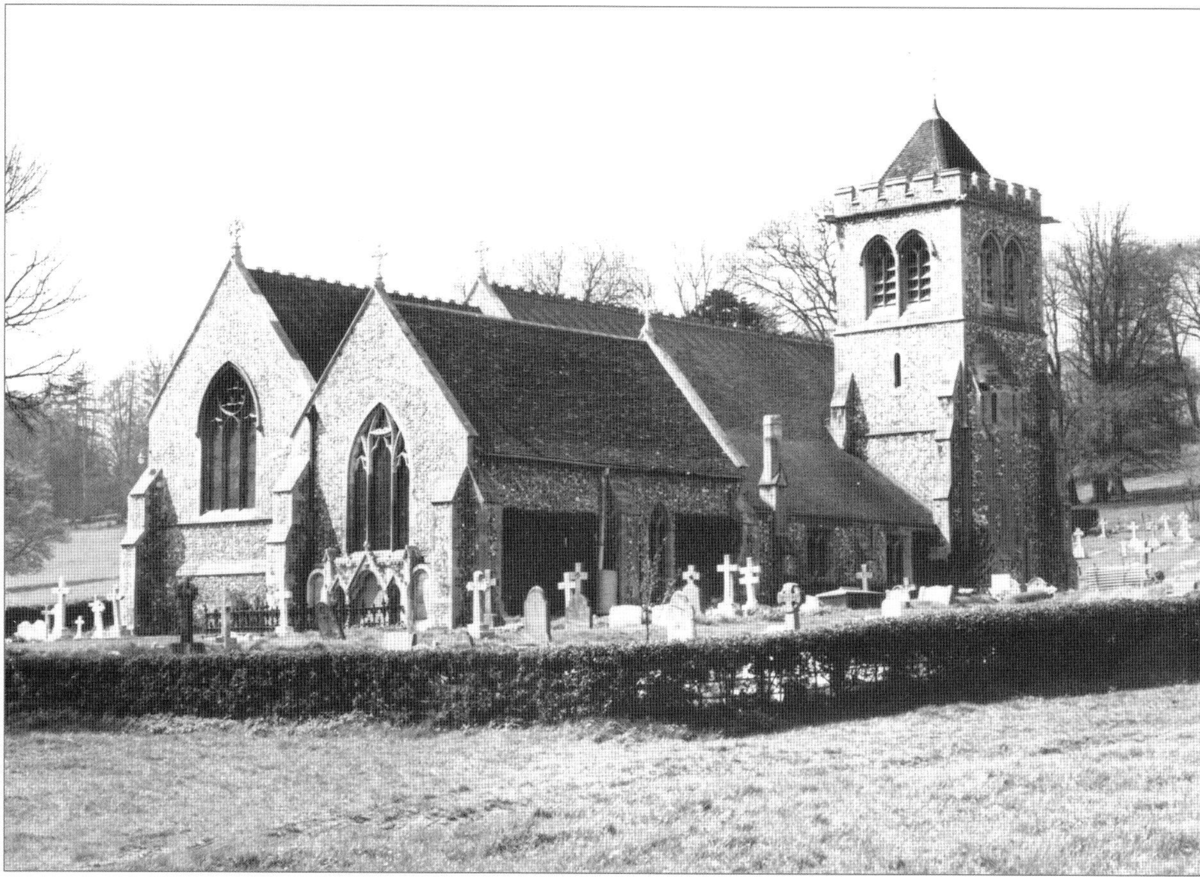

HUGHENDEN VALLEY, *The Church c1955* H471005

Heading east across a wooded chalk ridge, we reach the Hughenden Valley, which leads south back into High Wycombe. Here Benjamin Disraeli bought the manor; he enlarged and altered an 18th-century house, using the robustly original architect Edward Buckton Lamb to transform the house into its present appearance in the 1860s. The house and estate passed to the National Trust in 1946. The mansion is on the ridge behind the church, which is nearer the valley floor. Disraeli largely rebuilt the church; he is buried here in this beautiful valley, and his memorial inside the church was actually paid for by Queen Victoria, 'his grateful and affectionate Sovereign and friend'.

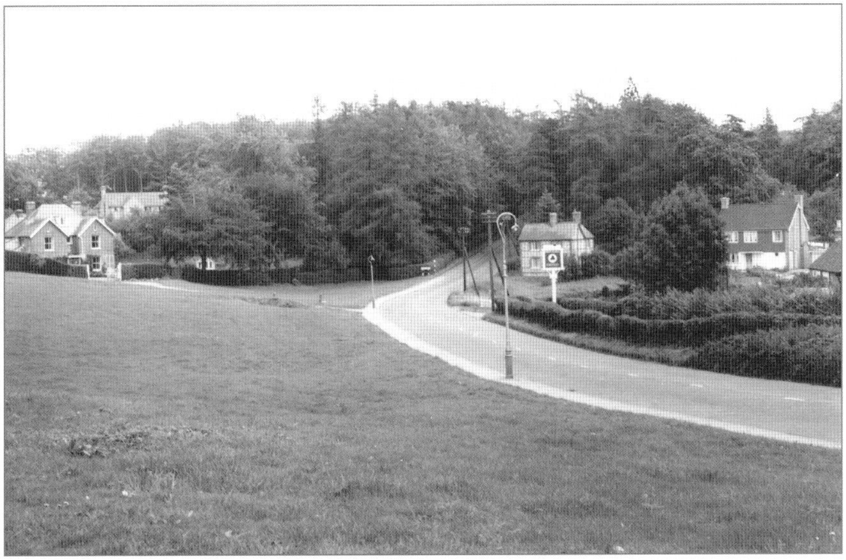

HAZLEMERE, *Terriers Green c1960* H470006

Climbing out of the Hughenden Valley eastwards onto the next ridge, we reach Terriers Green, north of High Wycombe on the Amersham Road, the A404. First noted in 1714 as 'Tarriers', it was a 'tarrying' or overnight resting place for sheep and cattle drovers, whose routes criss-crossed the Chilterns heading for local markets and London. In the dip to the right is the Beech Tree pub, its front garden now hedgeless. On the left the two-gabled house is Terriers Green, where in 1882 the great aeroplane maker Geoffrey de Havilland was born - his father was then the local vicar.

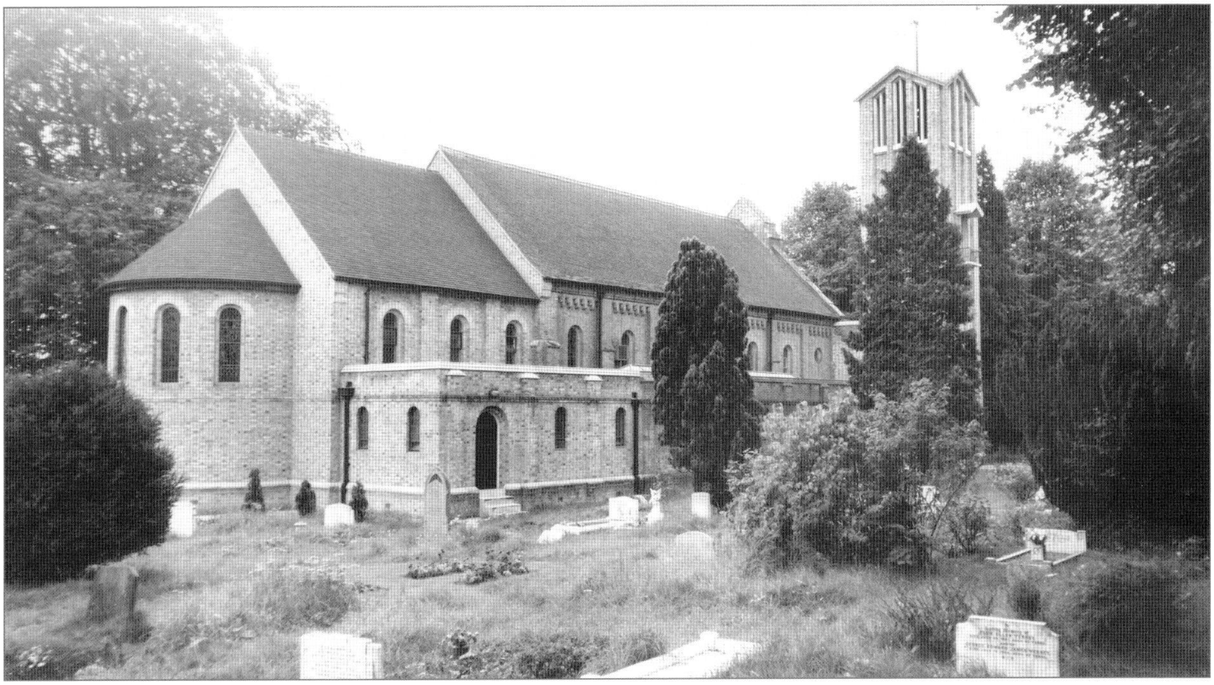

HAZLEMERE, *Holy Trinity Church c1960* H470002

Hazlemere was made a parish in 1845 to serve the small communities hemmed in by thick Chiltern plateau woodland, and it was provided with a yellow brick Romanesque-style church. In the 20th century, development swept north from High Wycombe and the church was progressively enlarged. In July 1938 the Bishop of Buckingham laid the foundation stone for the north aisle, partly hidden by conifers, and in the 1950s the chancel with its semi-circular apse was added, as well as the more exciting bell tower, seen here almost new. Since this view was taken, an octagonal parish room has been added (in 1978).

▼ **HAZLEMERE,** *Sandy Lane 1961* H470004

Protected from development by Green Belt status, the lanes and woods around Penn and east of Hazlemere survive little changed since the 19th century. The heavy, flinty clay soils of the plateau which cap the chalk lend themselves well to forestry, and there are extensive beech and oak woods here, as well as conifer plantations. Here the edge of the vast Penn Wood is on the right. The lane leads towards the Amersham to High Wycombe road, the A404, with the fields of Inkerman Farm on the left beyond the woods, now a golf course.

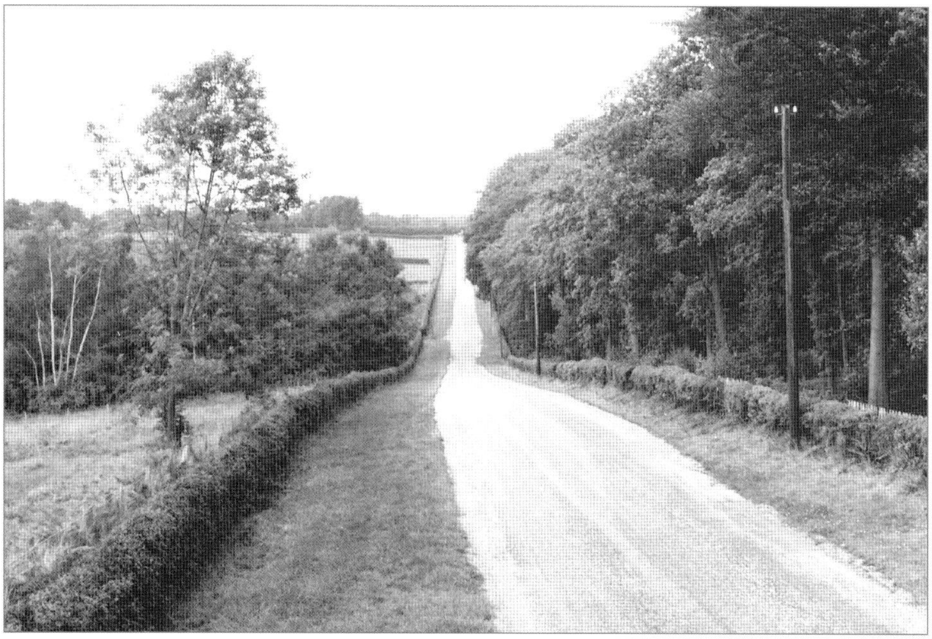

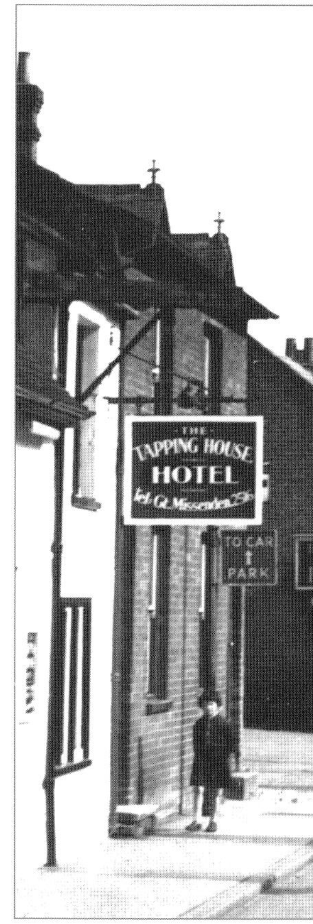

► **PRESTWOOD,** *Holy Trinity Church c1965* P281008

From Hazlemere we head north-east to Prestwood, whose parish church lies south of its 20th-century suburban growth which followed the opening of nearby Great Missenden railway station in 1892. Prestwood was created a parish in 1849, and the church complex is a delightful group on the west side of Wycombe Road: the church, the school (now the church hall), the school house (now Church Cottage) and the vicarage (flats since 1989). All were designed for the Frankland Russells of Chequers by Edward Buckton Lamb in 1848-50 – Lamb was Disraeli's architect at Hughenden Manor. The foreground is now the church car park.

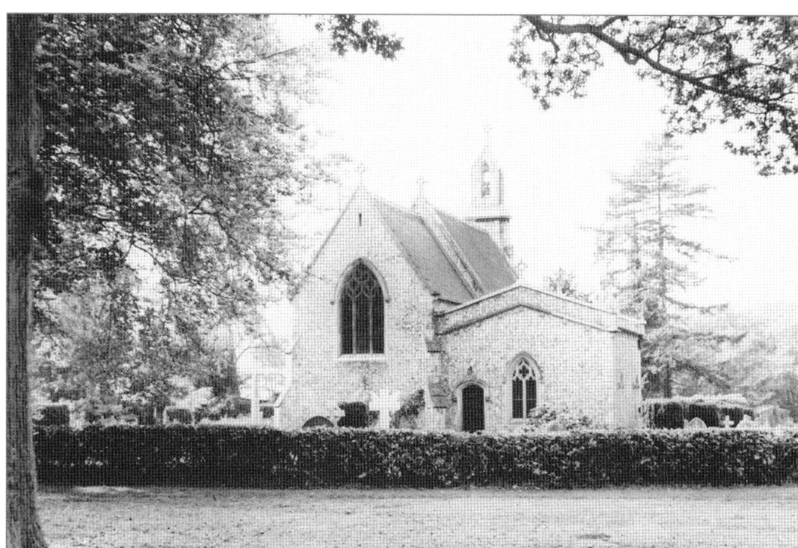

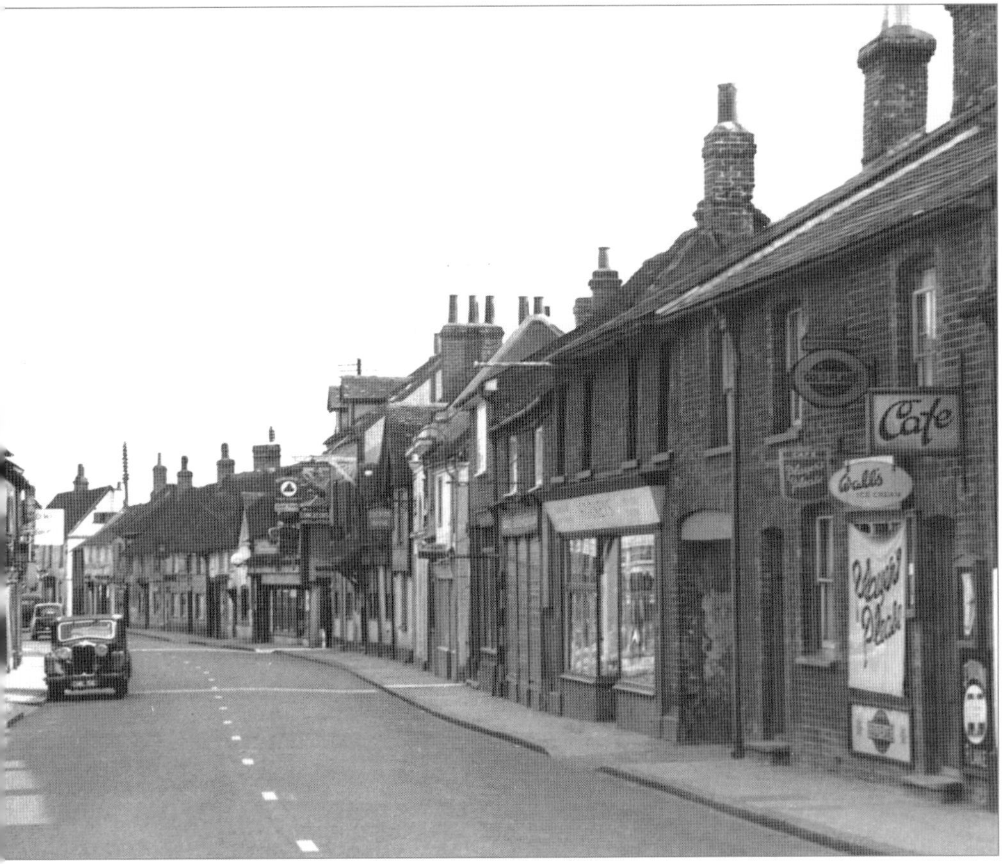

◄ **GREAT MISSENDEN**
High Street c1955
G241050

Descending from Prestwood into the valley of the River Misbourne, we reach Great Missenden, a town since the 1950s. It is by-passed by the A413 Aylesbury road, and its High Street traffic was calmed in the 1990s. This view looks south-east down the High Street, and captures well the back-of-pavement enclosed character of the town with its mix of timber-frames and 18th- and 19th-century brick fronts. The Tapping House Hotel has gone, rebuilt as a bank, and the White Lion beyond was rebuilt further back in the 1930s.

► **GREAT MISSENDEN**
High Street 1952 G241026

Frith's photographer now looks north-west, with the Station Approach turning on the left - this leads to the station, which opened in 1892. It is odd that Great Missenden itself did not grow much; perhaps this is owing to its valley location. Its main suburbs climb uphill towards Prestwood. The terrace on the right has since been rebuilt, but the Cross Keys opposite remains, and has incorporated the shop. Gilbert's (left) has long gone, while the fine Baptist Church of 1838 set back behind the left-hand gate pier thrives, as does the 1890s post office, the tall building beyond the pub.

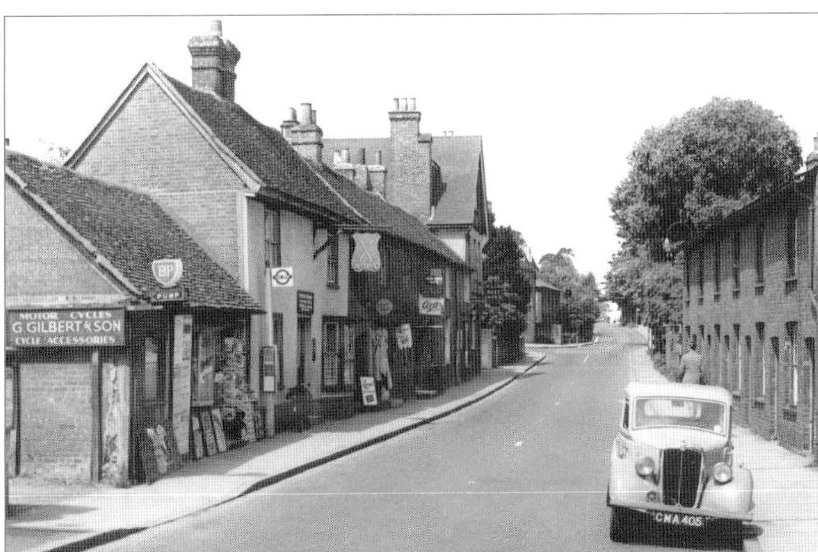

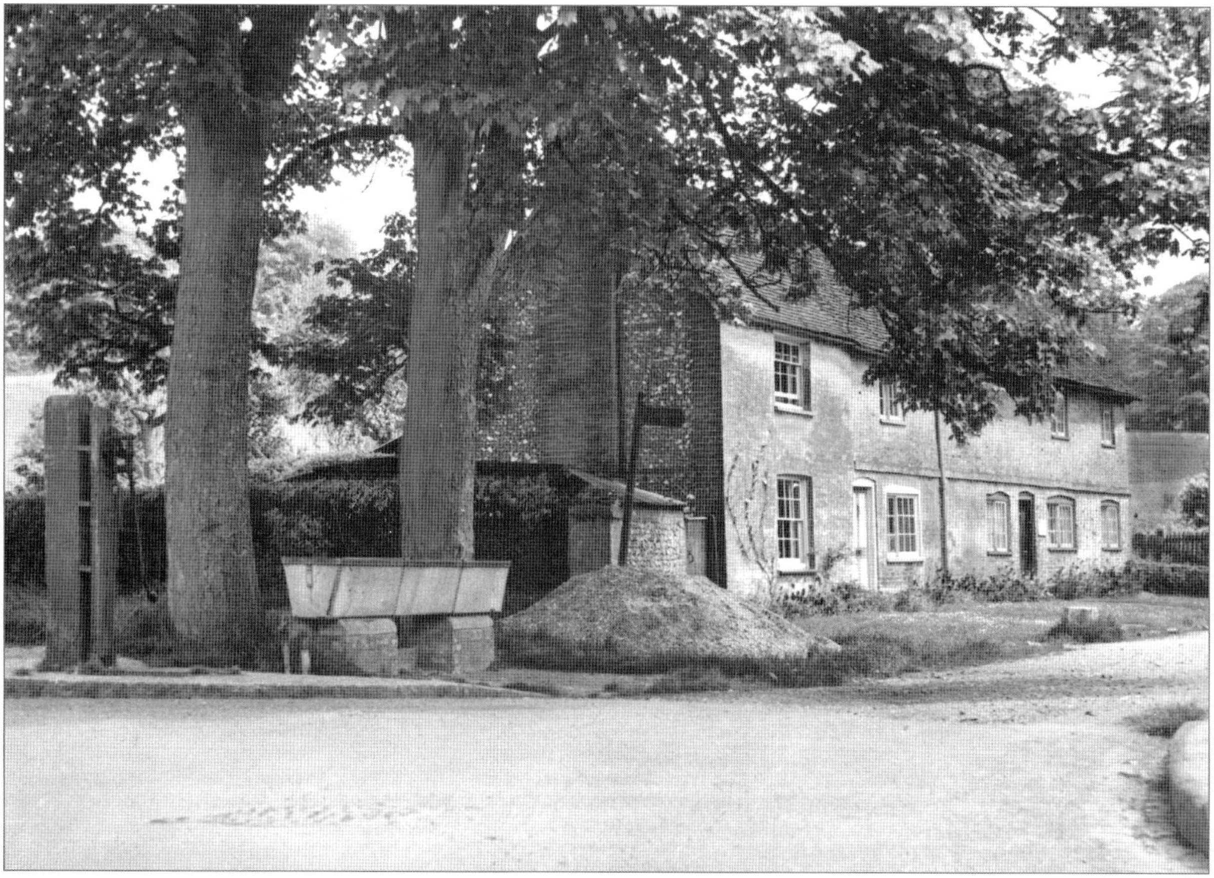

GREAT MISSENDEN, *The Old Pump and the Cottages c1955*
G241030

The delightful, winding Church Street runs east of the High Street, past the much altered former gatehouse to the Abbey and Abbey Farmhouse, to a green in front of the Victorian school. Church Lane bears right past these cottages, The Pound and Close Cottage, uphill to the isolated parish church. Behind the cottages is the by-pass, and Church Lane now crosses it on a high bridge, so the view is somewhat less rural. The drinking trough remains, but the parish pump has long gone.

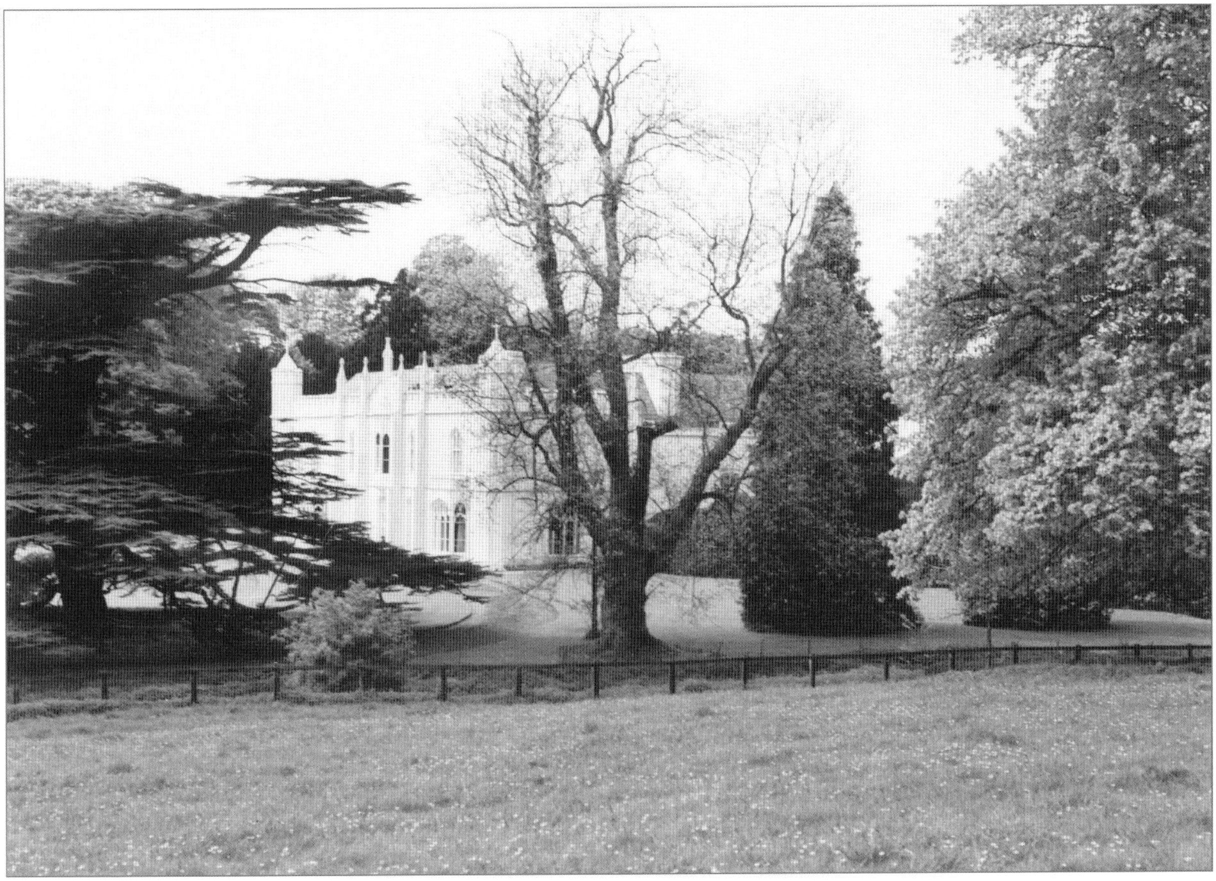

GREAT MISSENDEN, *The Abbey c1955* G241037

Great Missenden grew up at the gates of Missenden Abbey, founded in 1133 by William de Missenden. Dissolved under Henry VIII in 1538, some of its buildings survived to become a mansion; it incorporated some of the monastic buildings around the cloister, although the abbey church was totally demolished. There was a superb 15th-century roof to the dorter, but all this was destroyed by fire in 1985. Now a college and conference centre, the building was carefully restored. This view is now obscured by planting in the foreground to protect the Abbey from the embankment of Church Lane as it climbs to cross the by-pass.

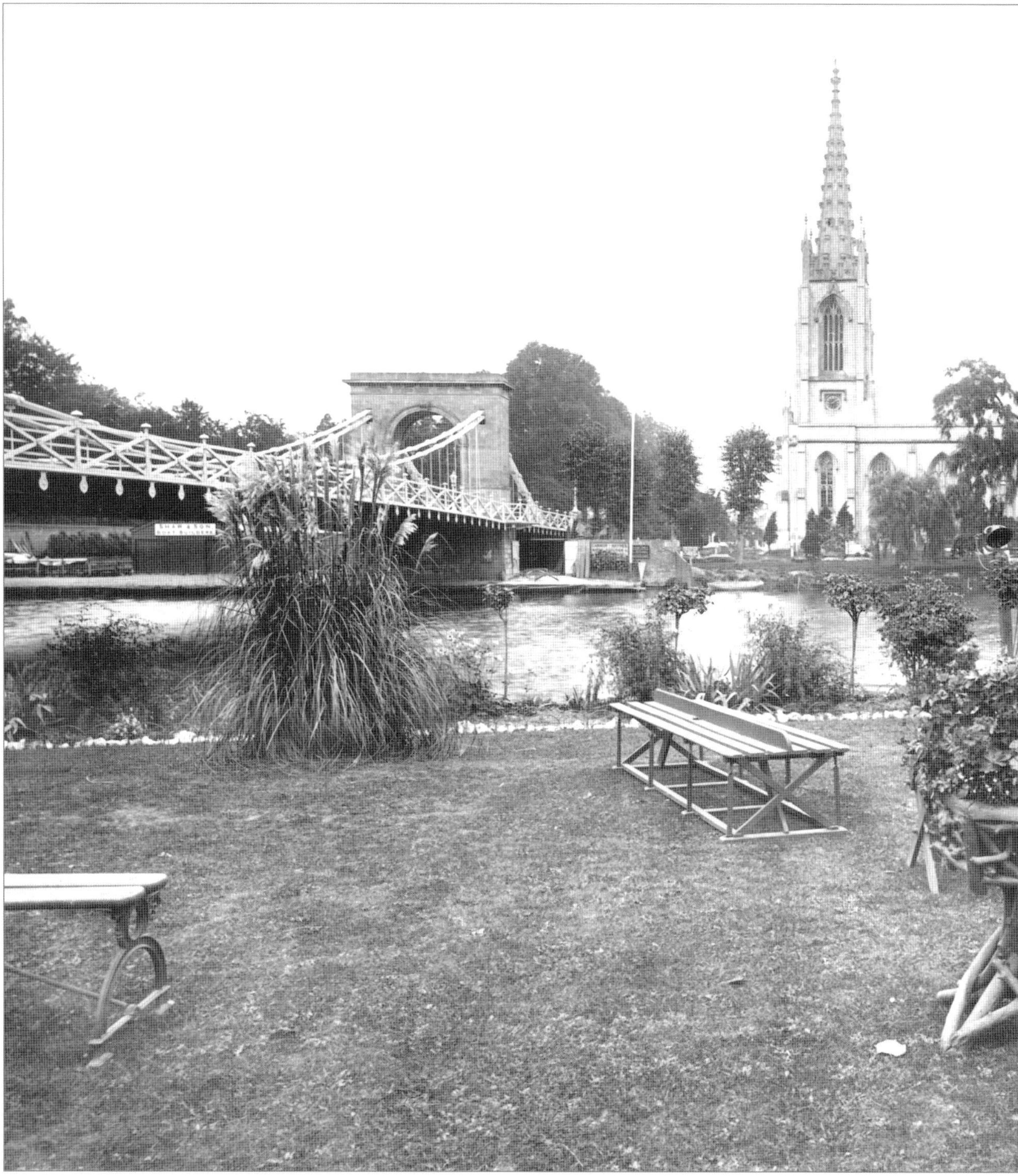

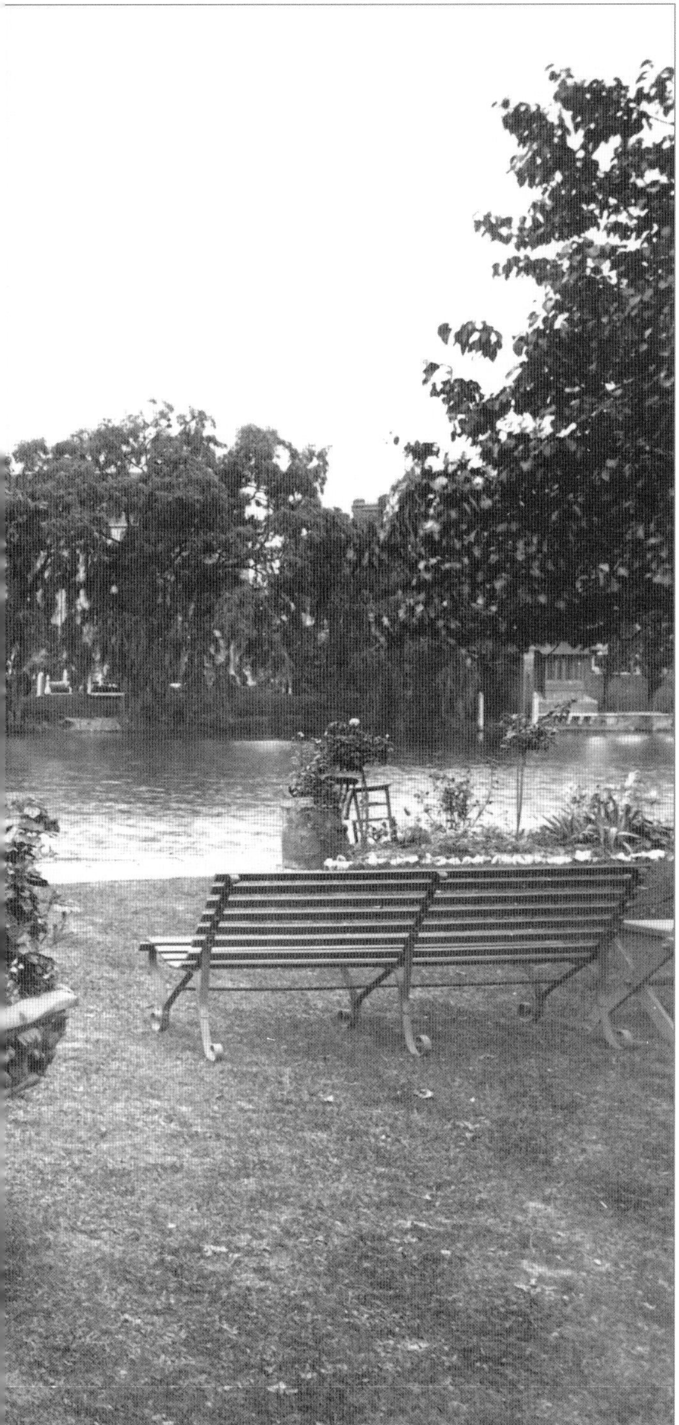

MARLOW AND THE THAMES VALLEY

MARLOW, *The Church and the Bridge 1890*
23674

This tour starts in the delightful and popular riverside town of Marlow, here seen from the Berkshire bank of the River Thames within the gardens of the Compleat Angler Hotel. At the left is the fine suspension bridge, which was designed by William Tierney Clark and opened in 1832. In 1860 it was widened by the footways on each side, and it was thoroughly repaired and restored in 2002. The church of All Saints replaced a medieval one that had partially collapsed in 1831. Here we see it with its original very knobbly 1830s spire, which was replaced in 1898.

MARLOW
The Boat Yard 1890
23678

Now on the suspension bridge, Frith's photographer is looking north-west across Shaw and Son's boatyard. The trees behind the houses are in the grounds of the mid 18th-century Court Garden House, now a public park, Higginson Park. The left-hand house has been replaced by a white rendered block of flats, Dunstable House, but the other two survive, albeit somewhat altered. To the right there used to be a great 13th-century stone barn, probably a tithe barn for nearby Bisham Abbey; it was demolished in 1862, and its site is now occupied by Tierney Court, good flats of 1972.

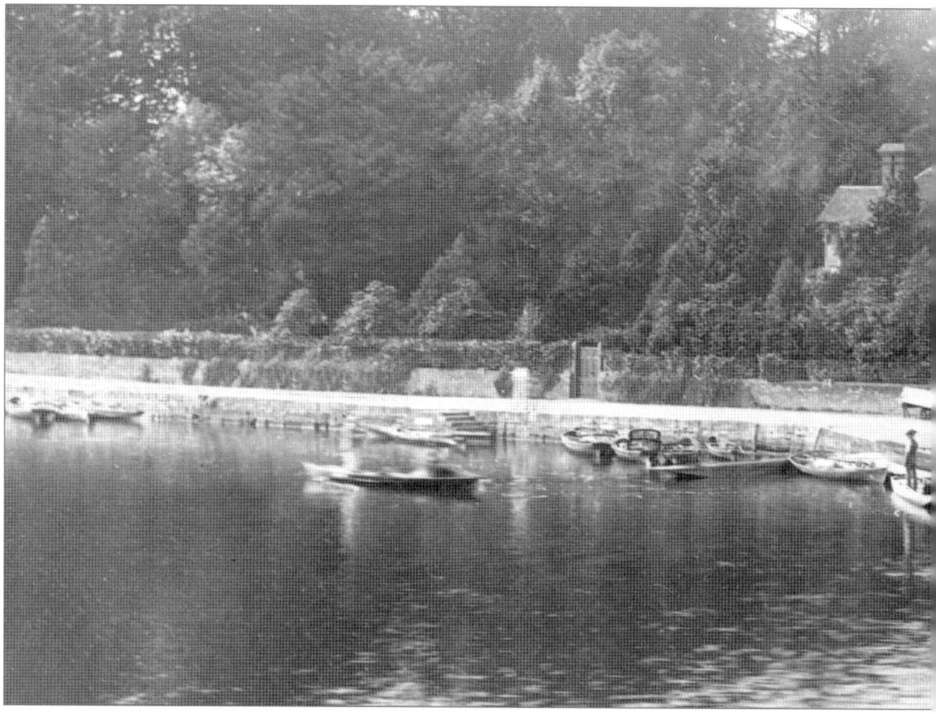

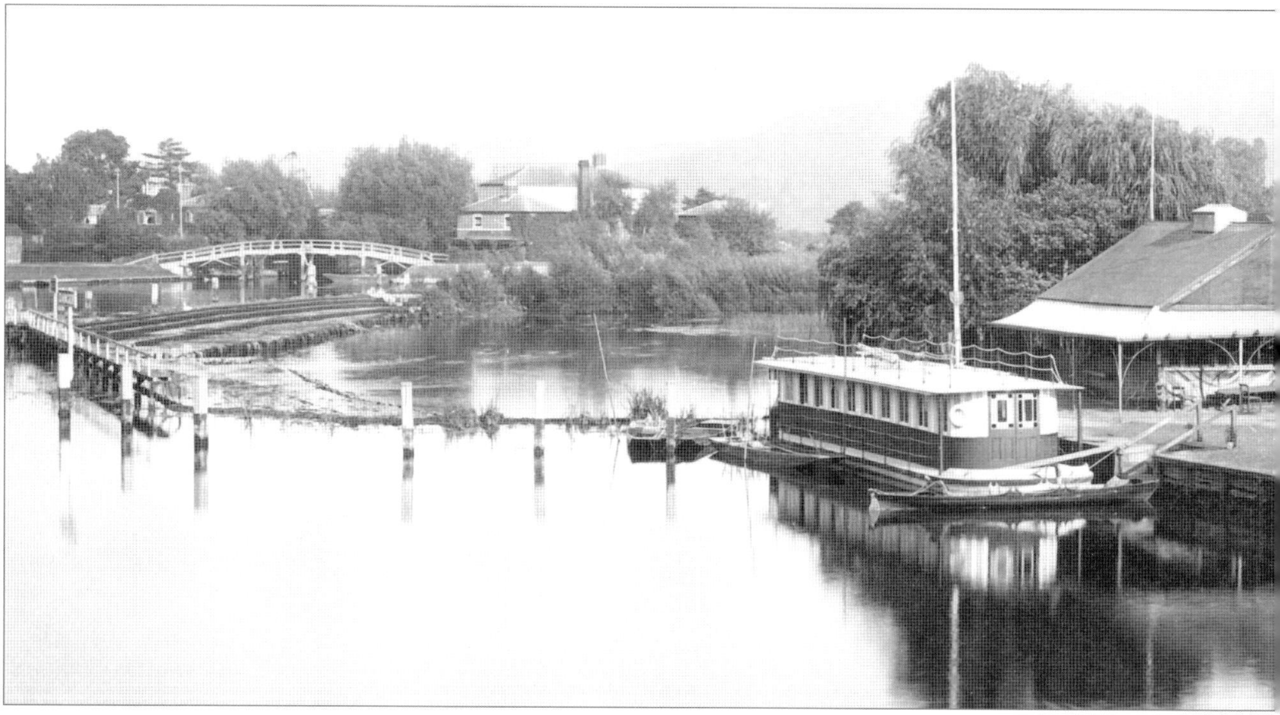

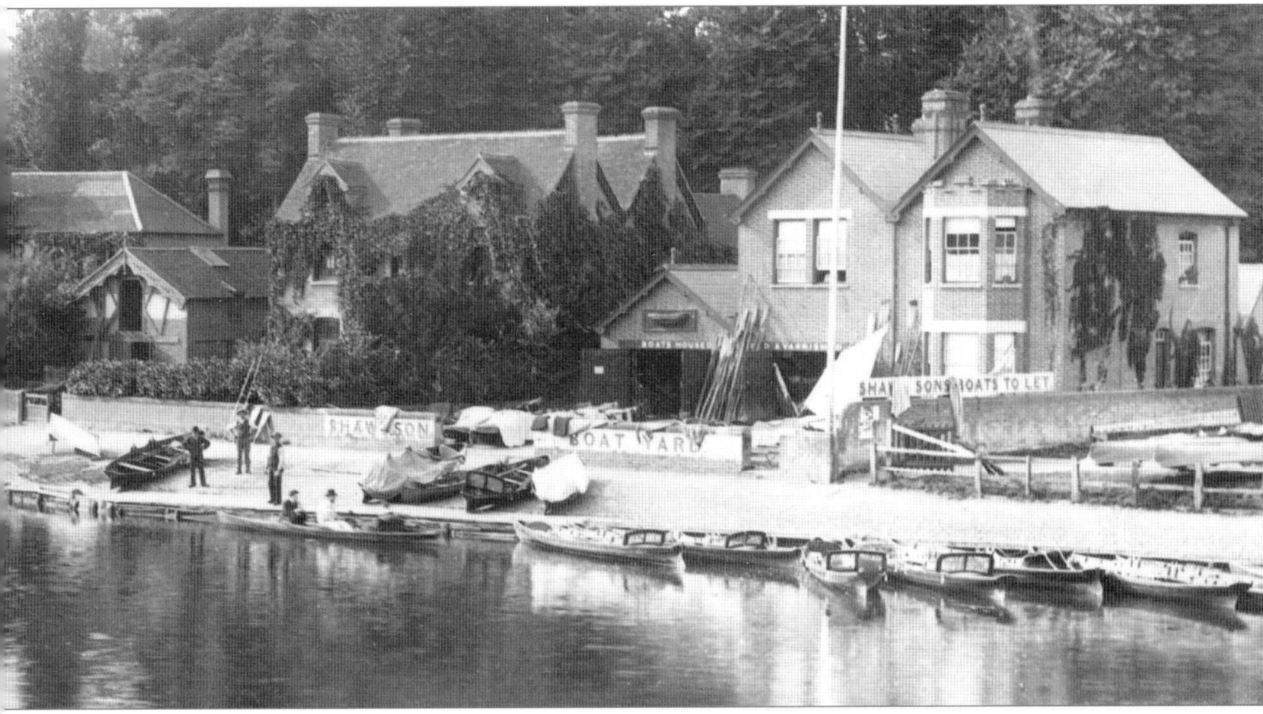

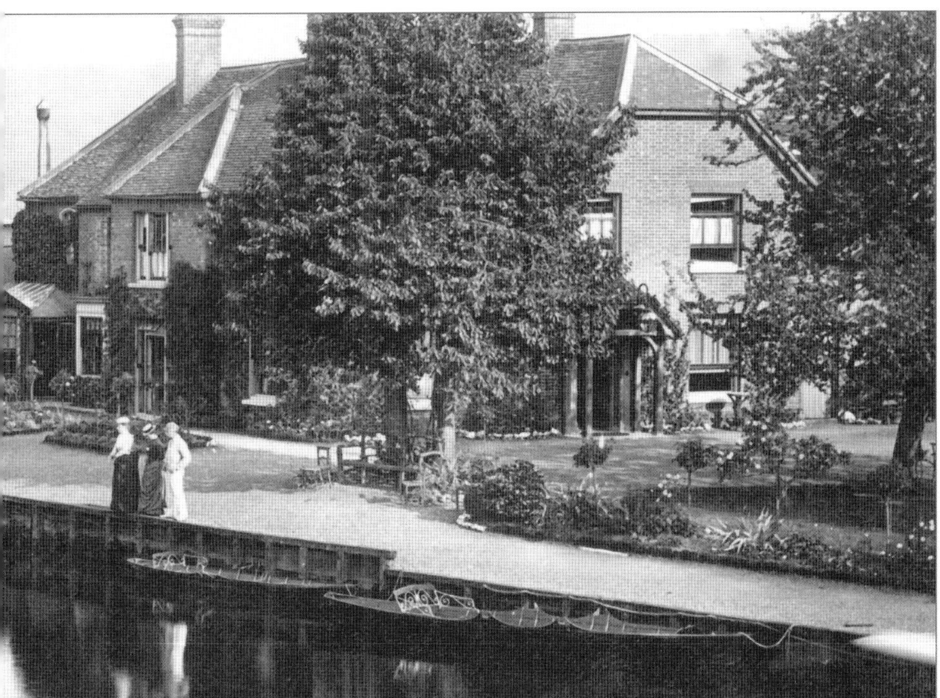

MARLOW

The Compleat Angler Hotel 1890 23679

Now looking south-west from the suspension bridge, the photographer looks into the gardens of the Compleat Angler Hotel, nowadays much enlarged, with conservatories and dining rooms replacing the single-storey structure to take advantage of the superb riverside views. The medieval bridge crossed here from Marlow's St Peter Street, so the road passed on the other side of the hotel. The bridge was renewed in 1789, and then replaced by the suspension bridge on a site further west. To the left we can see the weir and a footbridge (since rebuilt) leading to Lock Island.

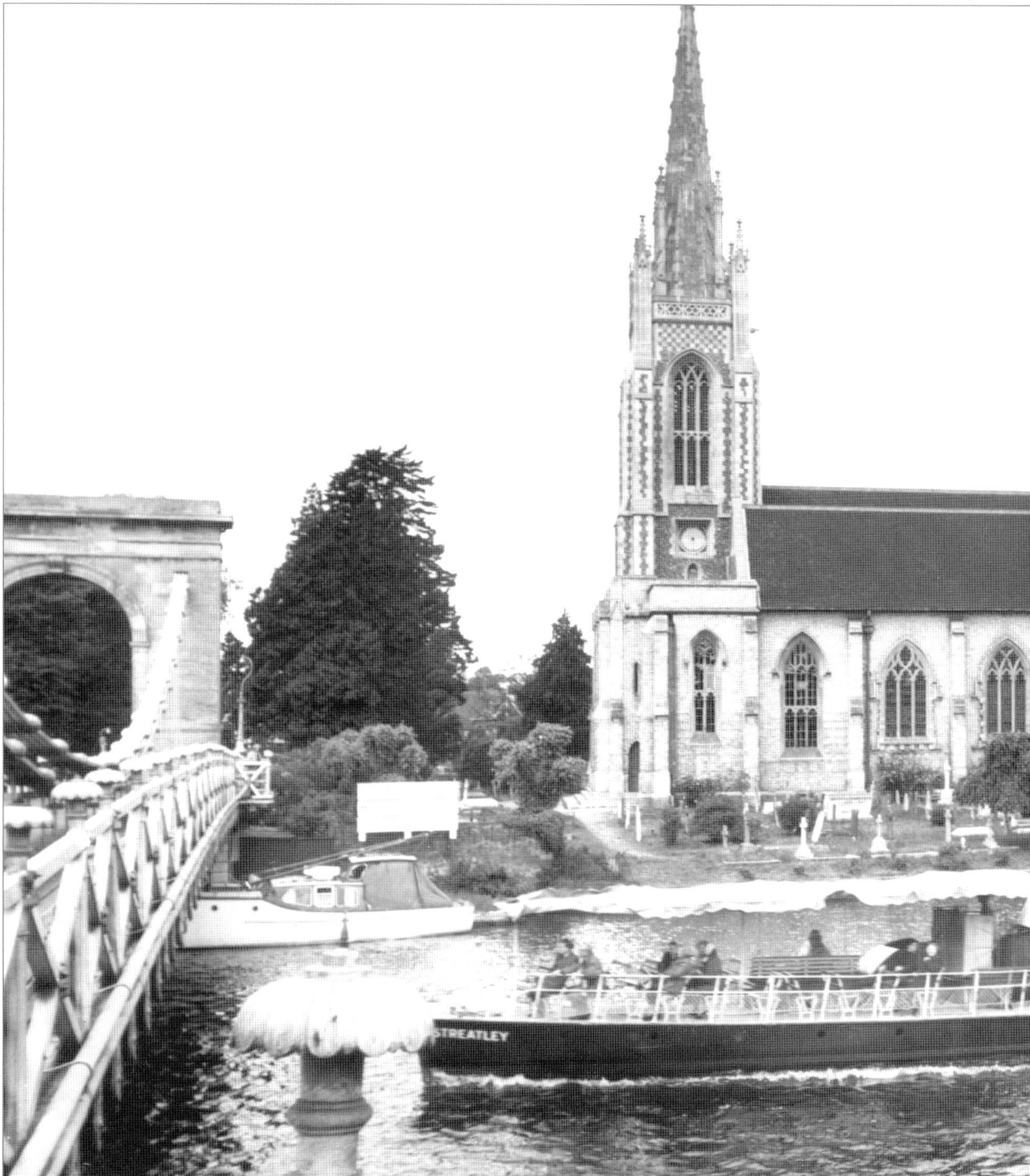
STREATLEY

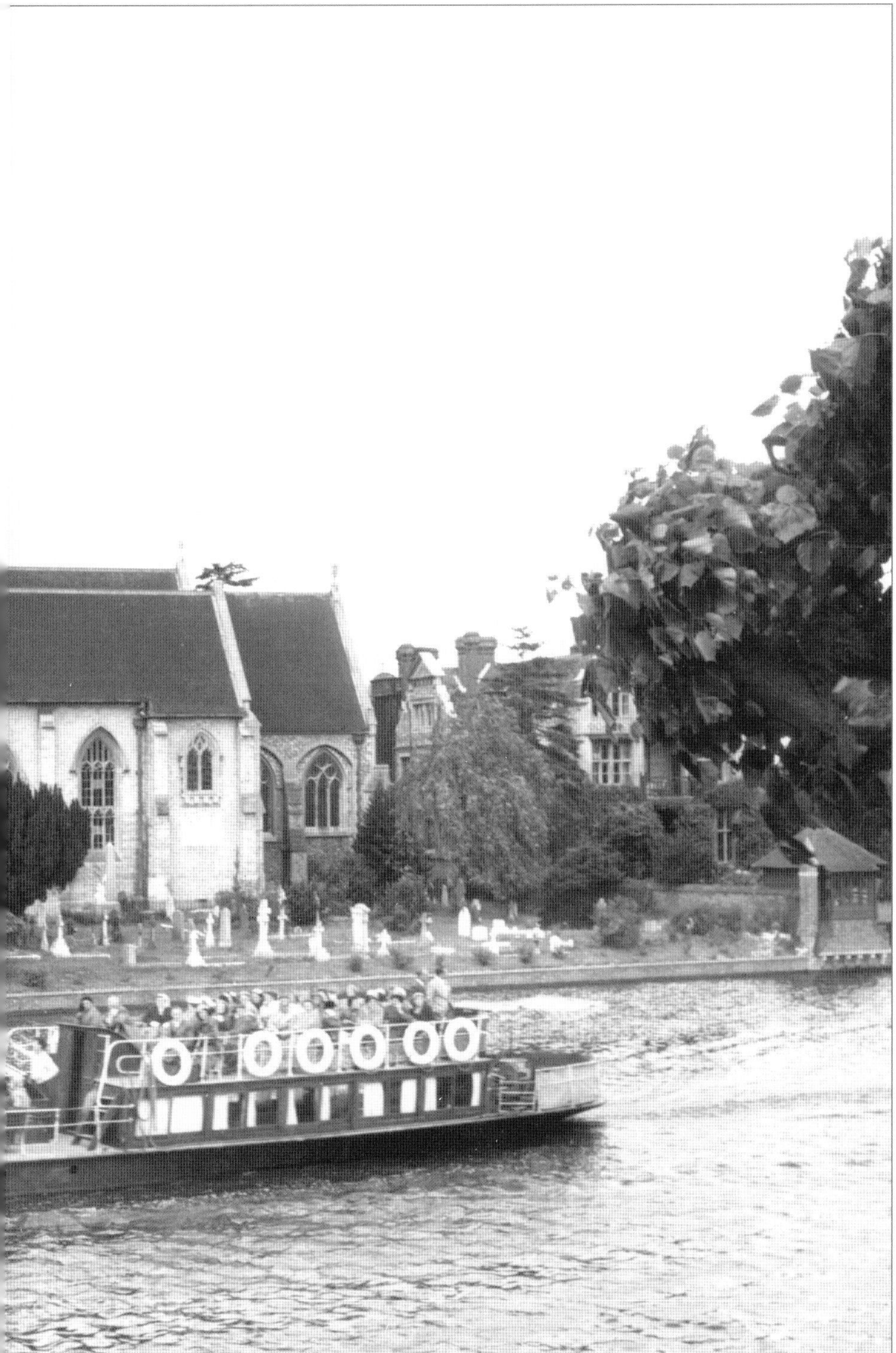

MARLOW, *The Church c1955* M35045

We have moved on to more recent times. This view, also taken from the suspension bridge, looks past the steam launch 'Streatley' towards the churchyard. The church was built in 1832 in brick, replacing the decrepit medieval one, but it was extensively reworked to bring it into more 'correct' Victorian taste, and a chancel was added. Internally it was completely recast, while outside new windows were inserted; but the intended flint skin for the whole exterior was never completed. The original 1830s spire, seen in view 23674, was replaced by this less knobbly one by John Oldrid Scott in 1899.

▼ **MARLOW,** *High Street c1955* M35015

Marlow's fine High Street runs north from the river. Many of the Georgian and later brick fronts conceal medieval and Tudor timber-framed houses built when the town was an important market and river port town, similar to Henley further upstream. On the right the buildings between the bracket clock and the chequerboard sign were demolished (apart from the one with window blinds and bay windows) and replaced by blander terraces, but on the left the two big houses have had their forecourts with iron railings reinstated in the 1990s.

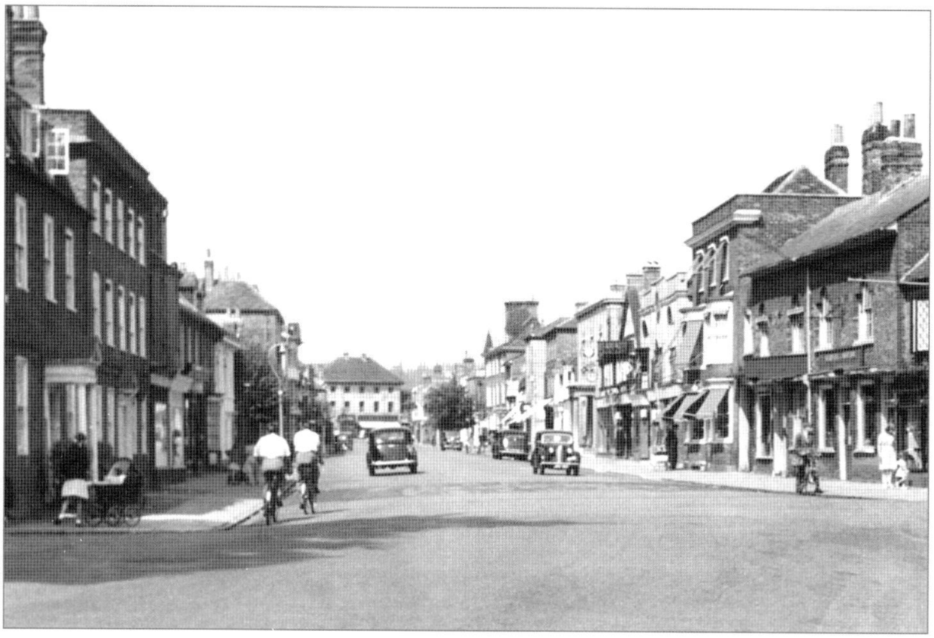

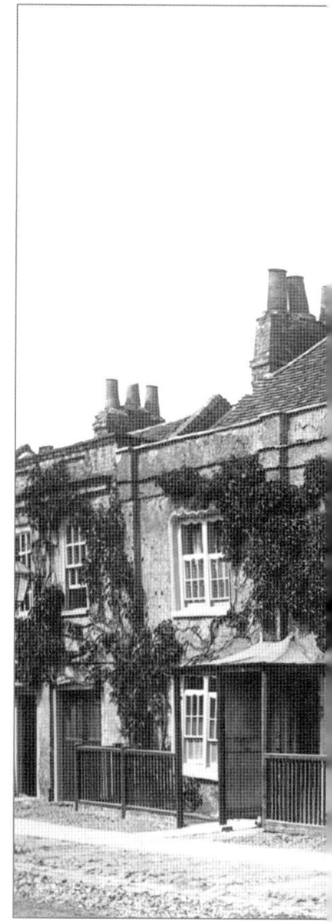

► **MARLOW,** *High Street c1965* M35119

Further north along the High Street is the 17th-century timber-framed Chequers Hotel (right). Beyond it we can see the pediment of Cromwell House, a fine mid 18th-century Georgian house that was for years the town's post office; since the 1990s it has been a fashionable clothes shop. In the distance is the hipped roof of the former Crown Hotel, now a Boots shop. Immediately to its left is the Town Hall, a stone building by James Wyatt of 1807, and now the Crown, which took it over before the middle of the 19th century.

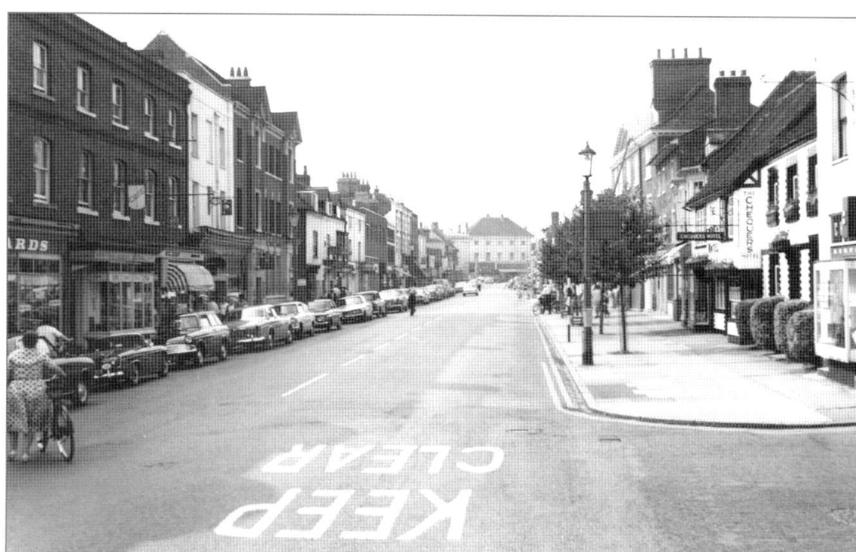

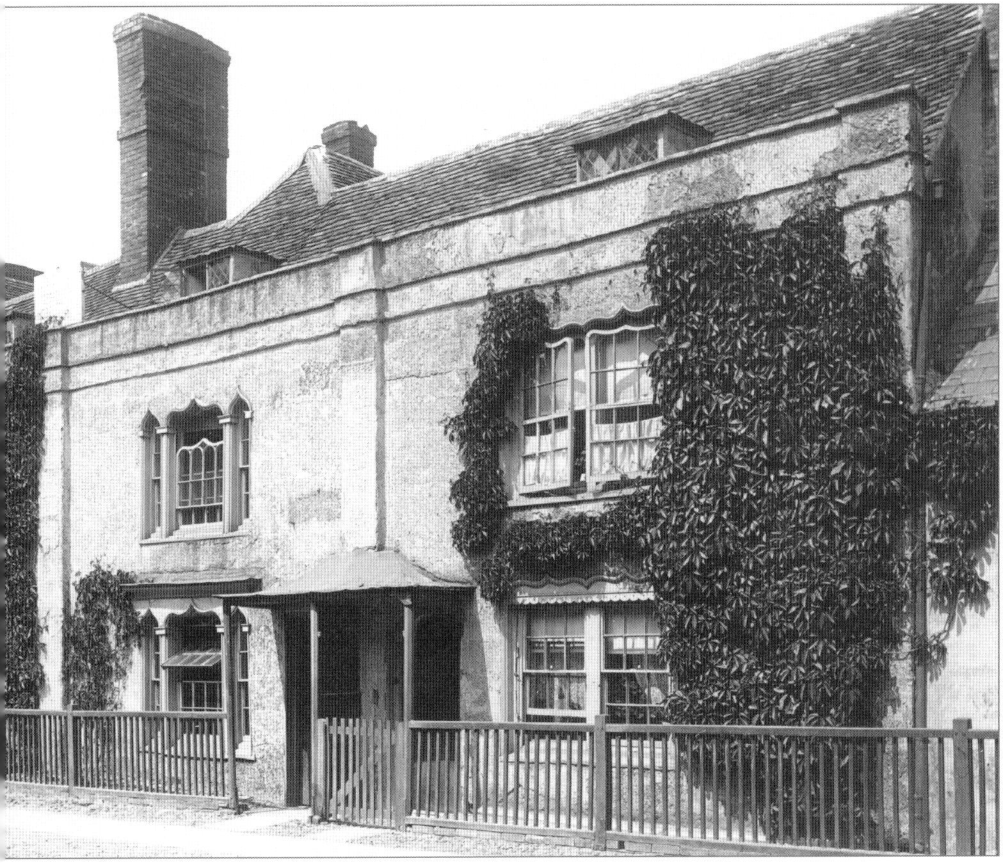

MARLOW
Shelley House, West Street 1893 31744

Turning left and west out of the High Street into West Street, the best street of the town architecturally, we reach at its west end Shelley House. This Gothick-fronted range, now subdivided into four houses, was rented by Percy Bysshe and Mary Shelley from March 1817 until February 1818; this was where Mary re-wrote and prepared her great horror novel 'Frankenstein' for publication. In 1893 the house looks run down, but the commemorative plaque installed on the parapet below the chimney in 1867 by the lord of the manor, Sir William Clayton, still looks fresh.

MARLOW
The Borlase Grammar School, West Street 1893 31745

Immediately to the west of Shelley House is the Borlase Grammar School, founded as a free school by Sir William Borlase, MP for Marlow, in 1624. The flint section with the three-storey porch is from the 1620s (the door is blocked), and beyond is a range built in 1892. The bays on the right are mid-19th century, and were rebuilt in grander flint and brick style in 1902, less than ten years after this view was taken. The school is now one of Buckinghamshire's leading grammar schools. Its street front was lengthened in the 1990s with a further very good flint and brick range.

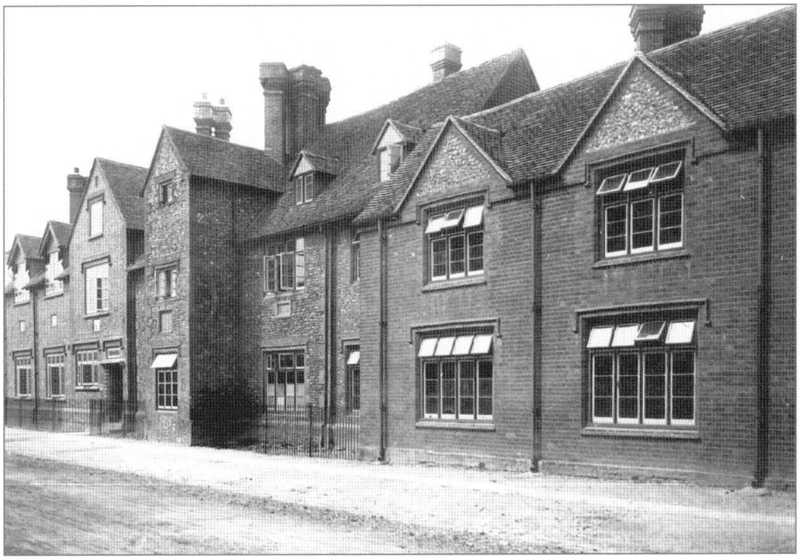

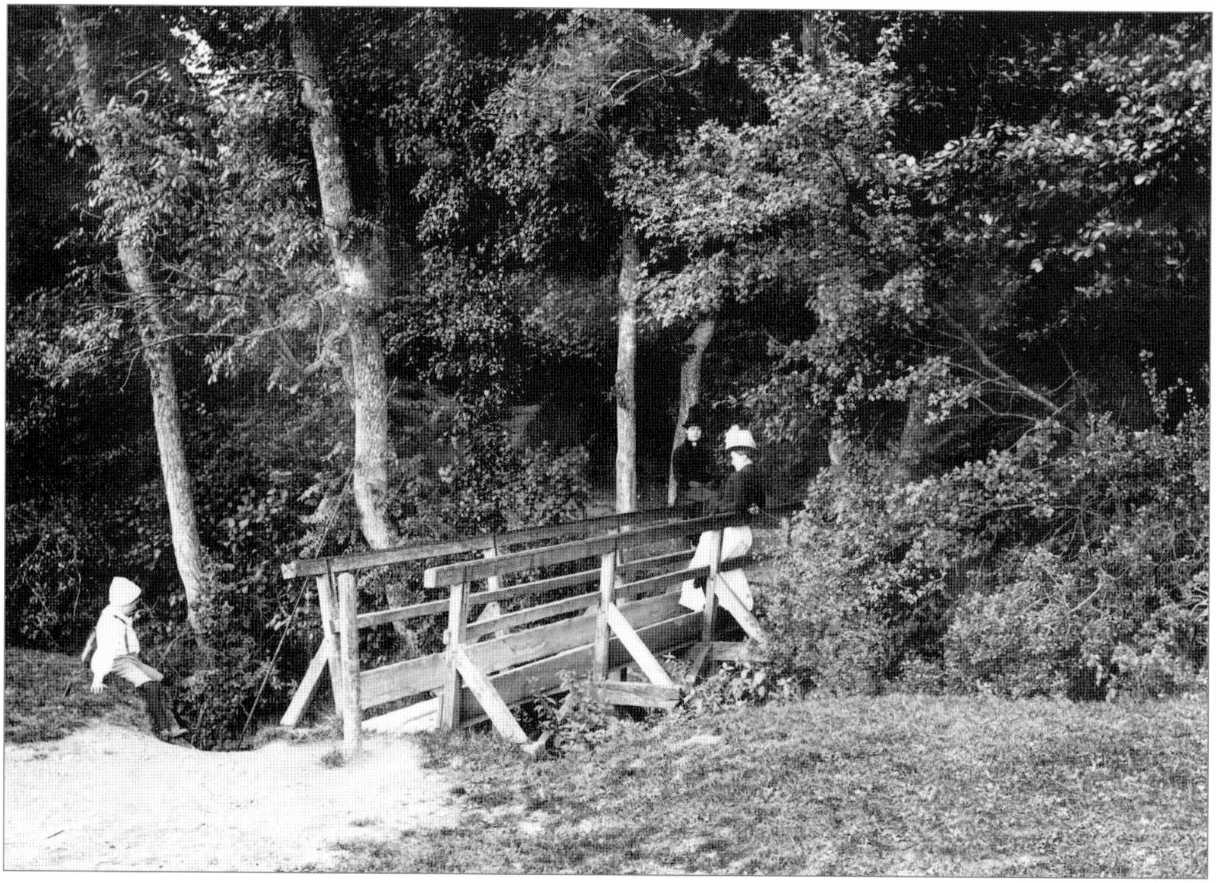

MARLOW, *Quarry Woods and the Rustic Bridge 1890* 23693

Frith's photographer has re-crossed the river Thames onto the Berkshire bank to Quarry Woods. These woods cloak the chalk ridge that rises steeply over 200 feet from the Thames valley flood plain. These woods and Bisham Woods, together with Winter Hill, were (and still are) popular with strollers and walkers. This view is from the meadow across one of the footbridges over the stream, giving access to the woodland paths. Close behind the camera is now the site of the Marlow Bypass, which relieved the old town of much of its north-south through traffic.

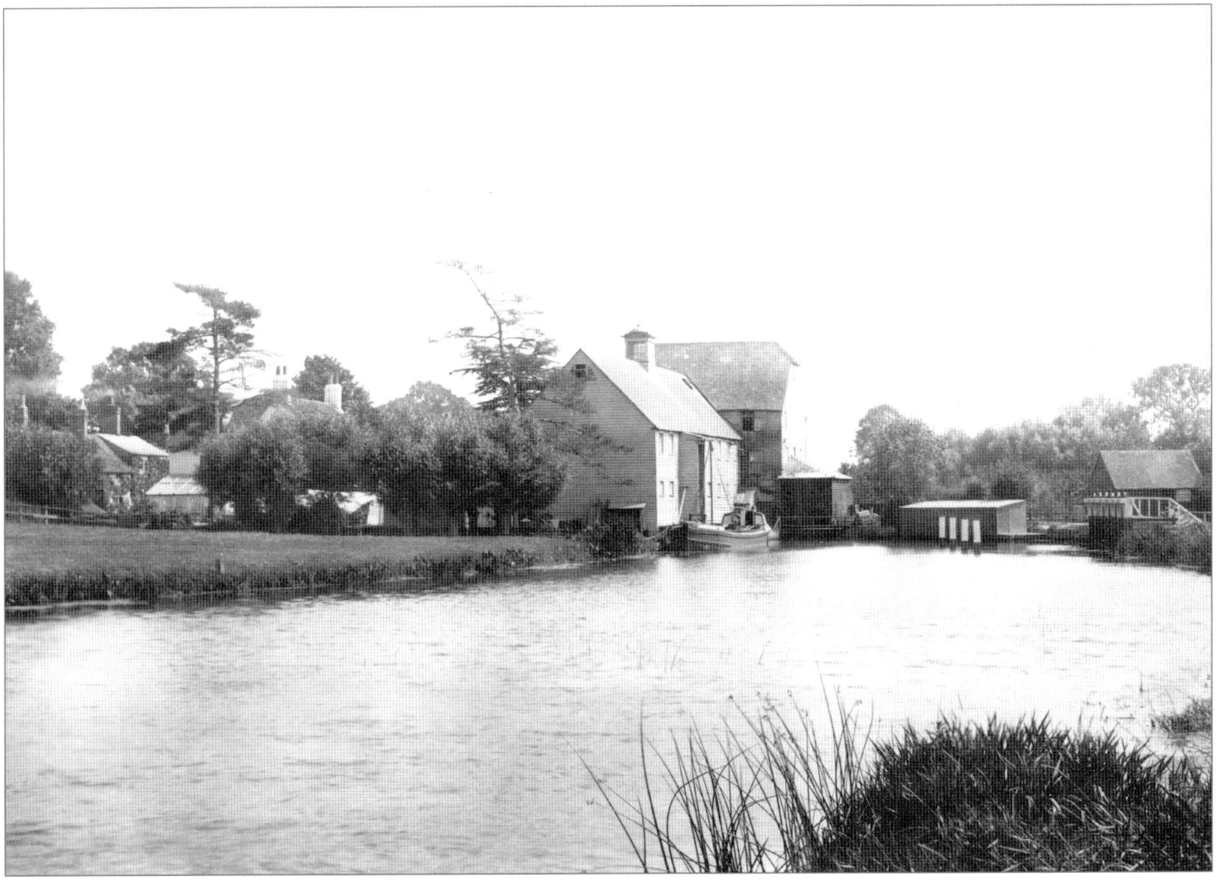

HAMBLEDEN, *The Mill 1890* 27221

West of Marlow we reach the beautiful Hambleden Valley, one of the county's main scenic delights; through it the Hambleden Brook, a winterbourne, flows to the Thames beyond the water mill. In 1890 the mill (the taller part beyond is 18th-century, the nearer and lower part with the cupola 19th-century) was grinding corn, and it carried on doing so until 1952, but in the 1980s it was converted into flats. The mill house's chimney-stacks rise to the left, and the river bank is more domesticated as gardens, while to the right is the start of the weir, the location for the climax of many 1950s and 1960s English films.

▼ HAMBLEDEN, *The Lock 1890* 27217

A little to the west of the water mill the weir is by-passed by Hambleden Lock, actually entirely within the Berkshire county boundary. The pound lock replaced a dangerous flash lock, the predecessor of modern locks: it had only one gate, and boats were 'flashed' through, or hauled upstream by a windlass. First installed in 1773, the lock has been reconstructed many times, most recently in 1993. The lock keeper's house we see here was rebuilt by the Thames Conservancy in 1928, long after this view was taken.

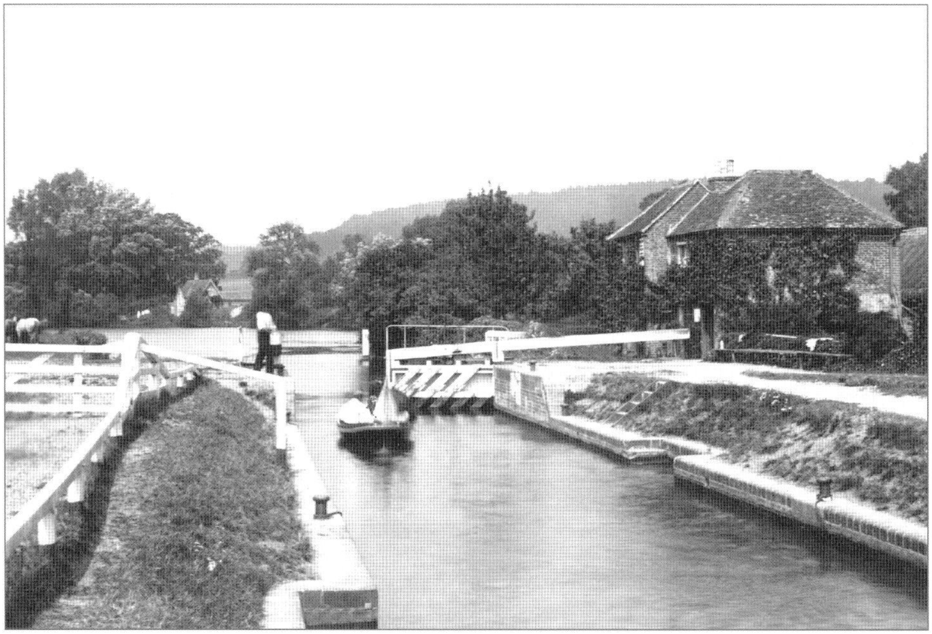

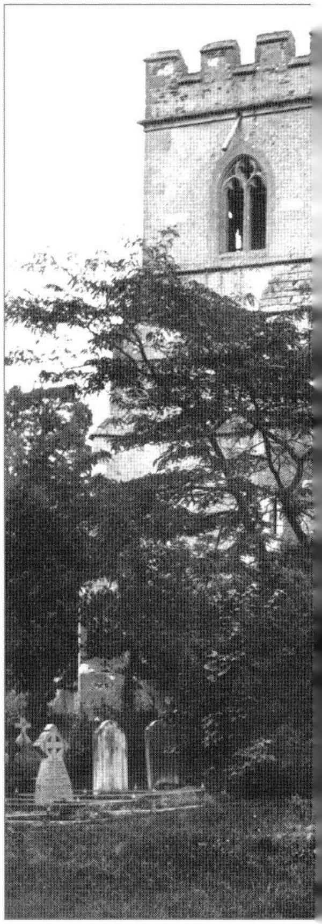

► HAMBLEDEN, *Eddying Waters 1890* 27216

The lock by-passed the weir, whose turbulent waters are good training for white-water canoeing or kayaking; on most weekends, canoeists cut in and out of the dangerous-looking waters watched by visitors. This 1890 view looks eastwards from the weir walkway, with the lock away to the right; it is typical of the rather fine views of natural phenomena taken by Frith's roving photographers, here dramatically, if somewhat inaccurately, entitled 'Eddying Waters'.

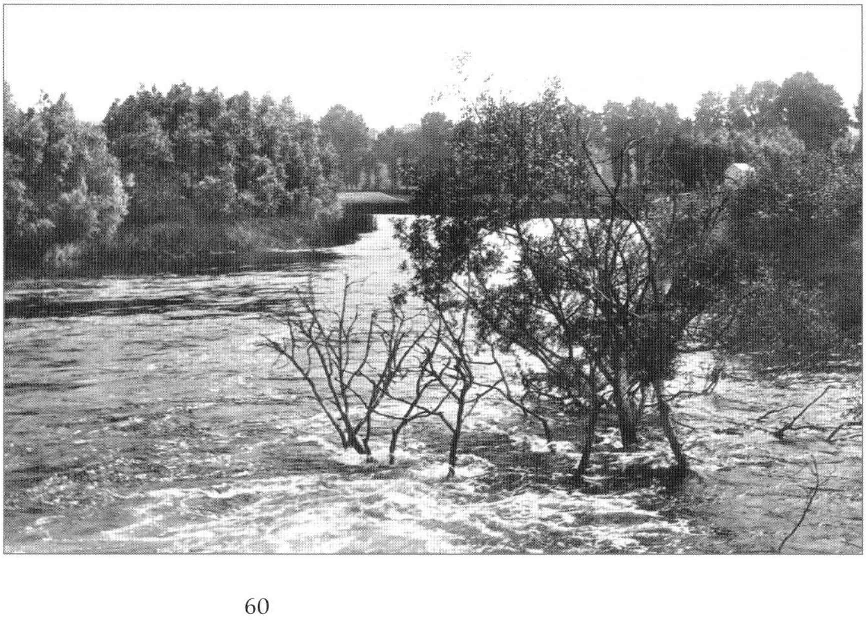

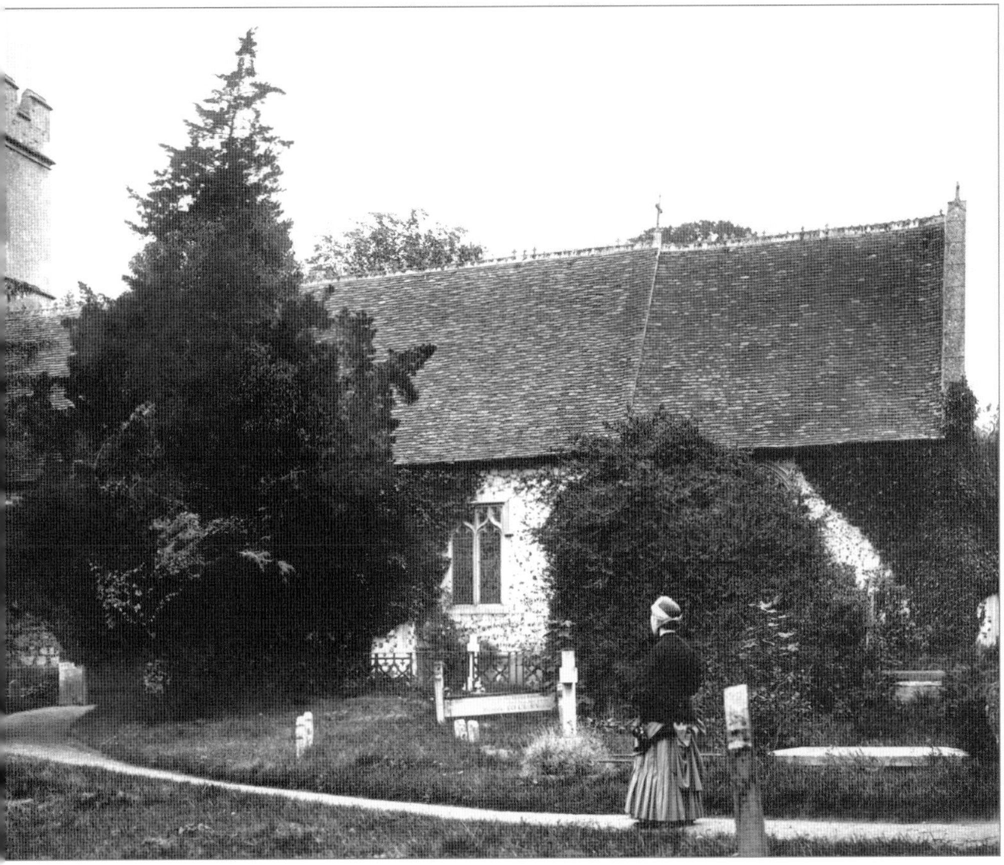

◄ **MEDMENHAM**
The Church 1890
23712

Halfway between Hambleden and Marlow, also on the River Thames, we pass through the village of Medmenham. Its church stands by the main Henley Road at the north end of the village, at the junction with Ferry Lane which leads south to the river. The ferry is long gone, of course, but the church survives in good heart; it is easier to see nowadays, for most of the trees have gone since 1890. The 15th-century tower was re-rendered in 1987, and the roofs were retiled soon after, but in this view we only get glimpses of the flint and chalk block walls of the church.

► **MEDMENHAM,** *The Church, the Interior 1890* 23713

The church was heavily restored by the lords of the manor, the Scott-Murrays of nearby Danesfield, most notably in 1839, when the earlier windows were replaced by more 'correct' ones. The woodwork, including the pews, was entirely replaced between then and 1876, apart from the 17th-century roof. A World War II bomb falling nearby destroyed the east window glass we see in this view. The present anaemic east window that replaced it is by Christopher Powell. The organ gallery has now gone, and the walls are more cheerfully whitewashed.

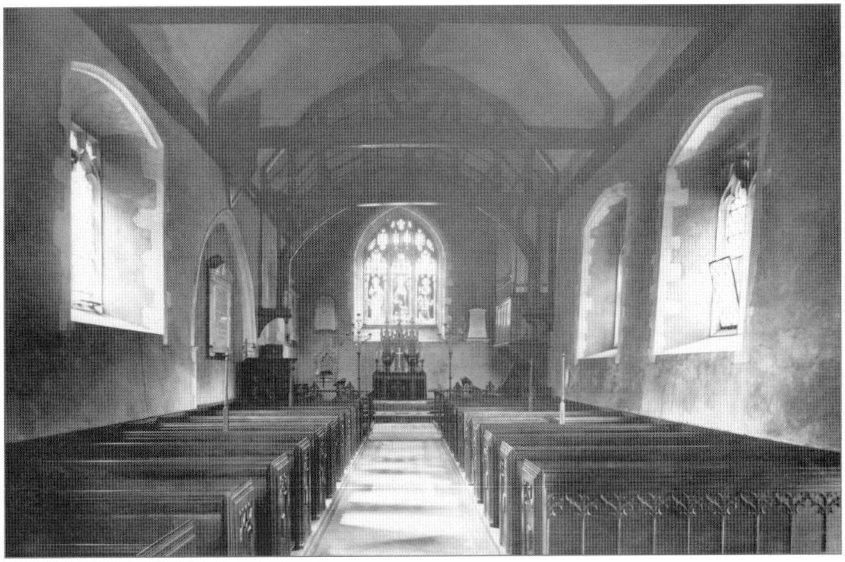

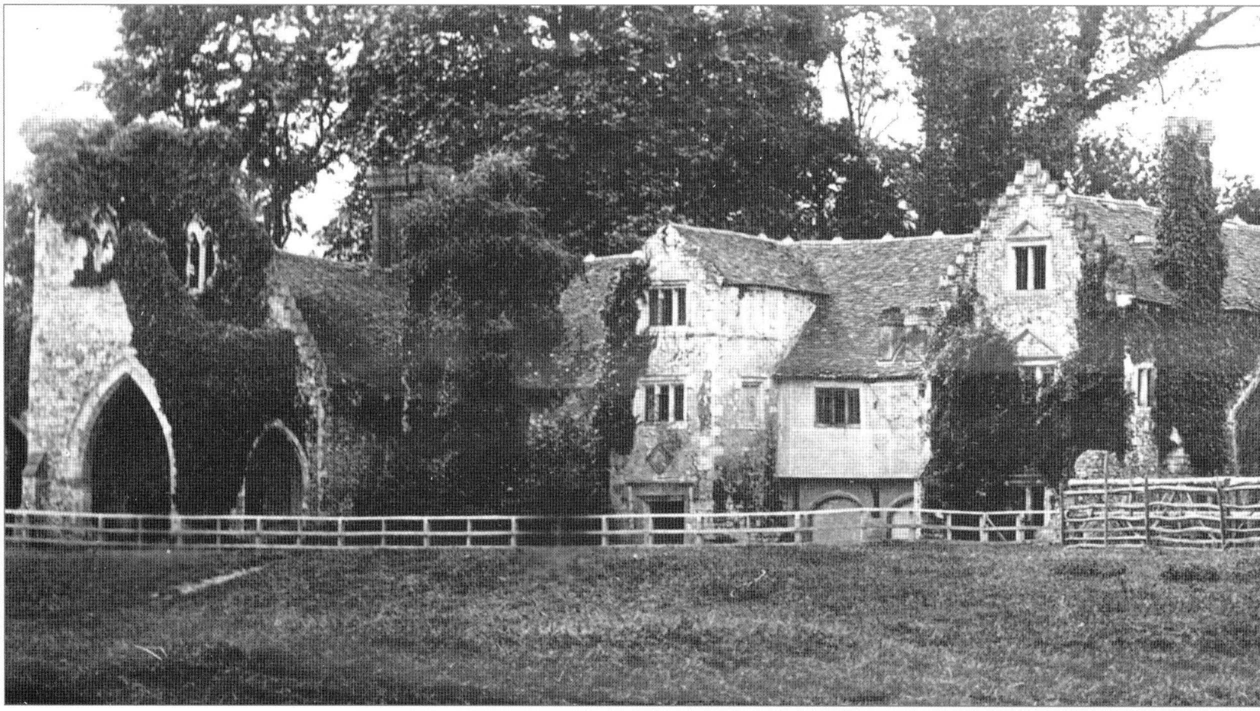

MEDMENHAM
The Abbey 1890 23715

Frith's photographer is now looking towards the abbey from the Berkshire bank of the River Thames, presumably having crossed on the now defunct ferry. The gardens extend to the right, and the house was enlarged to the left by Romaine Walker in the late 1890s, soon after this view was taken. The abbey achieved notoriety in the 18th century when it was rented by Sir Francis Dashwood of West Wycombe and used by his friends for the semi-blasphemous Order of St Francis of Wycombe, normally known as the Hell-Fire Club, who behaved like caricature Georgian rakehells. Their motto, 'Fay Ce Que Voudras', 'do what you will', sums up their approach, and is inscribed over the main doorway.

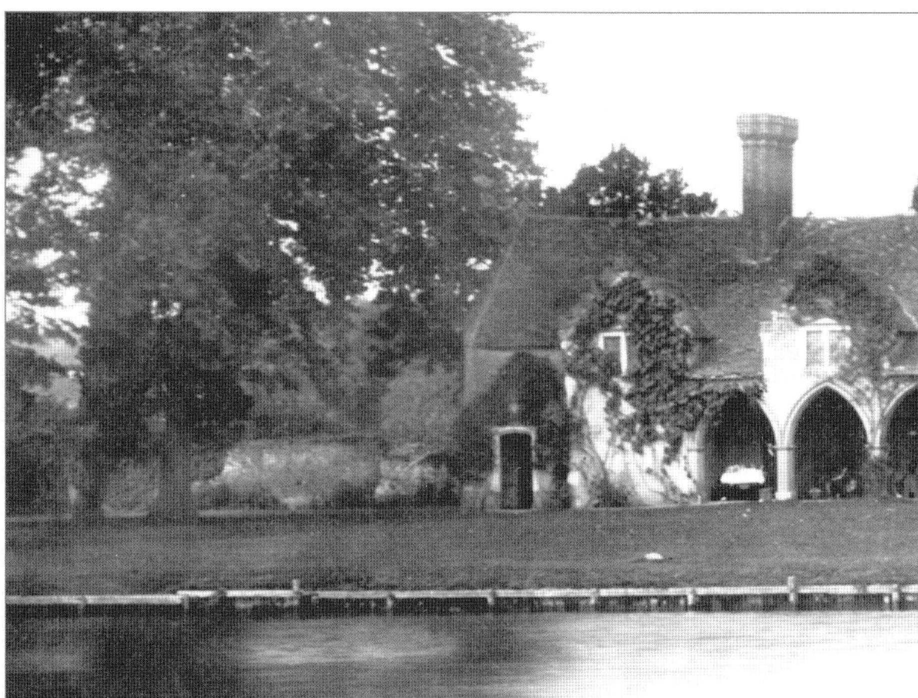

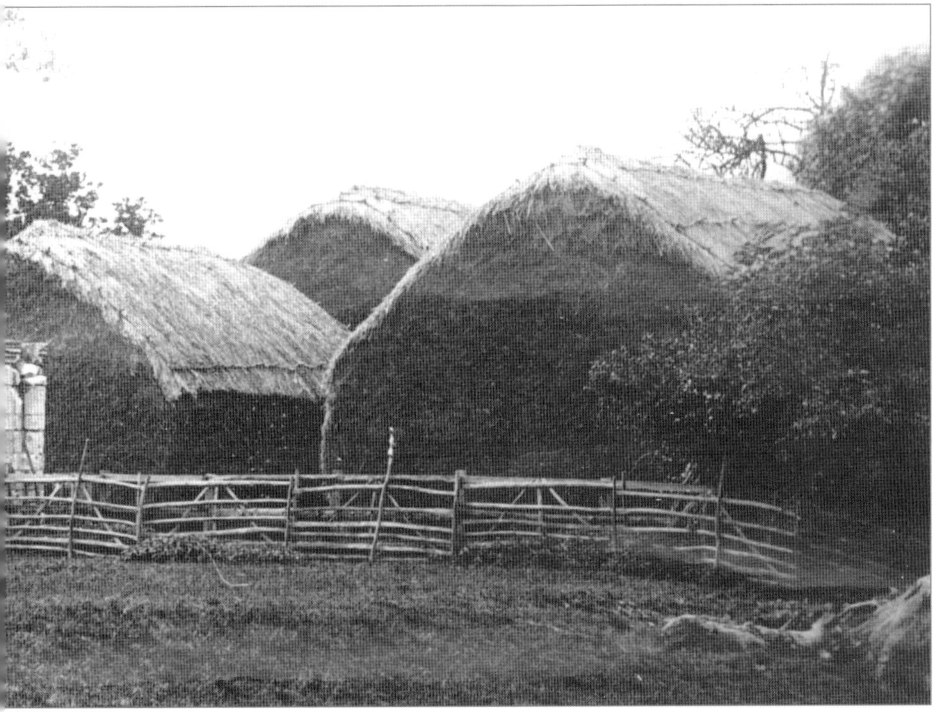

◄ **MEDMENHAM**
The Abbey 1890 23714

The house was built around 1569 for Sir Francis Duffield on the site of a small Cistercian abbey, which was founded in the 13th century. At the right, in front of a hayrick, we can see a column constructed from stonework found on the site, and to the left a mock medieval cloister, which also uses original stonework from the abbey. This view is of the house before Hudson of Danesfield, the soap king, had the house enlarged and improved by his architect Romaine Walker in 1898. There is now a road between the column and the house (no more hayricks) and a fine, well hedged garden to the left.

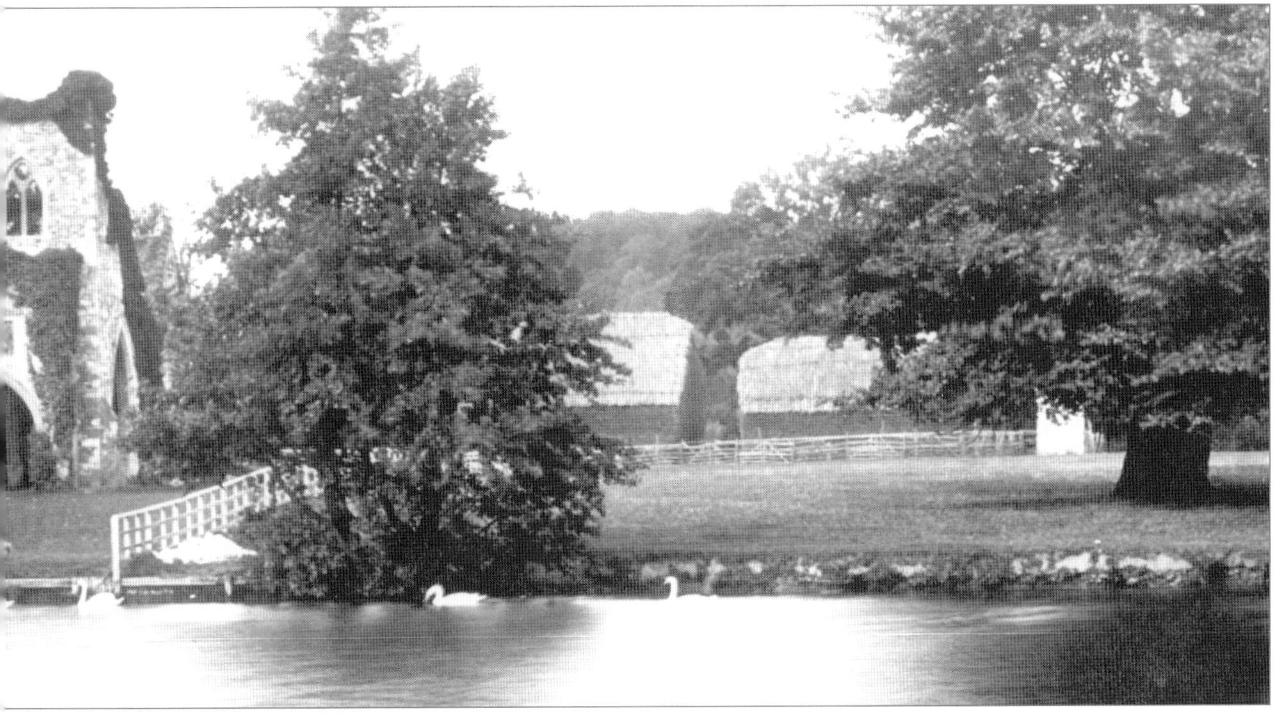

BOURNE END
Well End c1955 B160015

After this excitement, the tour heads east of Marlow along the Thames towards its big sweep south to Maidenhead. The first stop is the hamlet of Well End in the parish of Little Marlow at the north end of the Abbotsbrook, an Edwardian riverside estate built along a brook leading north from the Thames. This was the site of another small medieval priory, in this case a Benedictine nunnery founded before 1218 and dissolved in 1536. The hedge on the right belongs to Well End Farm, whose 18th-century house and weatherboarded barns face the cottages on the north or left side of the road, which are mostly refronted 17th-century timber-frames.

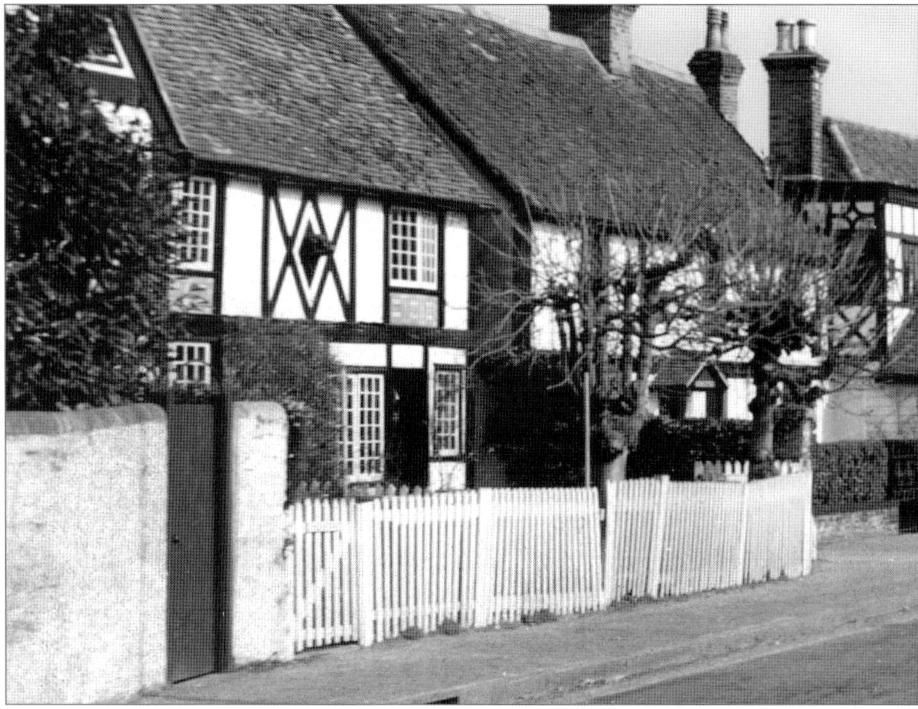

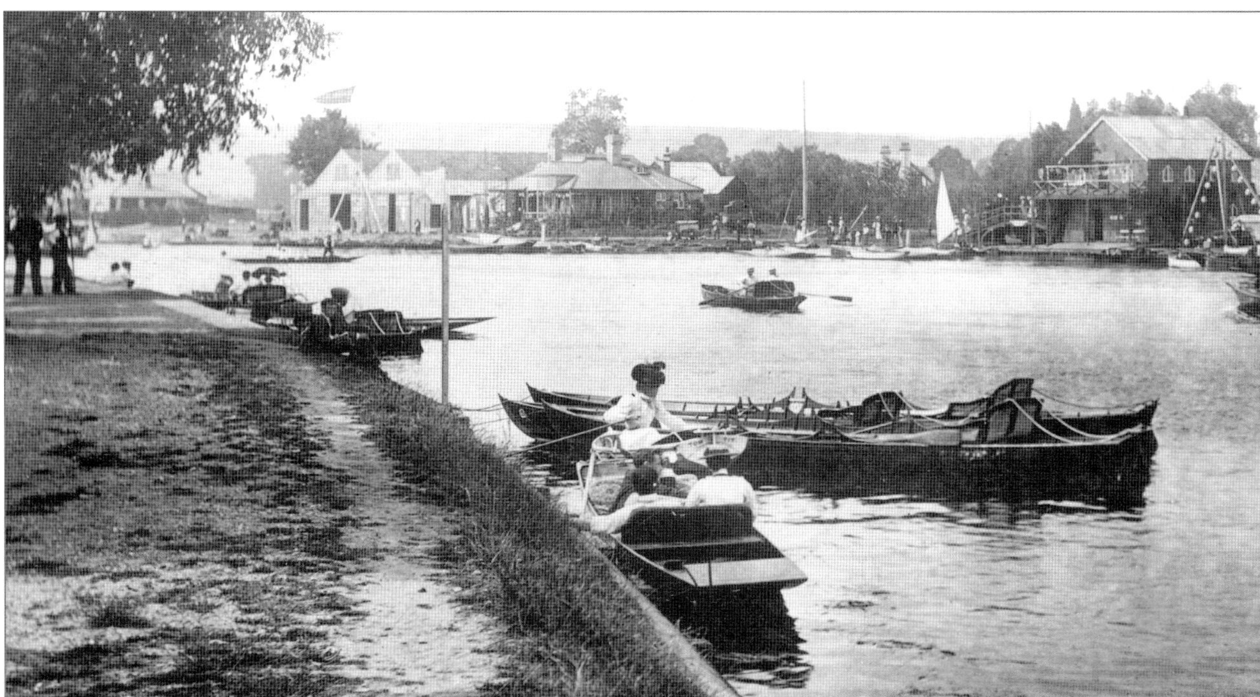

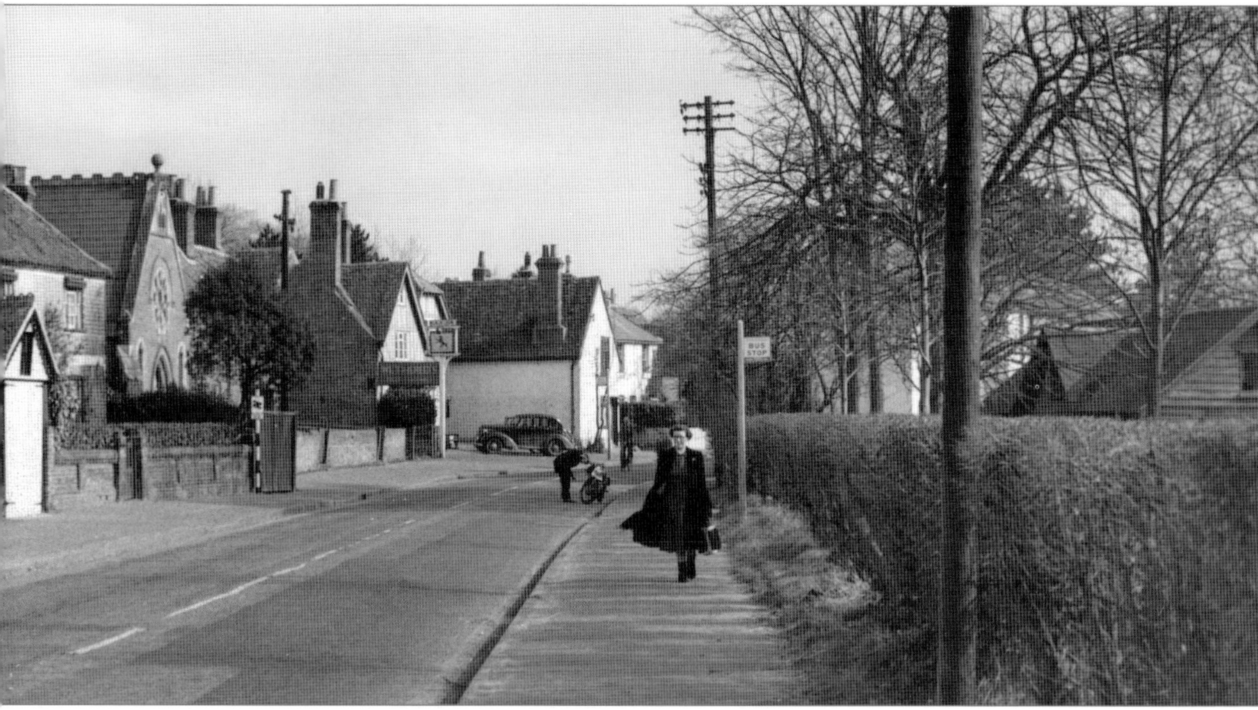

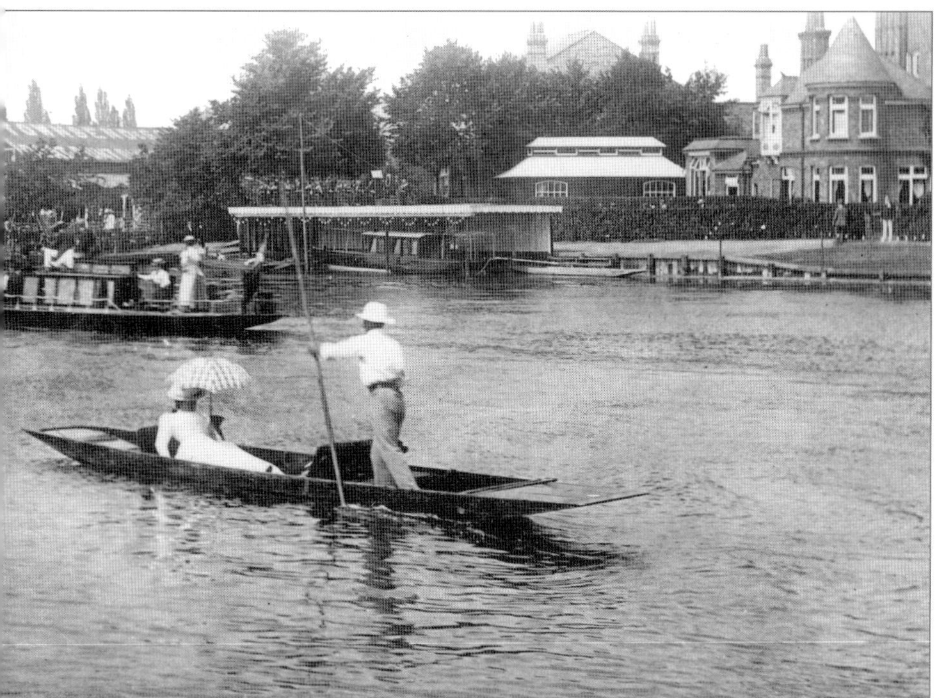

◄ **BOURNE END**

The Boat Yard 1899

43961

Back at the river, this view looks from the Berkshire bank across to Townsend's Boat Yard. The garden suburb of the Abbotsbrook Estate was started in 1902 in the fields and grounds of the old abbey beyond, soon after this view was taken. Behind the yard is the branch railway line from Bourne End to Marlow that runs alongside the river - it opened in 1873. The boatyard and the nearby riverbank were the base for the Bourne End Regatta, a major local event to rival Marlow's and Henley's, which was started in 1897.

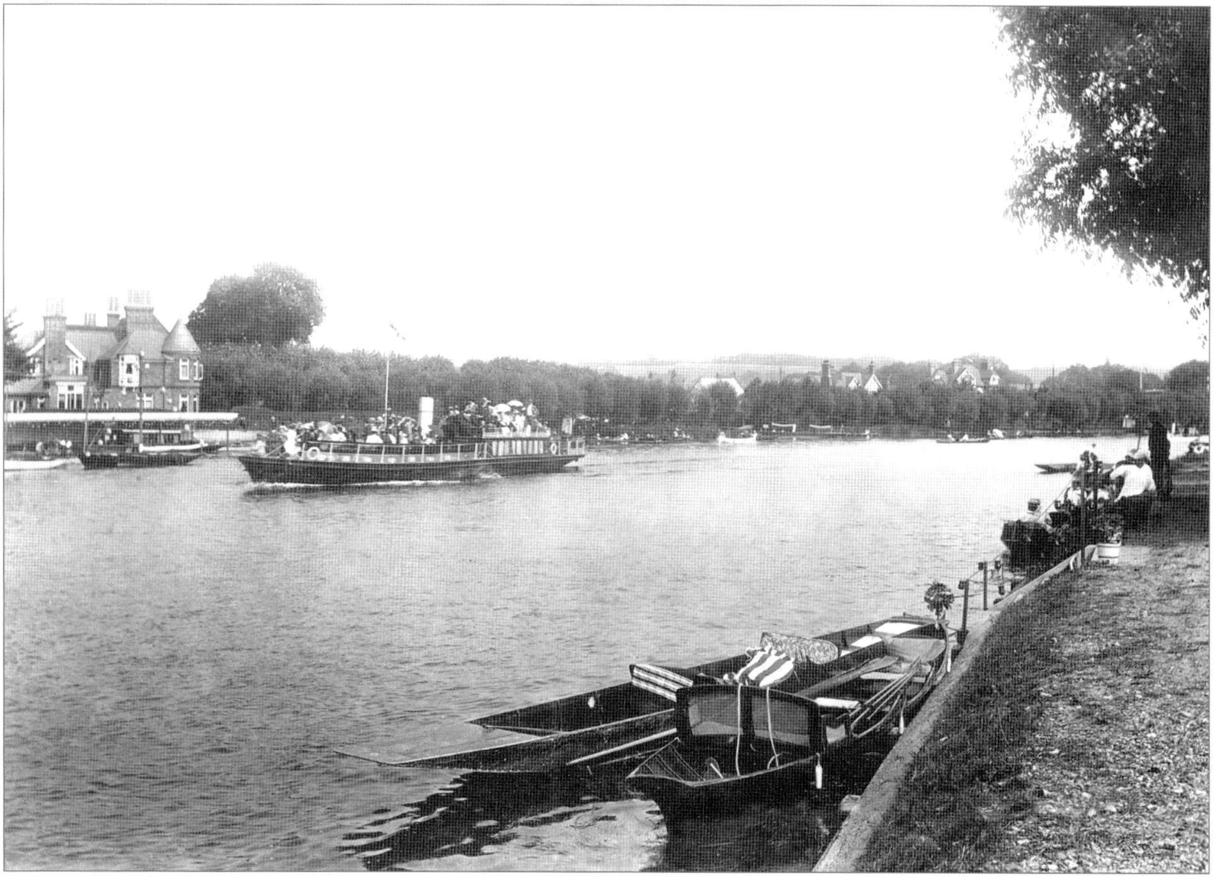

BOURNE END, *The River 1899* 43964

This view, like No 43961, captures well the late Victorian enjoyment of 'messing about in boats' - hired punts and rowing boats, yachts and steam launches are much in evidence. Boating was a joy celebrated by Jerome K Jerome in his 1889 comic masterpiece 'Three Men in a Boat'. Jerome had lived in Marlow and the area, and knew this stretch of river well. Here we see prosperous Victorian villas, one dated 1898, peering from the trees, the gaps now filled with more modern housing.

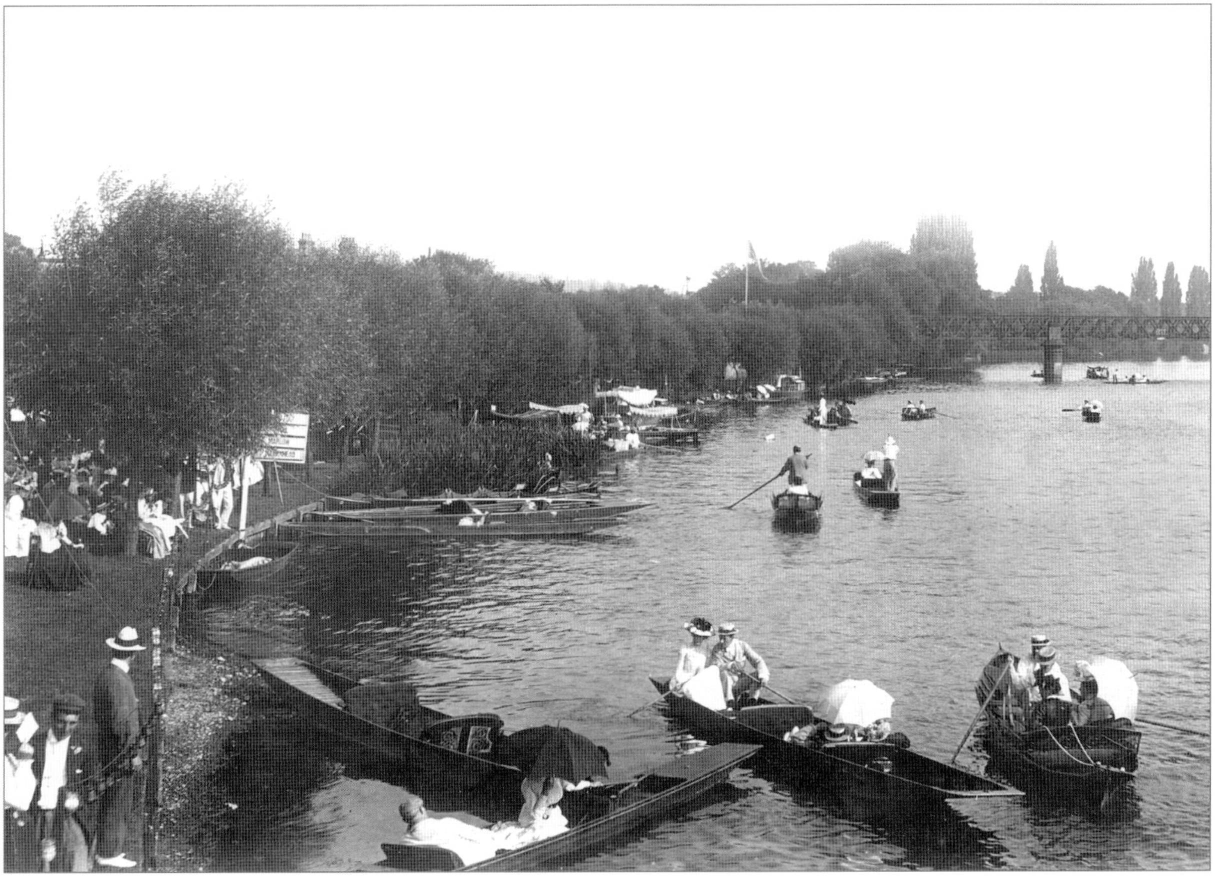

BOURNE END, *The River 1899* 43958

This view, probably taken during the 1899 Regatta, looks south-east down the Thames past the railway bridge. This steel bridge had been completed only four years before the photograph was taken, replacing the original 1853 timber bridge whose numerous piers made this stretch of the river hazardous for boats. This bridge was built for the Wycombe Railway, which opened in 1854 and ran from the main Great Western Railway line in Maidenhead to High Wycombe. It now terminates at Bourne End, where the branch line to Marlow starts.

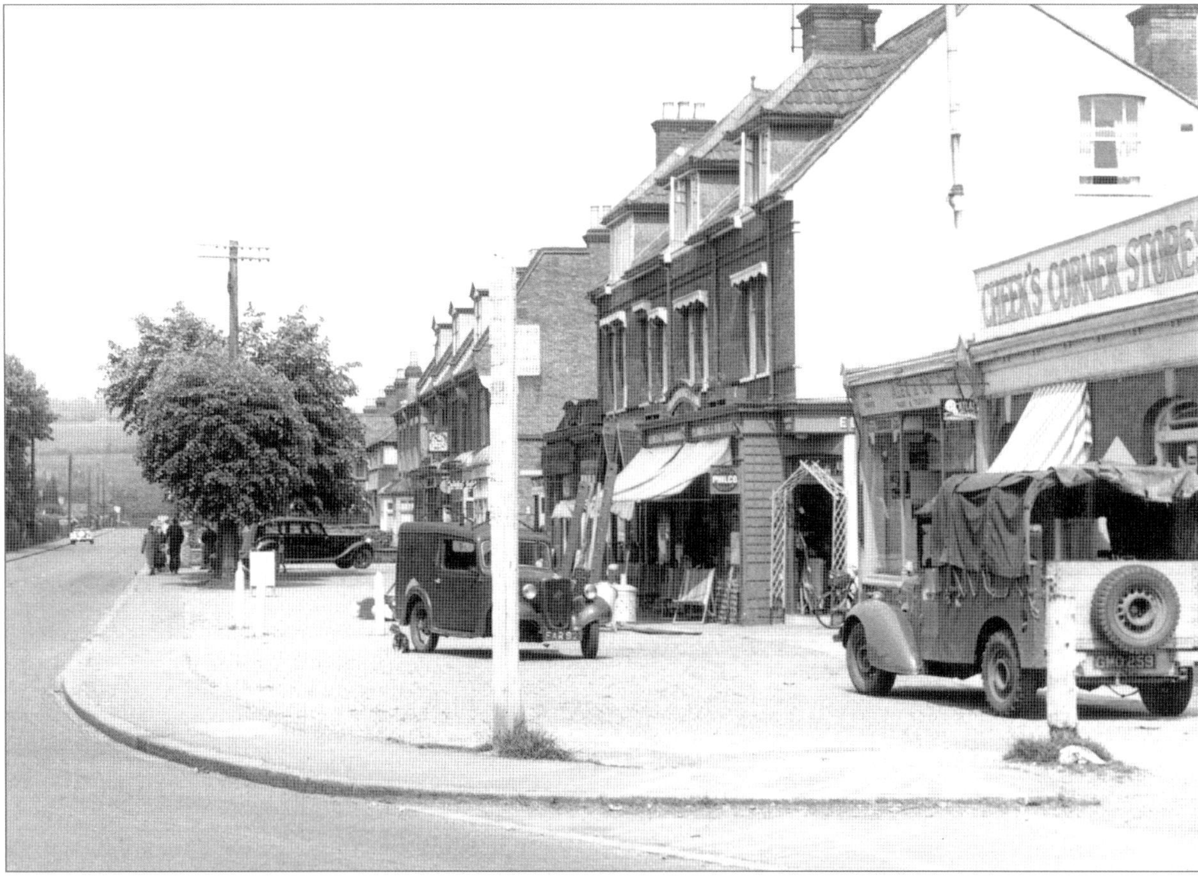

BOURNE END, *Furlong Road c1955* B160026

Bourne End's growth followed the arrival of the Wycombe Railway in 1854. Architecturally its amorphous development is disappointing, both until 1900 and throughout the 20th century. These Edwardian shopping parades of about 1902 were built when Furlong Road was formed from an old footpath, and give a good idea of Bourne End's style. These shops are a hundred yards from the railway station, and were intended as the new village's commercial centre.

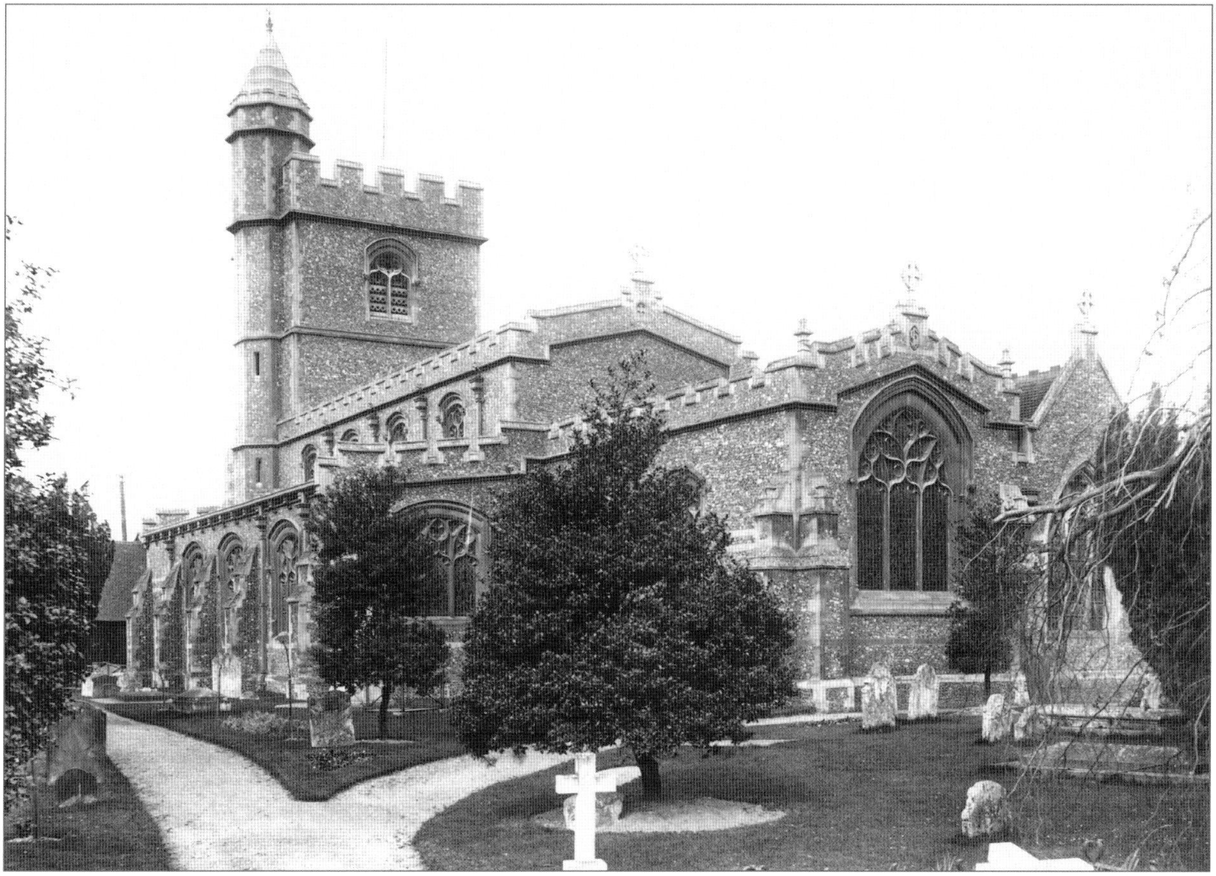

WOOBURN, *The Church 1910* 62232

The River Wye flows through Chapter 2's West Wycombe and High Wycombe, and curves down the Wooburn valley to join the River Thames below Bourne End. By the mid 19th century, the Wye was powering over 30 watermills and providing water for the Stag Brewery in Wooburn Town, as the area around St Paul's parish church was known. The medieval church was heavily restored, or largely rebuilt, in the 1860s. This view is little changed since 1910, apart from more tree growth. In the distance on the left is the roof of Deyncourt Manor, a fine medieval manor house almost entirely demolished in 1934 for road widening.

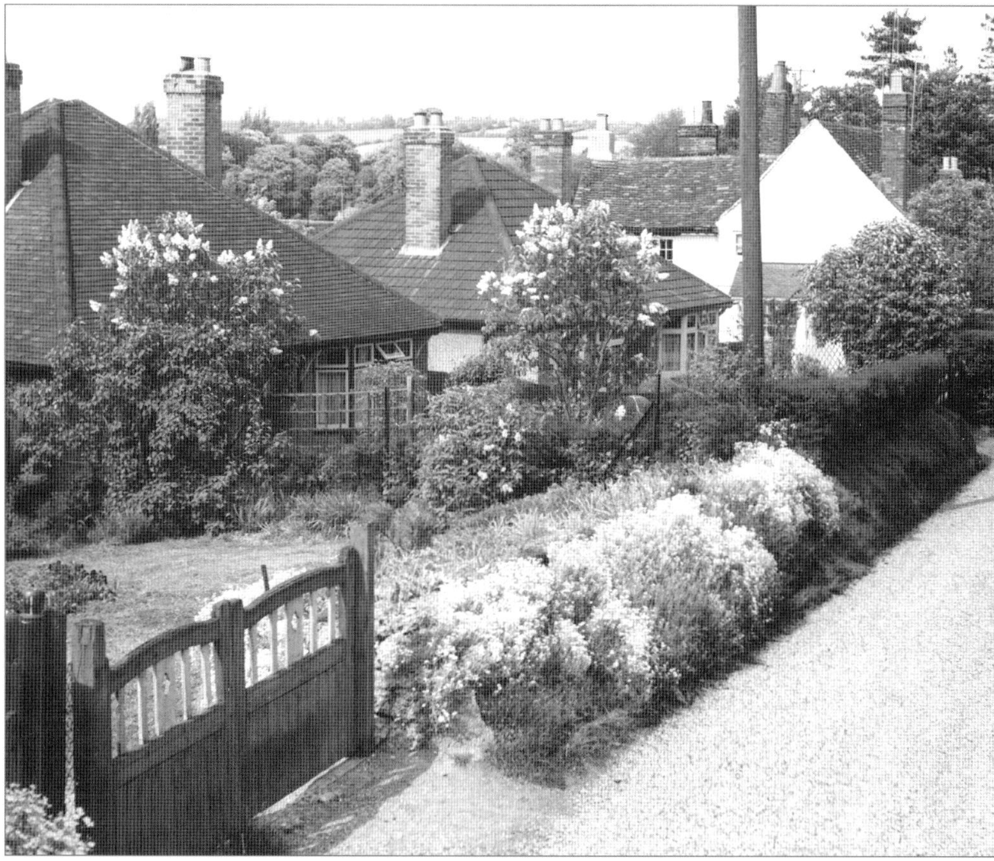

WOOBURN
Wash Hill c1960
W288004

South-east of the village centre, the lane called Wash Hill climbs out of the valley onto the chalk hills. Here the photographer looks downhill past 1950s bungalows towards the older part of the village, with the 1860s Dell Cottage at the bend. To the right, behind the hedge and set in an old chalk quarry, is Dell House, dated 1708.

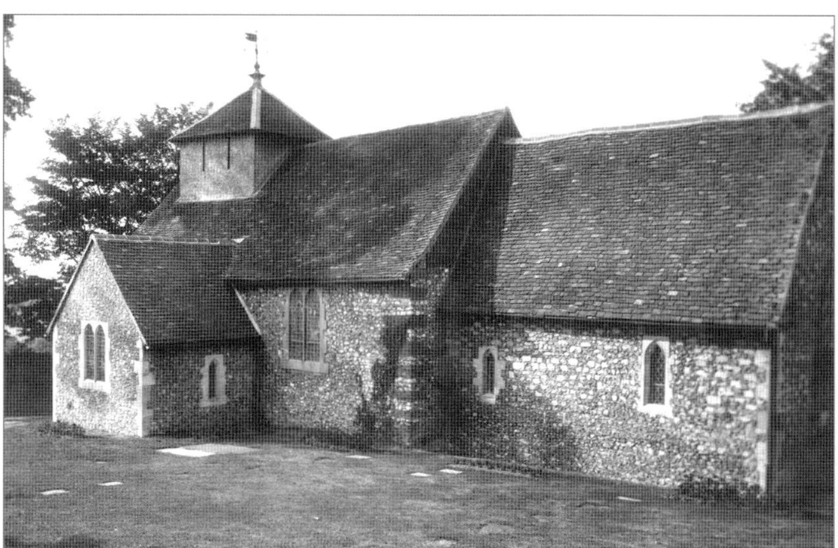

HEDSOR, *The Church 1890*
23656

Back near the Thames, on a chalk ridge overlooking the valley, St Nicholas's parish church is set near the Tudor brick and chalk chequered walls (dated 1583) to the former manor house - the church is in effect the chapel to the big house. This has gone; it was replaced by Hedsor Park further away, now used as offices. Here we look north-west, with the church unchanged since 1890. Basically medieval, it was restored in the 1860s, when a north aisle and vestries were added. The chapel at the left is a baptistery added in 1886, shortly before this view was taken.

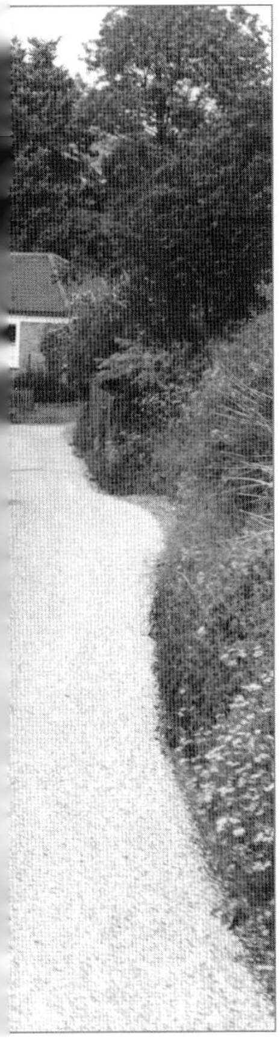

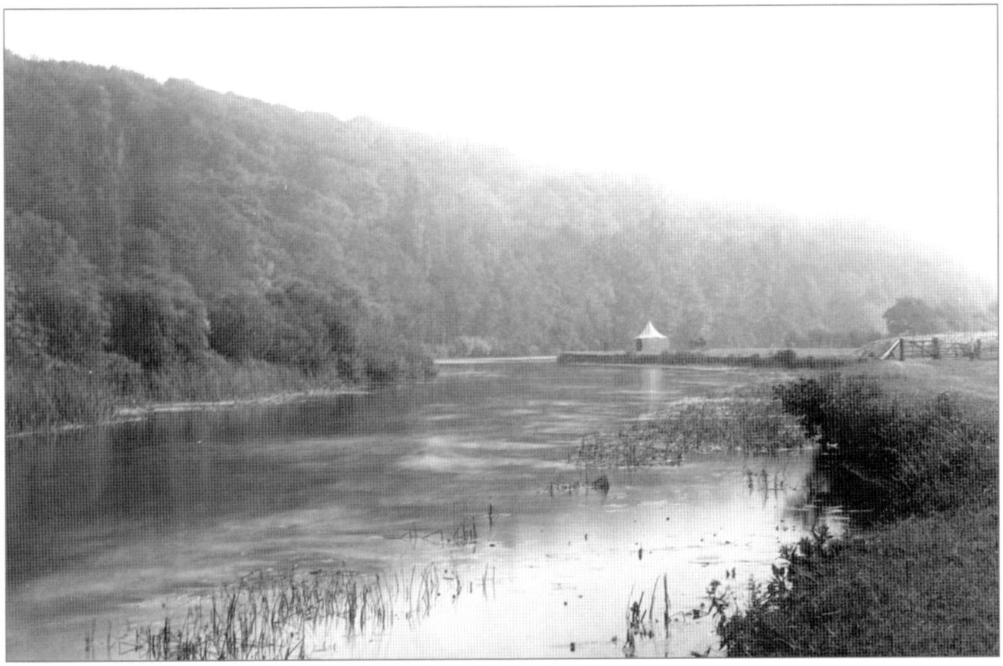

▲ **TAPLOW,** *Cliveden Reach 1890* 23639

Despite the caption on the photograph ('Taplow Woods, from Cliveden'), this view is taken from Cookham's river path along the Berkshire bank. This bank is now fringed with trees, and we cannot see this view today; but the great 'hanging' woods on the Buckinghamshire bank are still a very beautiful feature of this magnificent stretch of the River Thames, which is known as Cliveden Reach. Note the tent erected for a fisherman or a picnic party (centre).

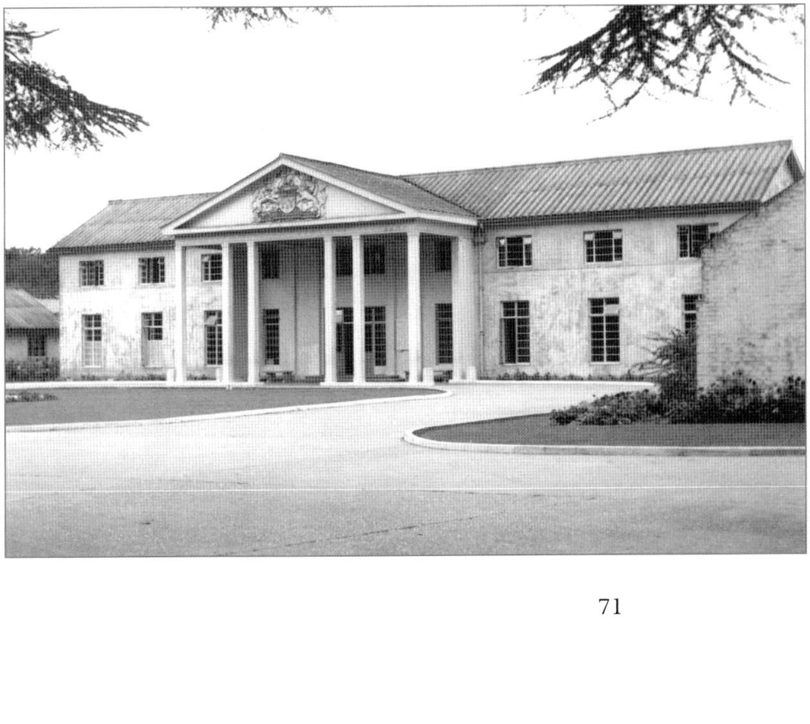

◄ **TAPLOW,** *The Canadian War Memorial Hospital c1955*
T11001

Up on the chalk ridge above Cliveden Reach are the grounds of Cliveden, a mainly 1850s mansion on older foundations that takes full advantage in its gardens and woodland walks of the views across the Thames valley below. Given to the National Trust by Lord Astor in 1942, the mansion is now a country house hotel of surpassing luxury. During World War I, buildings near Taplow Lodge were adapted and new ones added for the Canadian Army, later the Canadian Red Cross War Memorial Hospital. It treated over 24,000 casualties during that war. The buildings were demolished in 2006.

BEACONSFIELD AND THE CHILTERN HUNDREDS

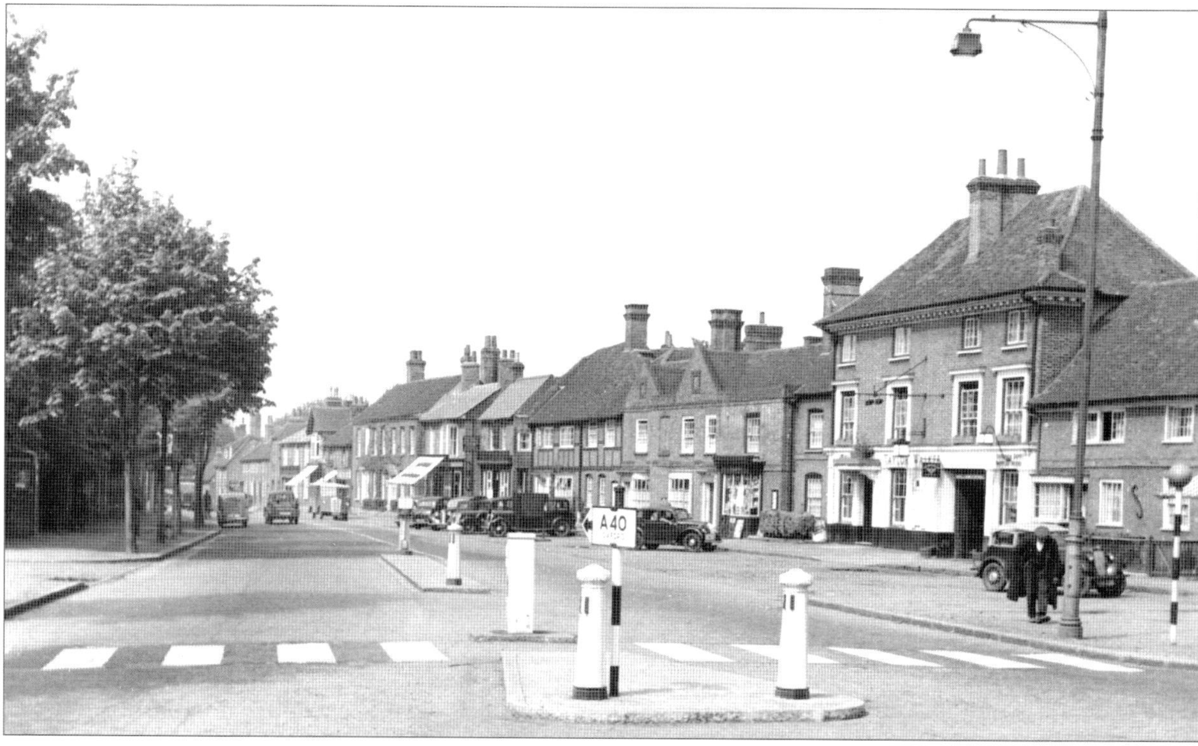

BEACONSFIELD, *Wycombe End c1955* B609010

Beaconsfield, where this chapter's tour starts, is another of the good historic towns in south Buckinghamshire's Chiltern Hills and valleys. It has four main streets that meet at the former market place, each an 'End' named after the town nearest to that compass point: Aylesbury, Wycombe, Windsor and London. Although now at the southern end of a vast 20th-century expansion after the railway arrived in 1906, the old town preserves its character almost completely. It was a coaching town on the London to Oxford Road, and this view shows the George Hotel, the Georgian hipped-roofed building on the right (without a pub sign in this view).

BEACONSFIELD
The Royal White Hart Hotel and Aylesbury End c1955 B609019

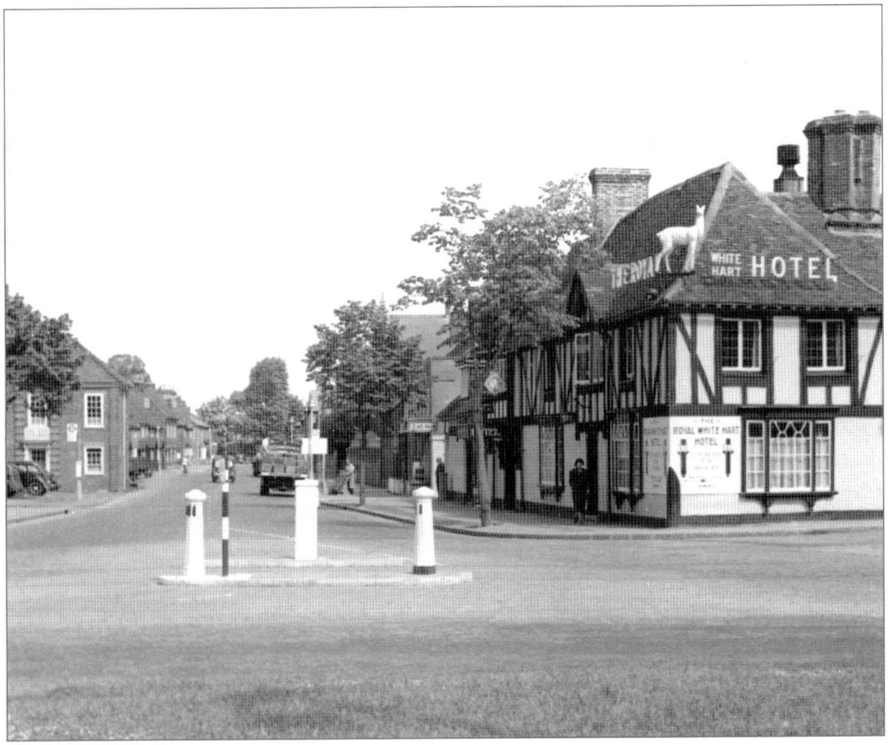

Frith's photographer now looks north along Aylesbury End past the roundabout (it is larger now) at the junction of the four Ends. On the right is another of Beaconsfield's old inns, the White Hart, its 19th-century fake framing concealing a 16th-century timber-framed interior. The building on the left behind the bus stop was the Hall Barn Estate Office, now private offices; it was built as a corn store and market house in the 18th century. Hall Barn is a mid 17th-century mansion built for the poet Edmund Waller in historic parkland south of the town, and now cut off from the town by the M40.

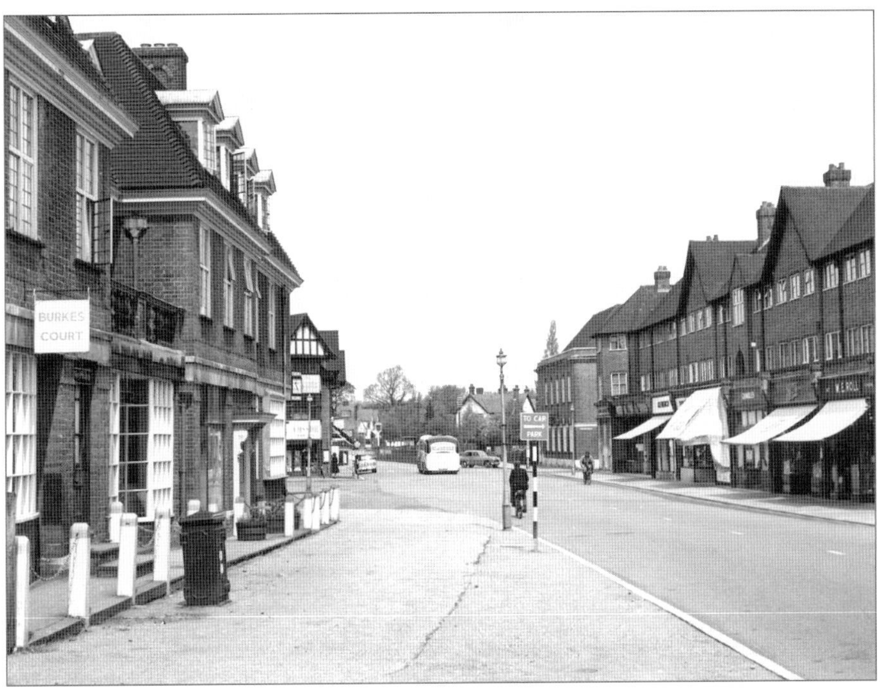

BEACONSFIELD
The New Town c1955
B609077

Beaconsfield's population before the railway arrived in 1906 was little more than 1,600, but it grew rapidly as the New Town developed to the north of the old town. The whole thing was and remains middle-class and prosperous, so the current population of about 13,000 occupies a large area. This view looks north along Station Road in the heart of the New Town; Highway Court of the 1920s stands on the right, with the railway bridge beyond the Post Office at the end. There are now two mini-roundabouts at these junctions. The parade on the left with half-timbered gables dates from 1913.

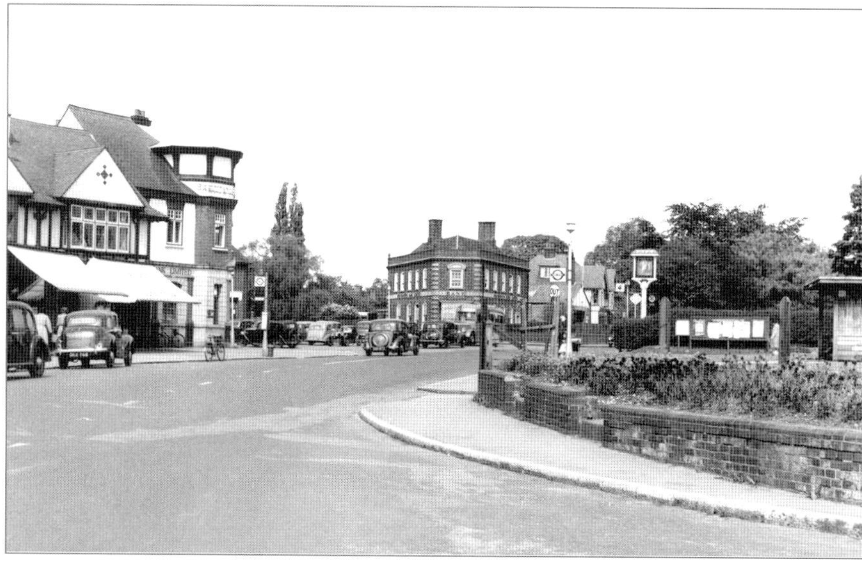

BEACONSFIELD, *Station Parade c1955* B609028

We are now north of the railway bridge, and looking towards Station Parade from the top of the station approach road leading down to the station's up platform. The neo-Georgian National Westminster Bank (now NatWest) in the centre of the view dates from the 1930s, while the pub whose sign we can see to the right was replaced by a 1980s Waitrose supermarket in tile-roofed vernacular style. Set well back behind the bus shelter is the 1914 Town Hall, originally built as offices and now the town council's headquarters.

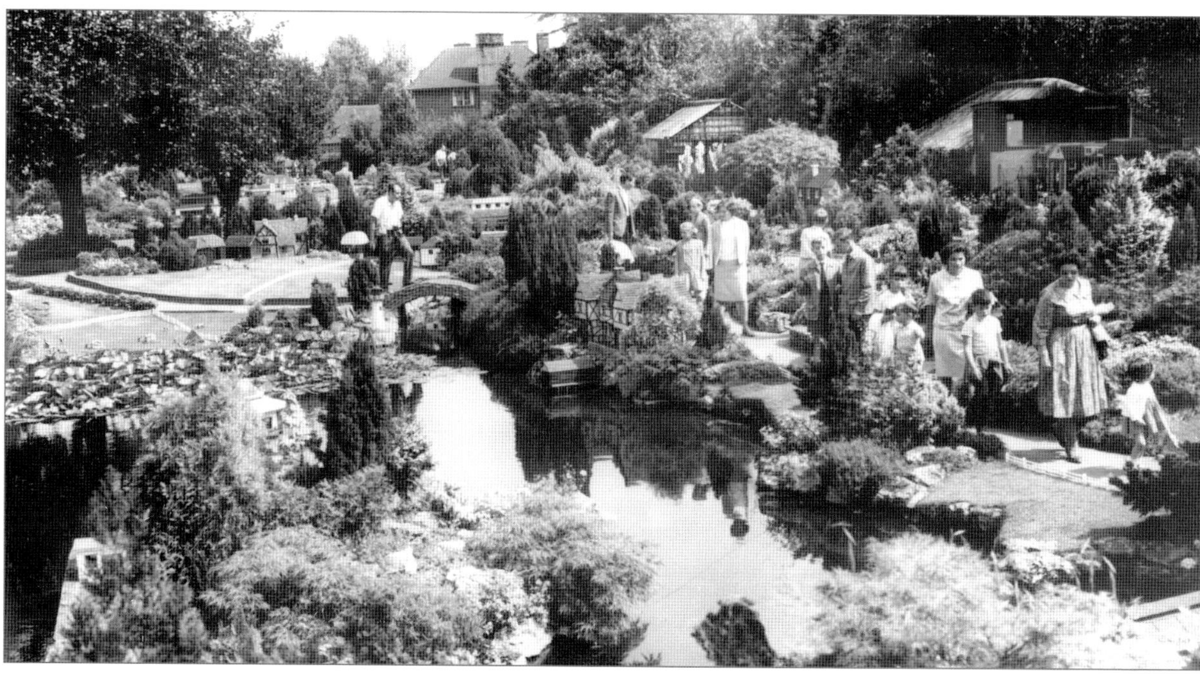

BEACONSFIELD, *Bekonscot Model Village c1960* B609123

Beaconsfield is famous for the model village of Bekonscot, which is in Warwick Road, a turning to the right beyond the Waitrose car park entrance. Here in 1929 a local accountant, Roland Callingham, started a scale model village in what was then a field. It is now surrounded by 1930s and 1950s houses (you can see one in this view) and is a quaint, charming and popular visitor attraction. A key feature is the miniature railway, which winds through the 'village'. Bekonscot now has nearly a hundred different buildings.

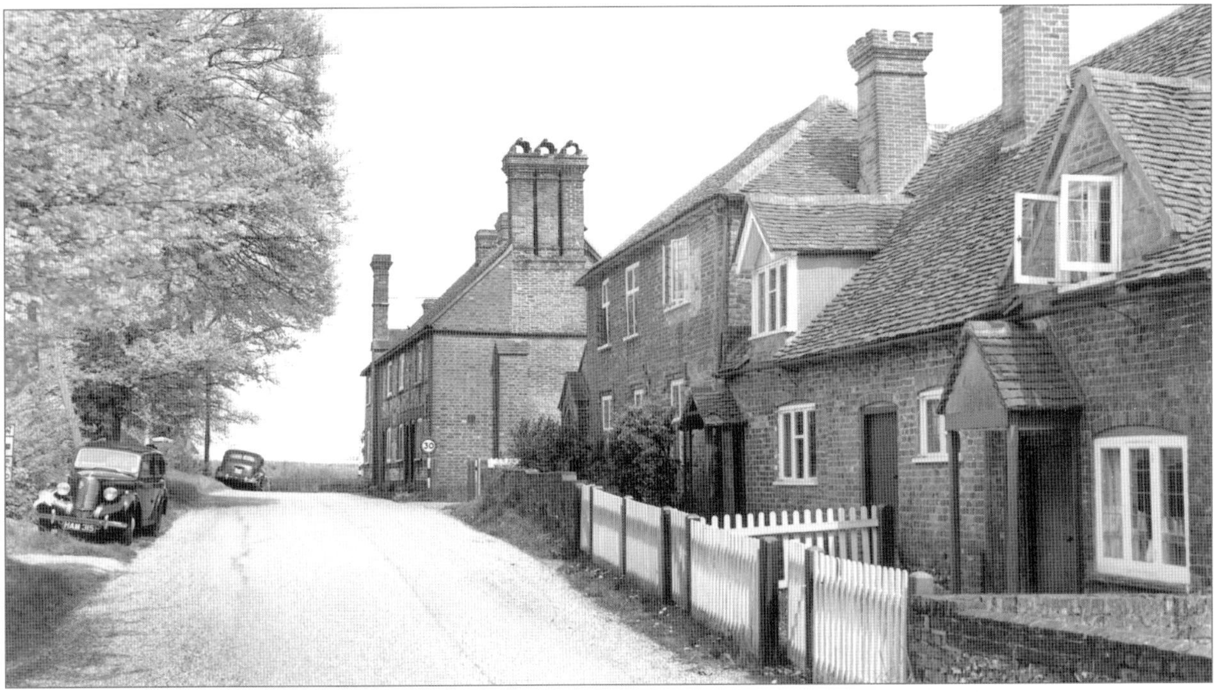

PENN, *Old Cottages c1955* P283001

Moving north from Beaconsfield and its smart suburbs we reach Penn, a superb village along the ridge with views north and south over the wooded Chilterns. Here Frith's photographer is looking up Paul's Hill towards the Church Street junction, with Holy Trinity's churchyard behind the trees on the left. At the top of the hill, Nos 1, 2 and 3 Church Cottages were once a single 17th-century timber-framed house, refronted in the 18th century; its original brick stack with three chimney shafts can be seen on the gable.

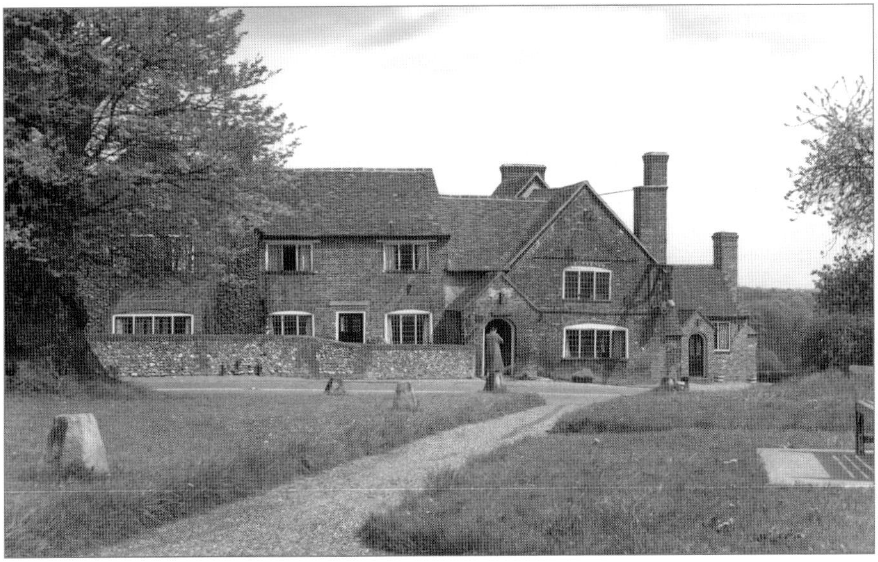

PENN, *The Crown c1955*
P283002

At the Church Street junction there is a small triangular green with a war memorial cross (out of view to the left); the large and ancient tree (left) has now been replaced by a young one. The bench and the former granary staddle stone bases that ring the green remain, and opposite is the Crown pub. This is also unchanged, having already expanded into the neighbouring cottages to the left. The core of the building is 17th-century, but the brickwork is mostly mid to late 18th-century, and there are 1930s additions by the brewery.

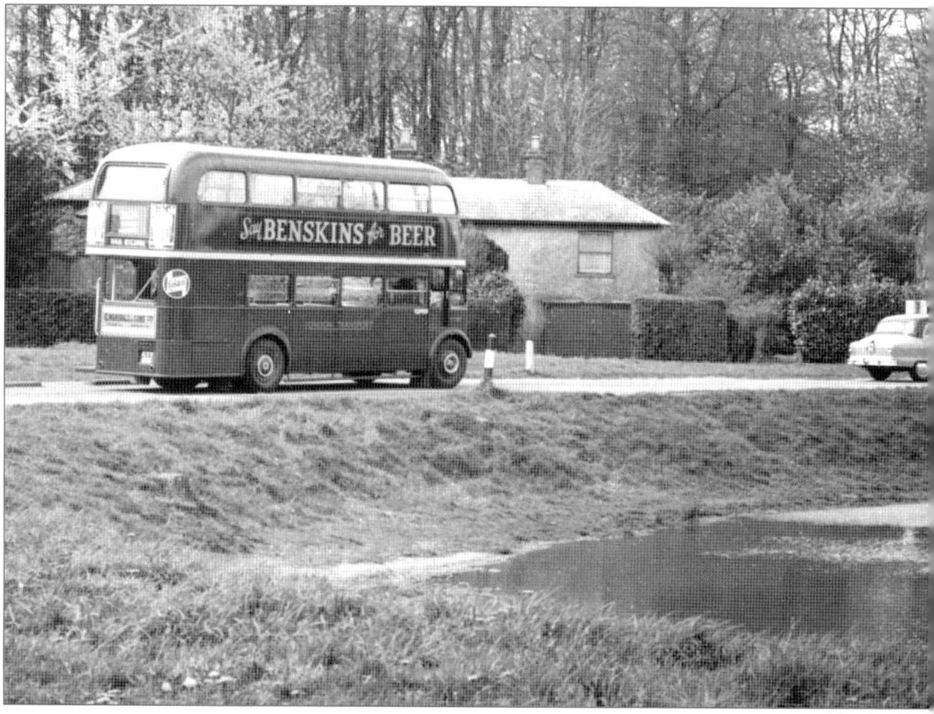

TYLERS GREEN
The Green c1960 T354005

Penn merges into Tylers Green; as its name suggests, it was once a centre for a floor and roof tile industry. Indeed, in the Middle Ages the decorative floor tiles were in great demand; they were used at Windsor Castle in the 14th century, and can still be found on the floors of numerous Chiltern parish churches. Cottages and more modern houses surround and divide in two a large and diverse green. This view looks across the east green with its pond. The shops were rebuilt in the 1980s, and at the right is the 1875 primary school with its bellcote.

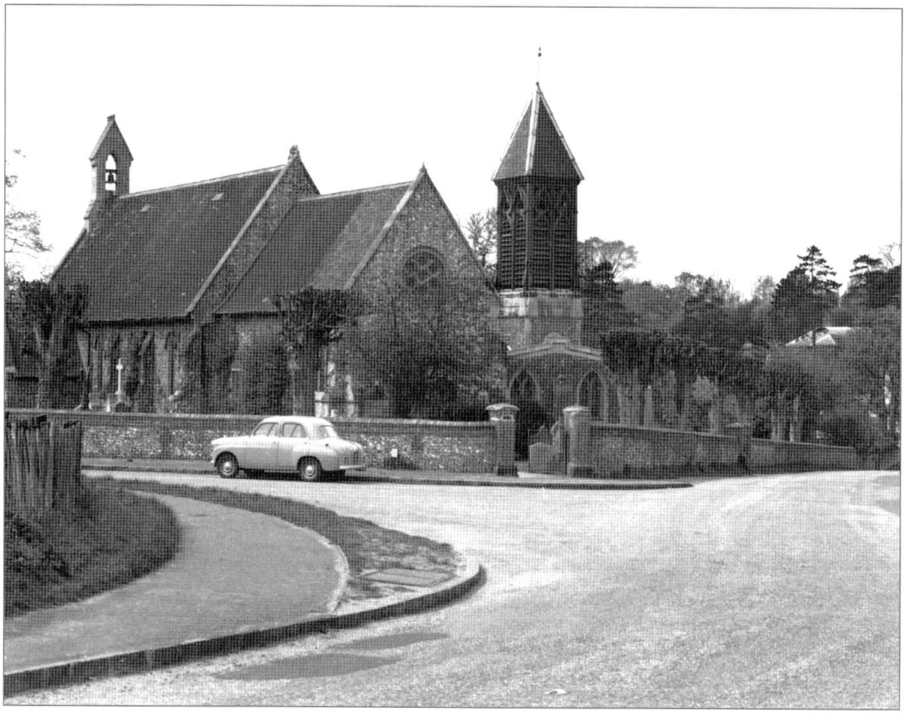

TYLERS GREEN
St Margaret's Church c1960 T354010

Formerly within Penn parish, Tylers Green got a church in 1854, but it did not become a separate parish until 1863. A simple and unremarkable two cell church by Brandon with a single bell bellcote and a porch, it was made considerably more interesting by the High Wycombe architect Arthur Vernon, who in 1891 added the north extension with the timber bell tower with its pyramidal roof. Most of the trees have been removed in the 1990s in an attempt to deal with spectacular subsidence of the graves and churchyard memorials.

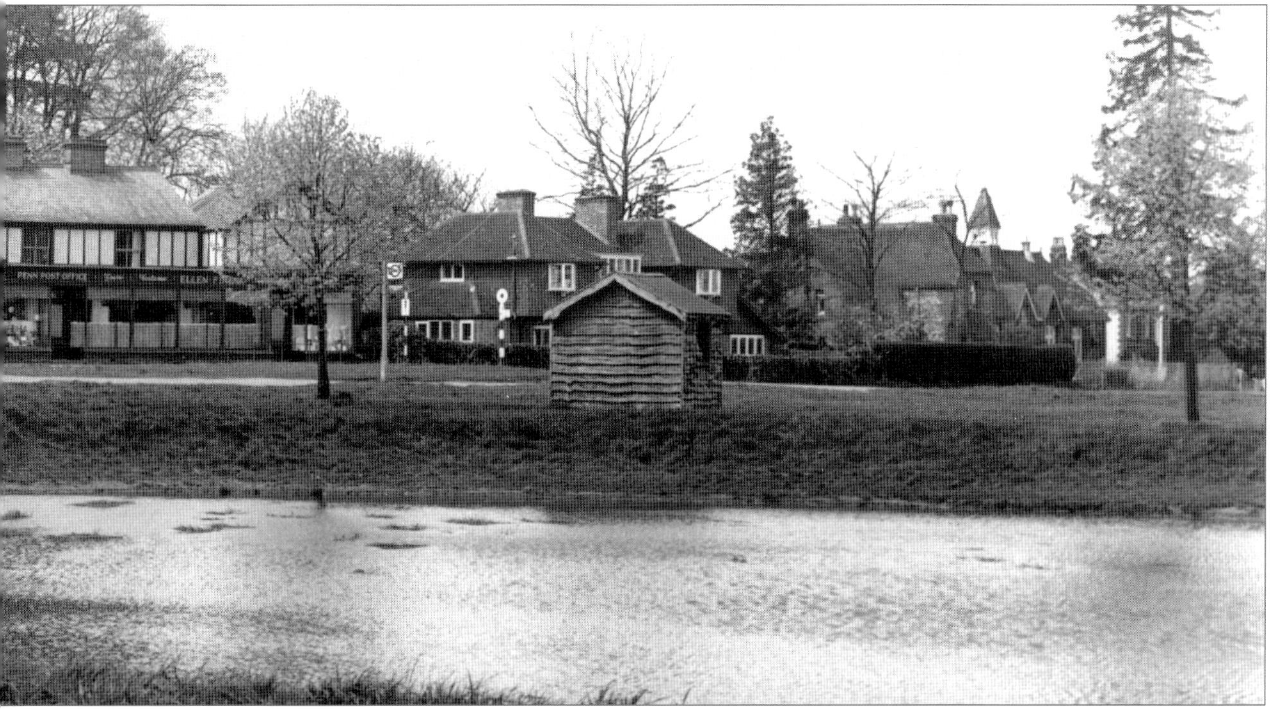

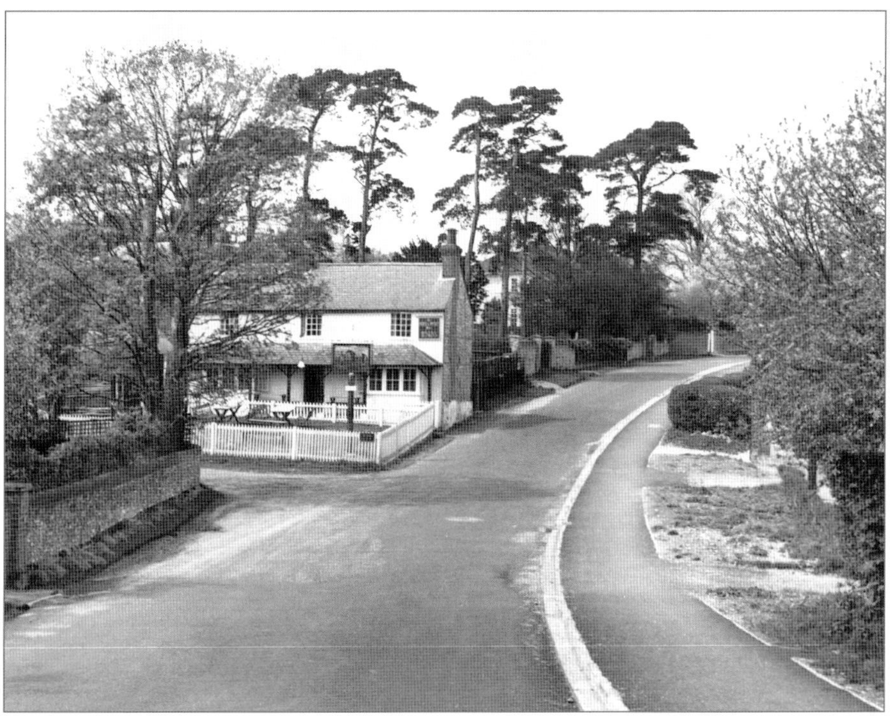

◄ **TYLERS GREEN**
By The Horse and Jockey c1960 T354009

Church Road descends past a group of the older houses of the village, including the Horse and Jockey pub. Behind and to its left is a good stucco Regency villa, formerly used as the rectory, while the tall pine trees surround the White House, a stucco neo-Georgian house of about 1910, now divided into three houses. The trees and hedge on the right, now replaced by brick and flint walls, conceal Dell Cottage of 1792, built in one of the numerous claypit depressions dotting this area - from these pits the raw material for the Penn tile industry was extracted.

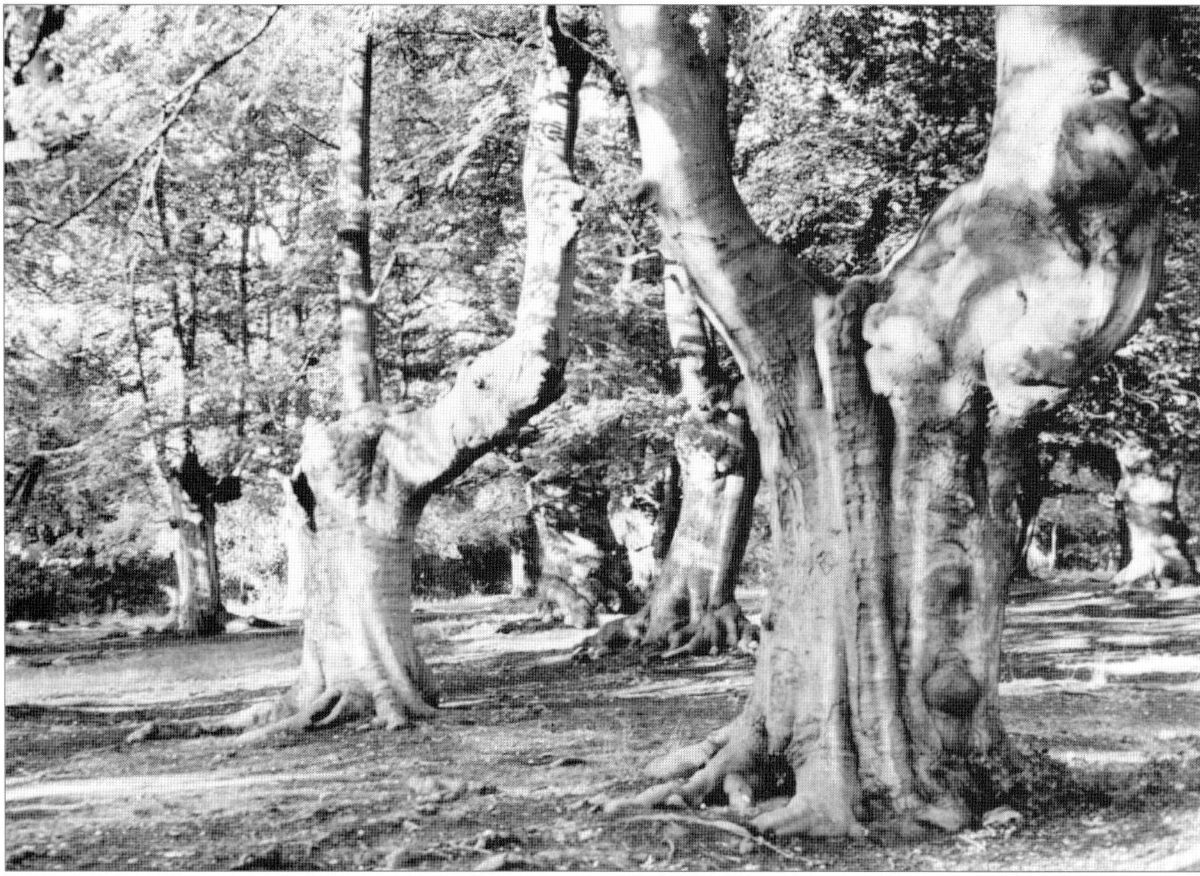

BURNHAM, *Burnham Beeches c1955* B250004

The second part of this chapter's tour moves south of Beaconsfield and starts in the one part of Buckinghamshire of which most people have heard: Burnham Beeches. These are about 80 hectares of ancient woodland commons here, which were bought by the Corporation of the City of London in 1880 for the benefit of Londoners (they also bought Hampstead Heath and Epping Forest as other London 'green lungs'). Many of the majestic beeches are over three hundred years old. They were pollarded for firewood for London, until wood was supplanted by coal in the 19th century. Now the beeches are a beautiful and much-loved asset for walkers and visitors.

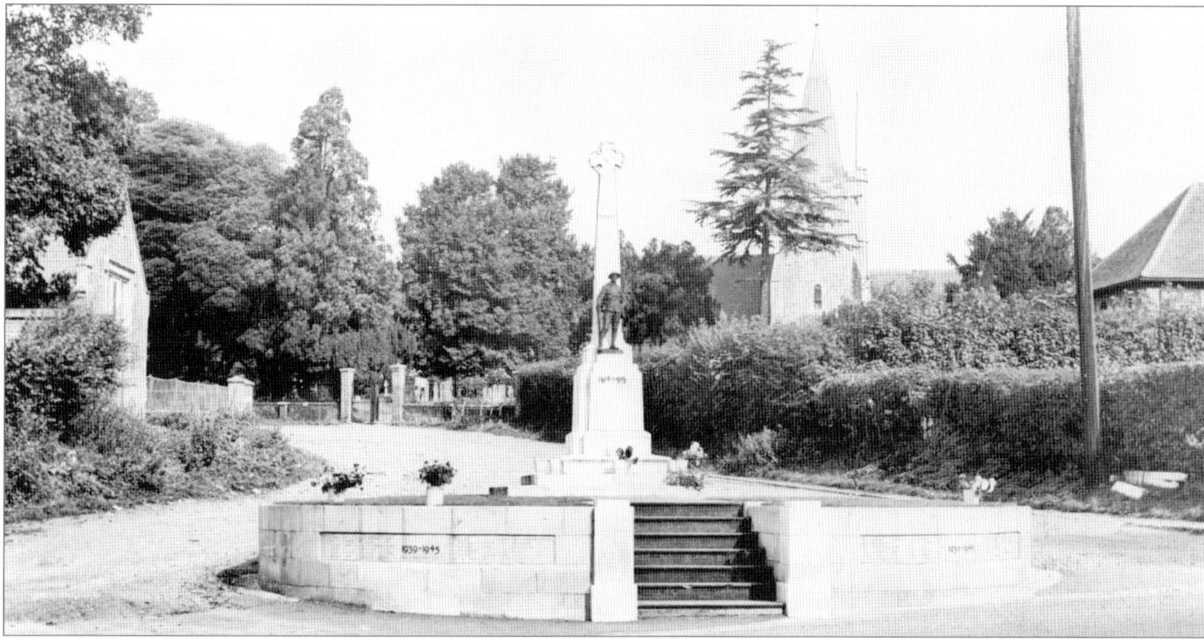

▲ **BURNHAM,** *The War Memorial and the Church c1955* B250006

In the 1950s Burnham still looked like a rural Buckinghamshire village, but within 15 years it had been swamped by housing estates. This view is particularly evocative, for the Infant School of 1844 on the left was demolished in 1962 and the fine Georgian vicarage behind it in 1965, both replaced by housing estates. The war memorial of 1920 was moved to the green at the south end of the High Street as part of these 1960s improvements. To the right, the Working Men's Club of 1903 and the churchyard walls survive. The church spire only dates from 1892.

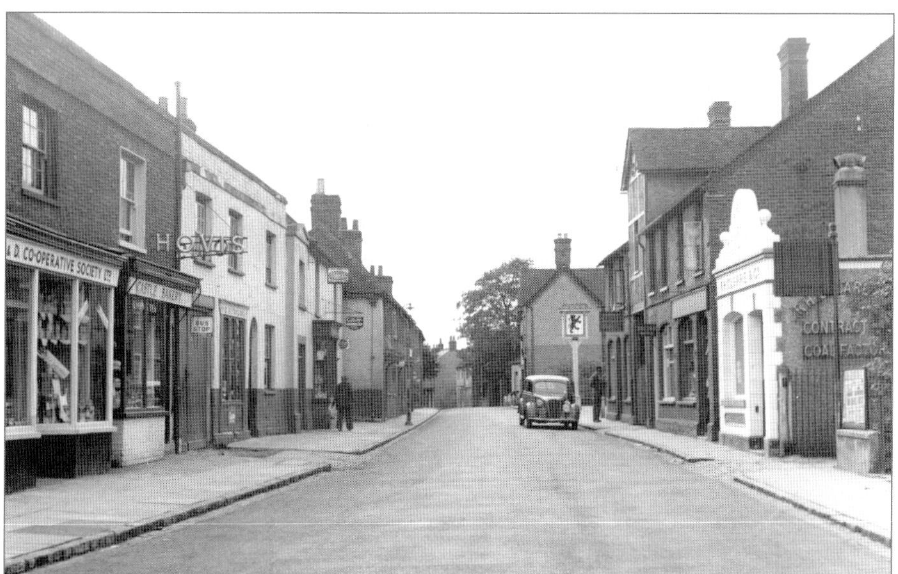

◄ **BURNHAM,** *High Street c1955* B250011

The next four views show the High Street before the 1960s 'regeneration' of Burnham, and so are very much an archive. That said, a good deal survived the modernisers. This view looks south down the High Street with most of the buildings on the right surviving, but only the Co-op and the bakery surviving on the left. The white gabled building on the right was the late Victorian office of R H Cleare, coal and coke merchants and building contractors, whose yard was behind. It is now a smart restaurant. The Red Lion was rebuilt about 1940 further back from the road frontage.

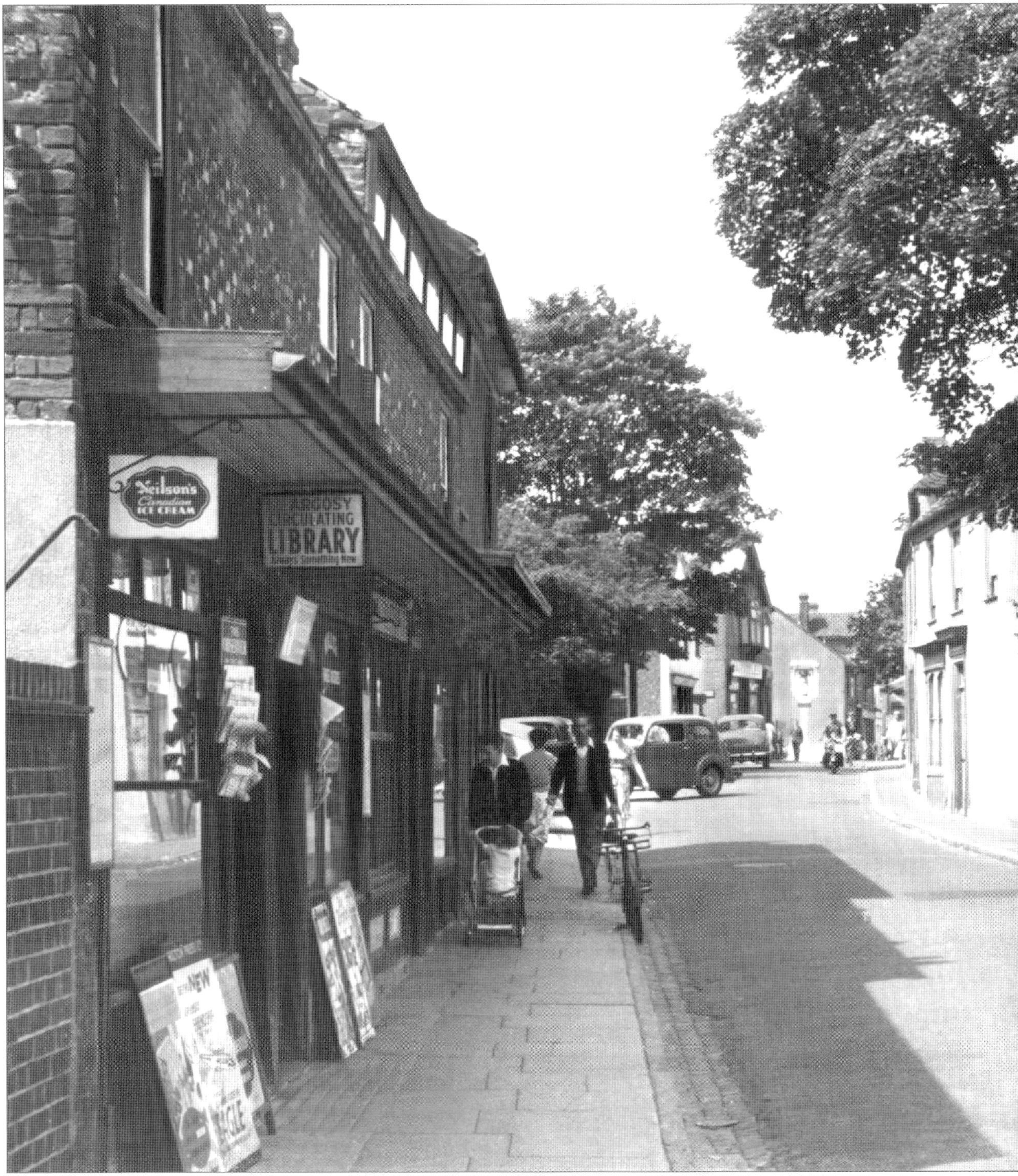
Neilson's
Canadian ICE CREAM
CIRCULATING
LIBRARY

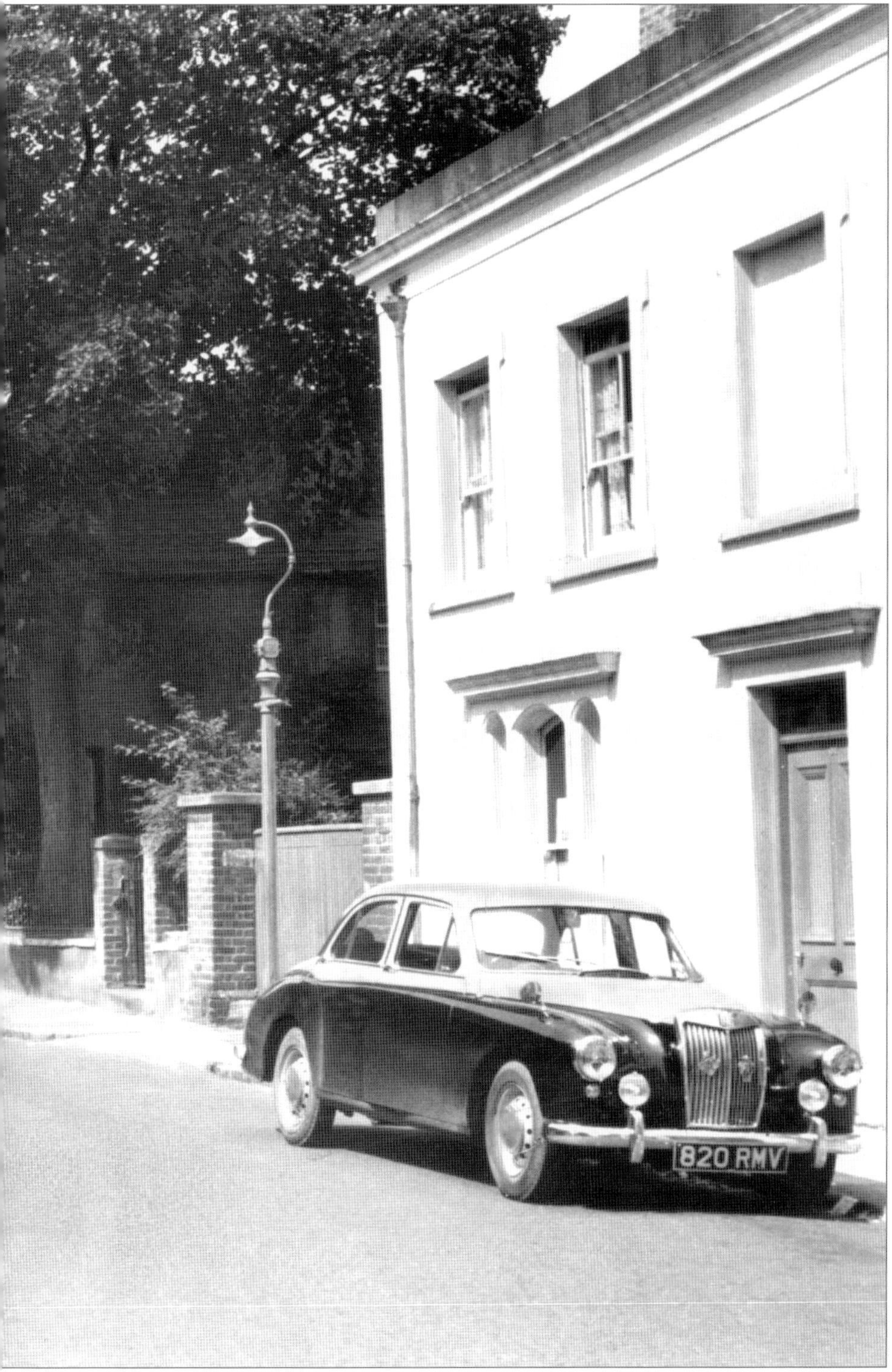

BURNHAM
High Street c1955
B250051

Further down the High Street, Frith's photographer is now looking back past the Red Lion pub sign. The stucco house on the right and the tree beyond disappeared in the 1960s for Budgen's supermarket and the formation of a new road, Jennery Lane. The shops on the left survive, despite a fire in the 1980s, and this section of road has been traffic-calmed with bollards and is a one-way street.

BURNHAM
High Street c1955
B250039

We are looking southwards again. The hedge on the left is now the entrance to Jennery Lane and its car park. In 1955 Sands traded out of the former Rose Brewery buildings as an Austin dealer (there are a few Austins in this view), but in more recent times flats have been built on its site. Sands later traded out of a modernistic 1960s Sands Garage building on the corner, its style suiting the up-to-the-minute image of its Citroen car dealership. Beyond are some of the best timber-framed buildings surviving in the High Street.

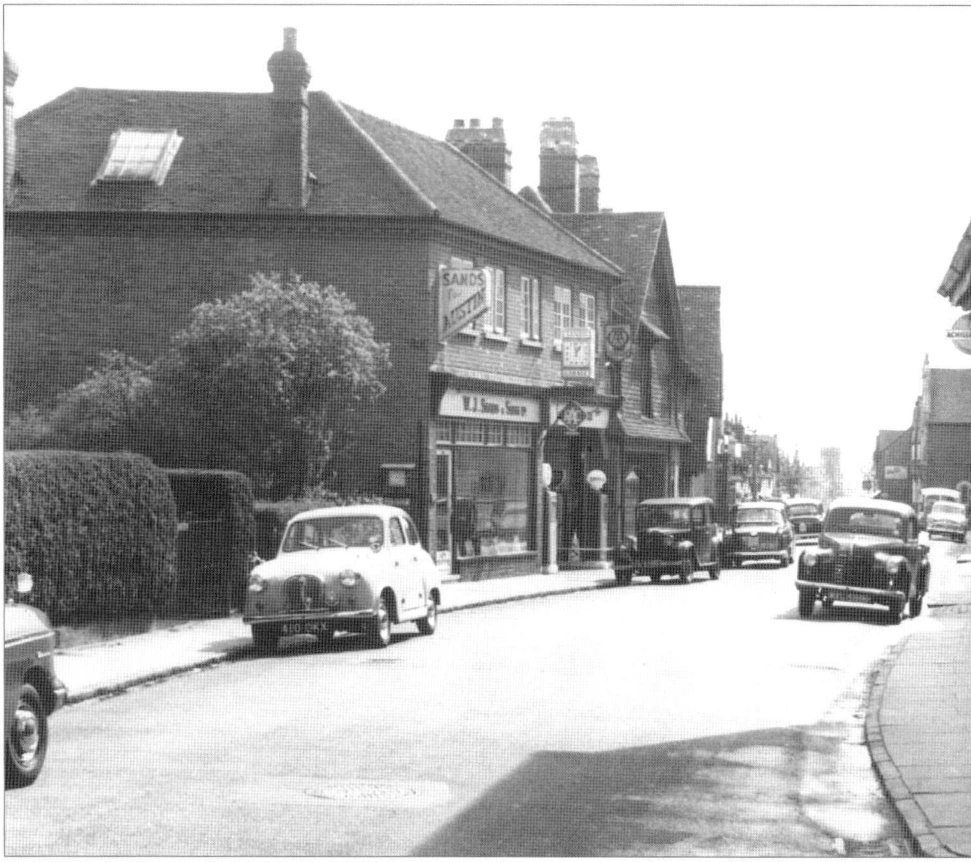

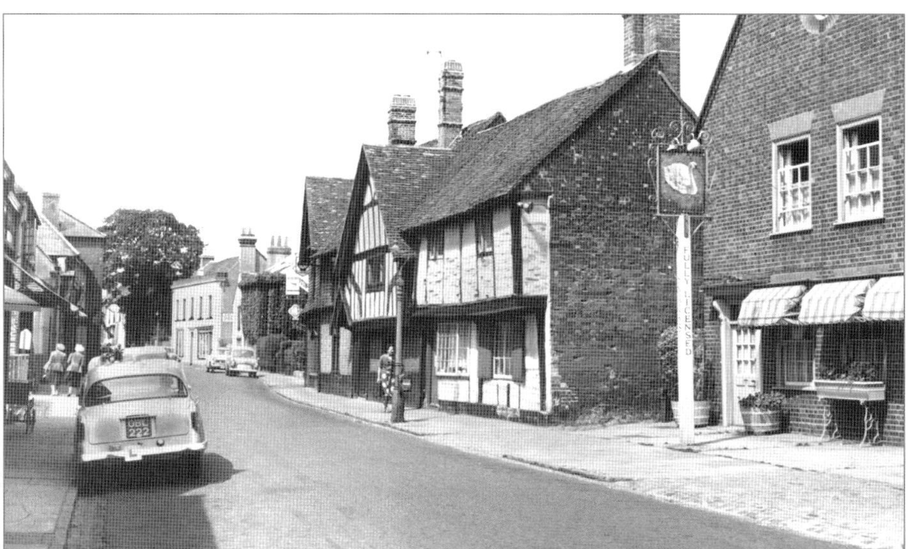

BURNHAM, *High Street c1955* B250049

Another fine archive view: the middle distance is now occupied by an architecturally poor Budgen's, the entrance to Jennery Lane and Sand's garage. All is not lost, however, for the fine 16th- and 17th-century timber-framed group survive, now used as a commercial premises. To the right is Ye Olde Swan, another of Burnham's pubs that was rebuilt, this time in the 1950s.

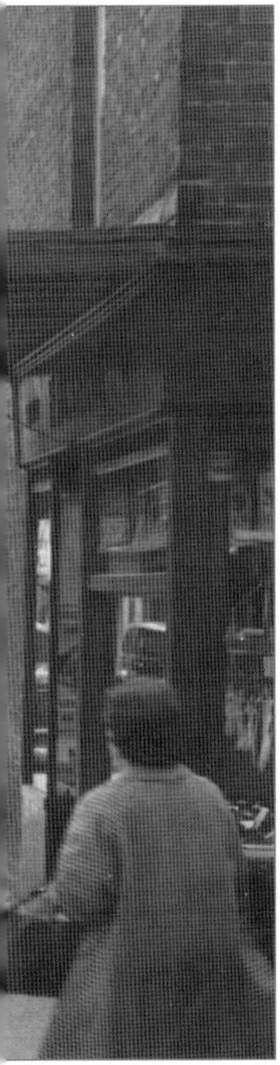

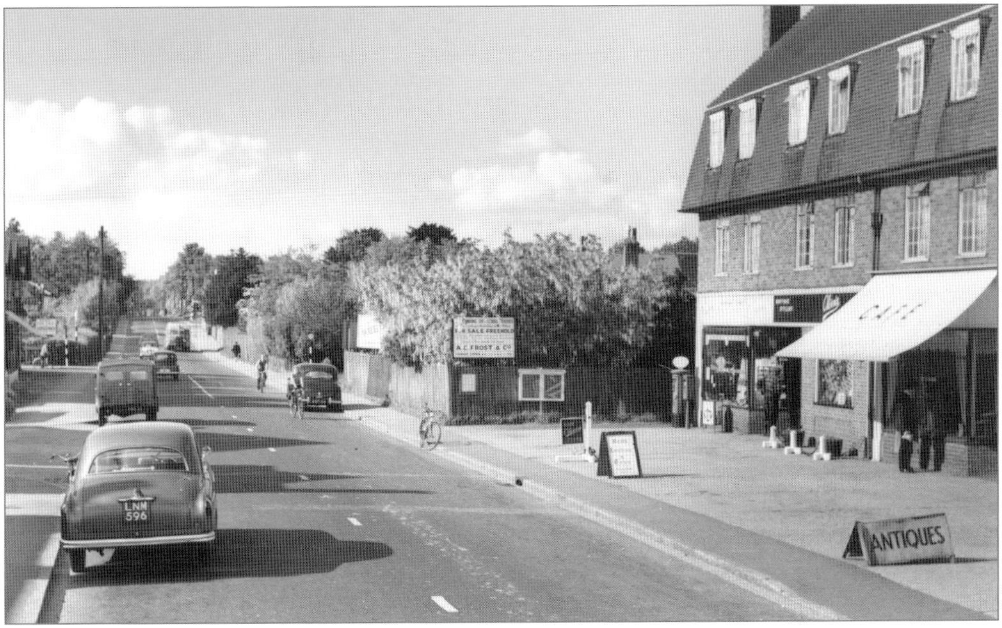

▲ **FARNHAM COMMON,** *The Parade c1955* F196001

From an historic, if battered, town we move to Metroland suburbia. Burnham and the Farnhams are within Slough's orbit, a Buckinghamshire town generously donated to Berkshire by local government re-organisation in 1974. The amorphousness of Farnham Common village, on the eastern edge of the delights of Burnham Beeches, is well captured by this view and No F196017. A new road, Rosewood Way, was formed beyond the 1950s shops and flats on the right, and further shops were added (we can see the For Sale sign on the fence).

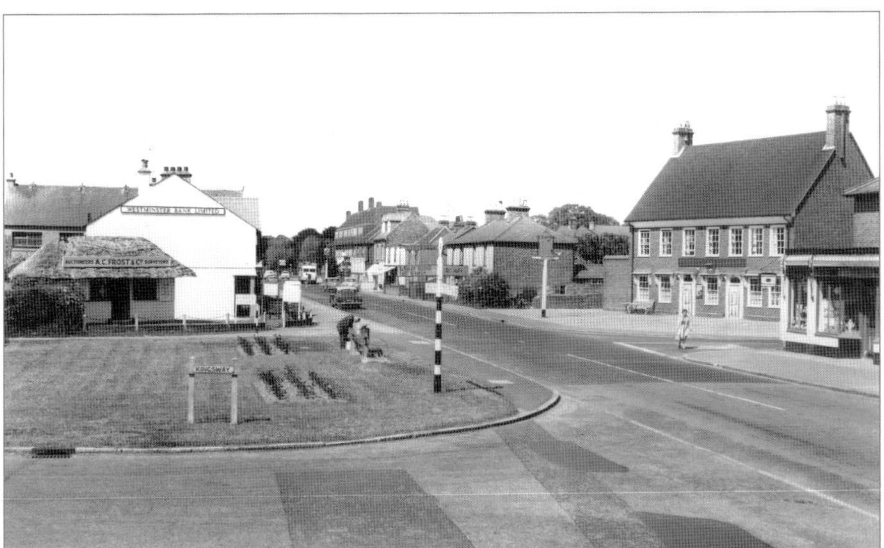

◄ **FARNHAM COMMON**
The Parade c1965 F196017

The village grew up along the Slough to Beaconsfield road, and its shopping centre was a mix of Victorian houses converted to shops and more recent shopping parades. The shops on the far right were replaced by flats in the 1980s, and the terrace and shops to the left of the 1930s the Foresters (now a café-bar and restaurant rather than a simple pub) were replaced by shops and offices, also in the 1980s. The Metroland-style thatched estate agents on the left is still an estate agency.

FARNHAM ROYAL
The Village c1955 F195010

Further south and on the north edge of Slough, Farnham Royal strives to keep its separate identity. These next three views were taken at the crossroads in the centre of the village; the church is isolated to the south-east. The scene is much changed since the 1950s. There are mini-roundabouts to both junctions, and the building on the right has been demolished for road improvements. The benefit is a small green formed from the left-over land. The old pump house, renewed in 1928, has been shifted 50 yards west out of harm's way onto this green.

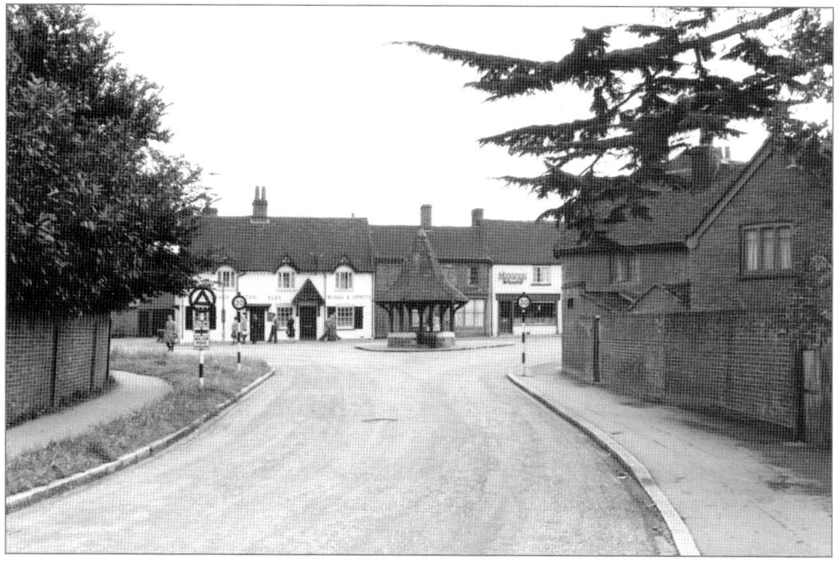

FARNHAM ROYAL, *The Village c1955* F195011

This view, also taken from Farnham Lane, looks across the Beaconsfield Road into Park Road, which leads to Stoke Poges. The Jolly Butcher (centre right) has now been renamed the Farnham Pump in honour of the pump house, which is now, of course, further away from the pub. On the left are the surviving gate piers to Farnham House, which was rebuilt in the 1970s as neo-Georgian offices. The cedar tree and the cottages beyond remain virtually unchanged.

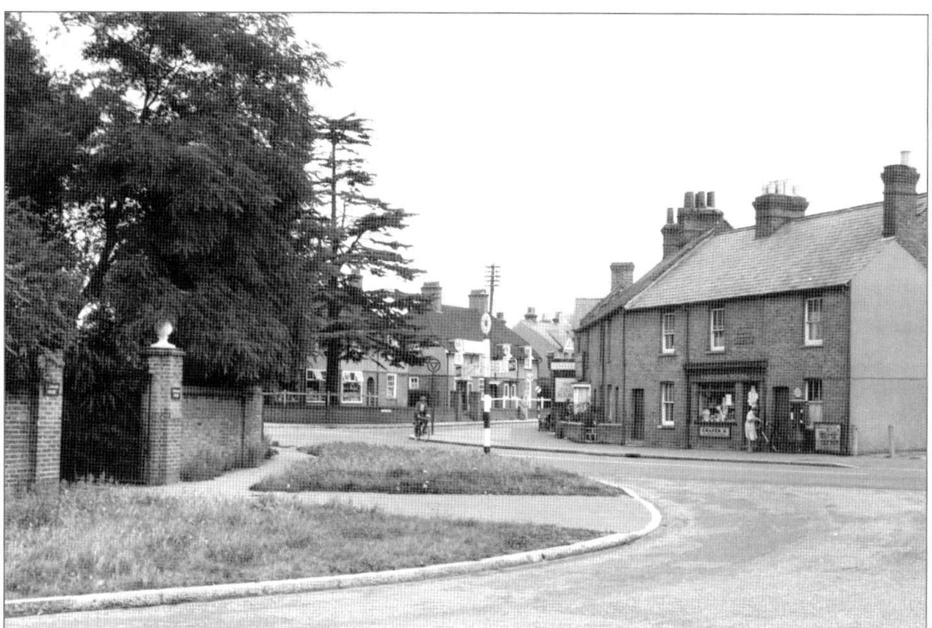

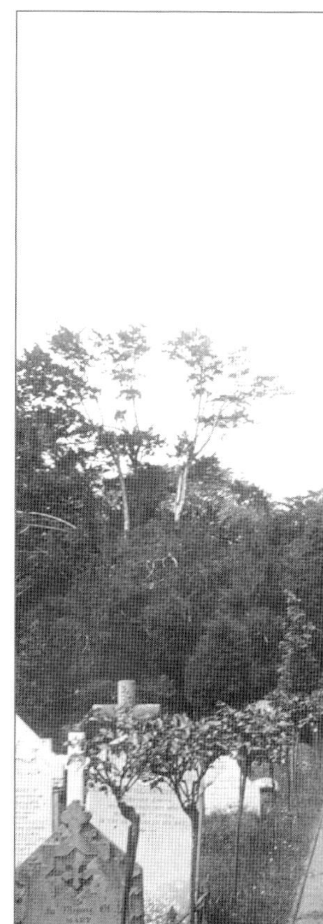

FARNHAM ROYAL
The Village c1955
F195008

This view looks south towards Slough with the Crown pub on the left. The shop beyond survives, now incorporated into the Crown, but all the buildings beyond have been demolished. They have been replaced by houses and flats. On the right is the Duke's Head pub, whose side and rear elevations now look out onto the new green with the relocated pump house.

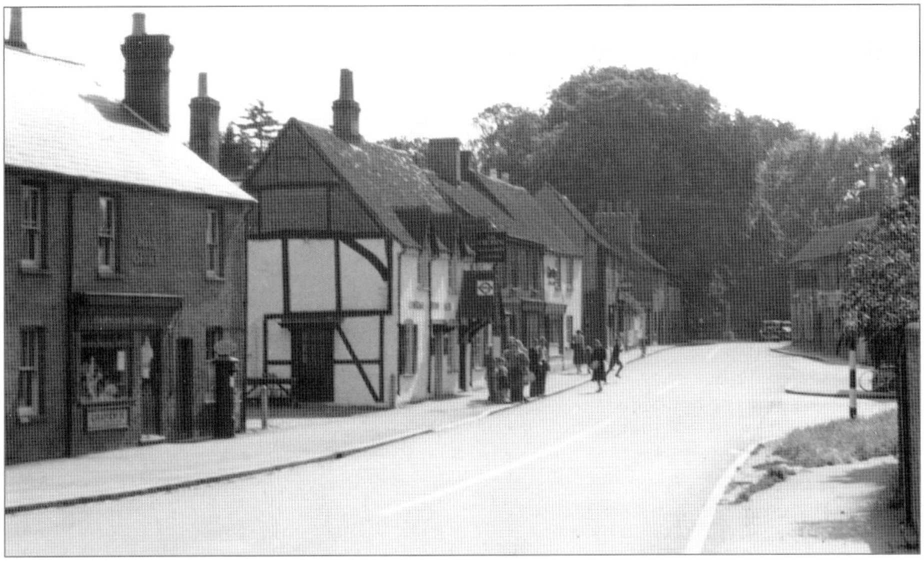

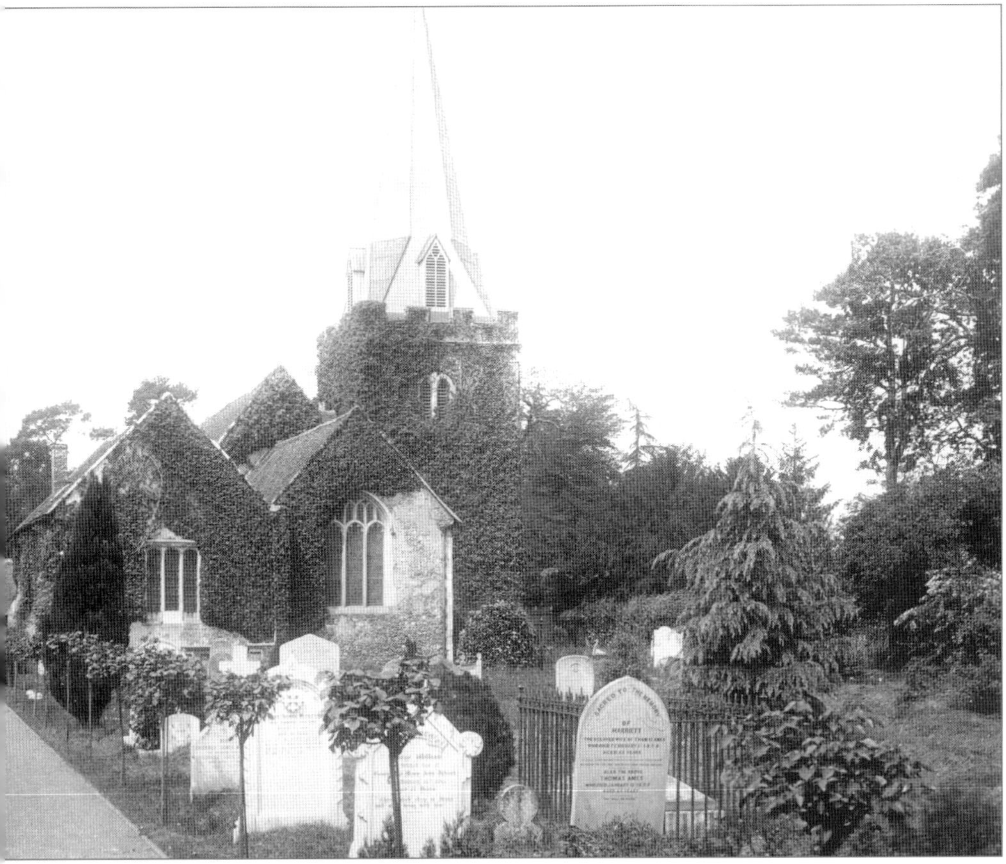

STOKE POGES
The Church 1895
35458

The parish church of St Giles looks much the same in this photograph as it would have done to Thomas Gray, whose great poem 'Elegy Written in a Country Churchyard' was set here. He was indeed buried here in 1777 with his parents, near the brick Hastings Chapel of 1558, the left-hand gable in this view. The church underwent considerable change after this view was taken, and extensions to the north for a vestry and passageway were added in 1907. The spire, a timber replica built in 1831, was removed in 1924, and there is now a low pyramidal tiled roof in its stead.

STOKE POGES
The Churchyard, Sandy's Grave 1929 82276

Here Gray's 'rude forefathers of the hamlet sleep'. How many 'mute, inglorious Miltons here may rest'? Most of the gravestones post-date Gray, of course, and Frith's photographer had his eye caught by this rather unusual one that features a ship's capstan, rope and anchor, as well as a model railway engine and a yacht, the favoured toys of John Alexander McCrea Collie, 'Sandy', who died aged 10 in 1922. Others of his family, including his parents, are also commemorated here. An unusual and poignant monument.

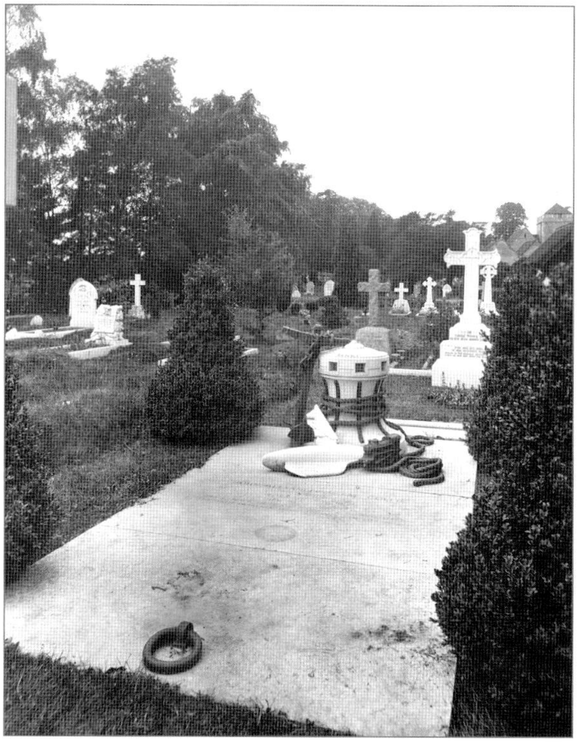

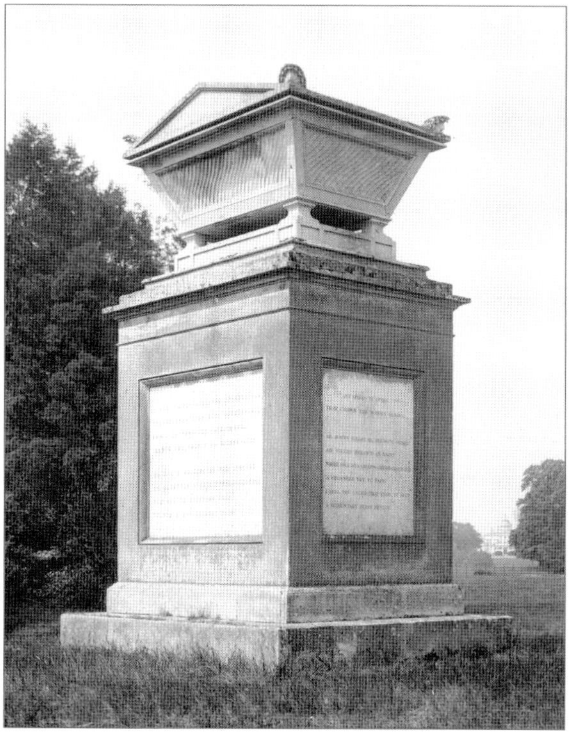

STOKE POGES
Thomas Gray's Cenotaph 1895 35462

South-east of the churchyard, a path through a National Trust-owned copse winds to the fine memorial to Thomas Gray erected by his friend, John Penn of Stoke Park, in 1799. Designed by James Wyatt, it is a classical sarcophagus on a 20ft-high pedestal. The monument was deliberately designed this high so that it could be clearly seen from Penn's house, whose domed front we can just see in this view to the right of the cenotaph (now no longer possible because of tree growth). Indeed, Penn had the old vicarage demolished and relocated to provide an uninterrupted view. The pedestal panels are, not surprisingly, inscribed with lines from Gray's 'Ode on a Distant Prospect of Eton College' and his 'Elegy' – 'The paths of glory lead but to the grave'.

▼ **DENHAM,** *The Village c1965* D183017

Denham, separated from the sprawl of Greater London only by the River Colne and the Grand Union Canal, preserves its beauty and a superb range of historic buildings in a remarkable way. To the left of this view are the grounds of the important Denham Place, built in 1688-1701. The River Misbourne, one of Buckinghamshire's trout-rich chalk streams, flows through the village on its way to join the Colne; this view looks across the river bridge towards the green, which is opposite the four-gabled Blacksmiths Cottage. By the 1960s the smithy had become a garage, but it is now part of the house.

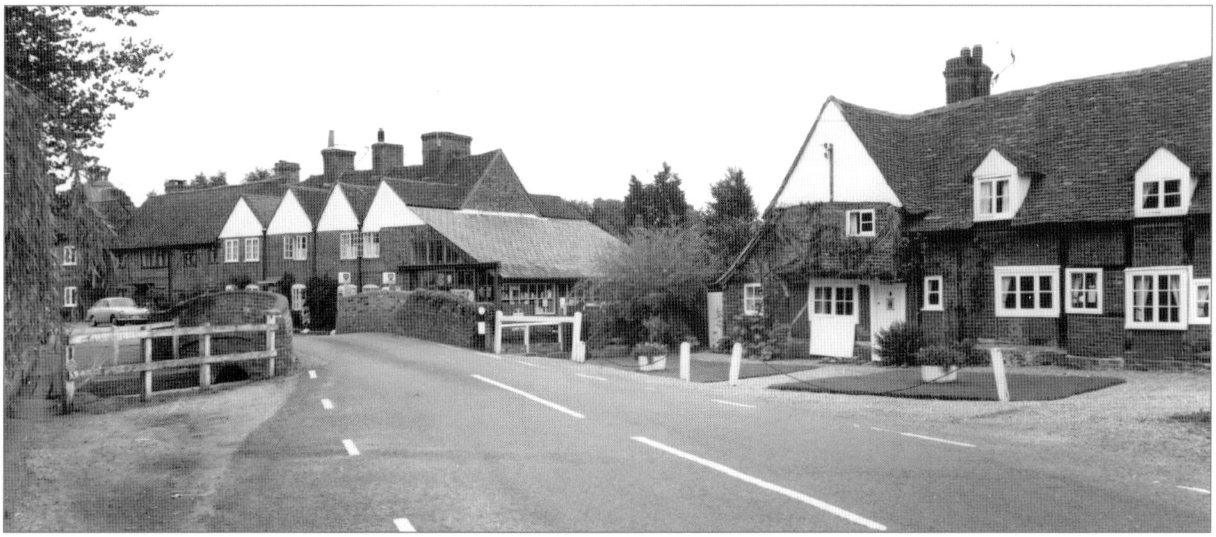

▼ **DENHAM,** *The Airfield c1965* D183015

To the south, the Misbourne suburbs fill the gap to the A40, while Denham Green grew up north of Denham railway station, which opened in 1910. Beyond Denham Green on the chalk plateau, Denham Aerodrome still thrives, although helicopters now fly from here as well as light aircraft. Originally a World War II airfield, it became a civilian one after the war, and is remarkably little changed since the 1960s. Behind the aircraft at the right is Tilehouse Lane; the aerodrome access road runs behind the bungalow and the hangars, all of which survive, along with some additional ones.

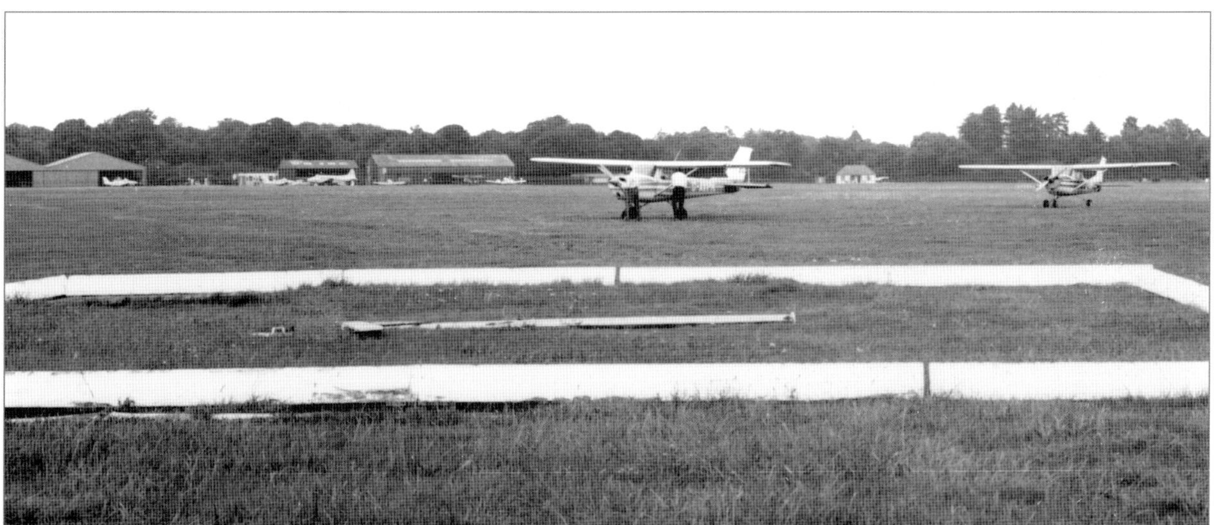

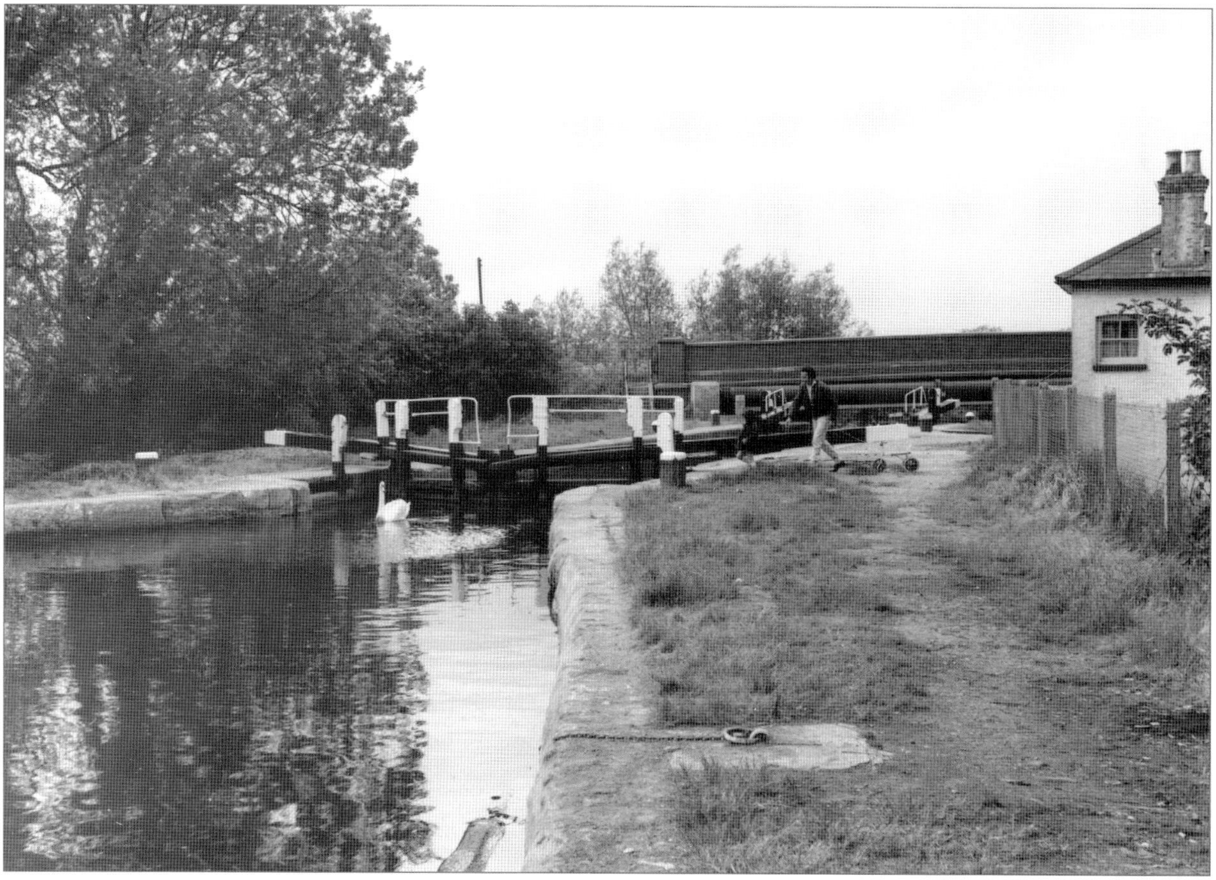

DENHAM, *Widewater Lock c1965* D183003

The eastern county boundary mainly follows the River Colne, with the Grand Union Canal sharing its valley immediately to its east. This view is on Moorhall Road, north-east of Denham Green and within the London Borough of Hillingdon, looking past Widewater Lock towards Moorhall Road bridge. The canal was built as the Grand Junction Canal, and fully opened in 1805. It is hardly surprising that locks were frequently rebuilt, and this one bears the dates 1876 and 1910. The former lock-keeper's cottage is on the right. Beyond the bridge is Harefield Marina, full of canal boats which are now mostly used for leisure.

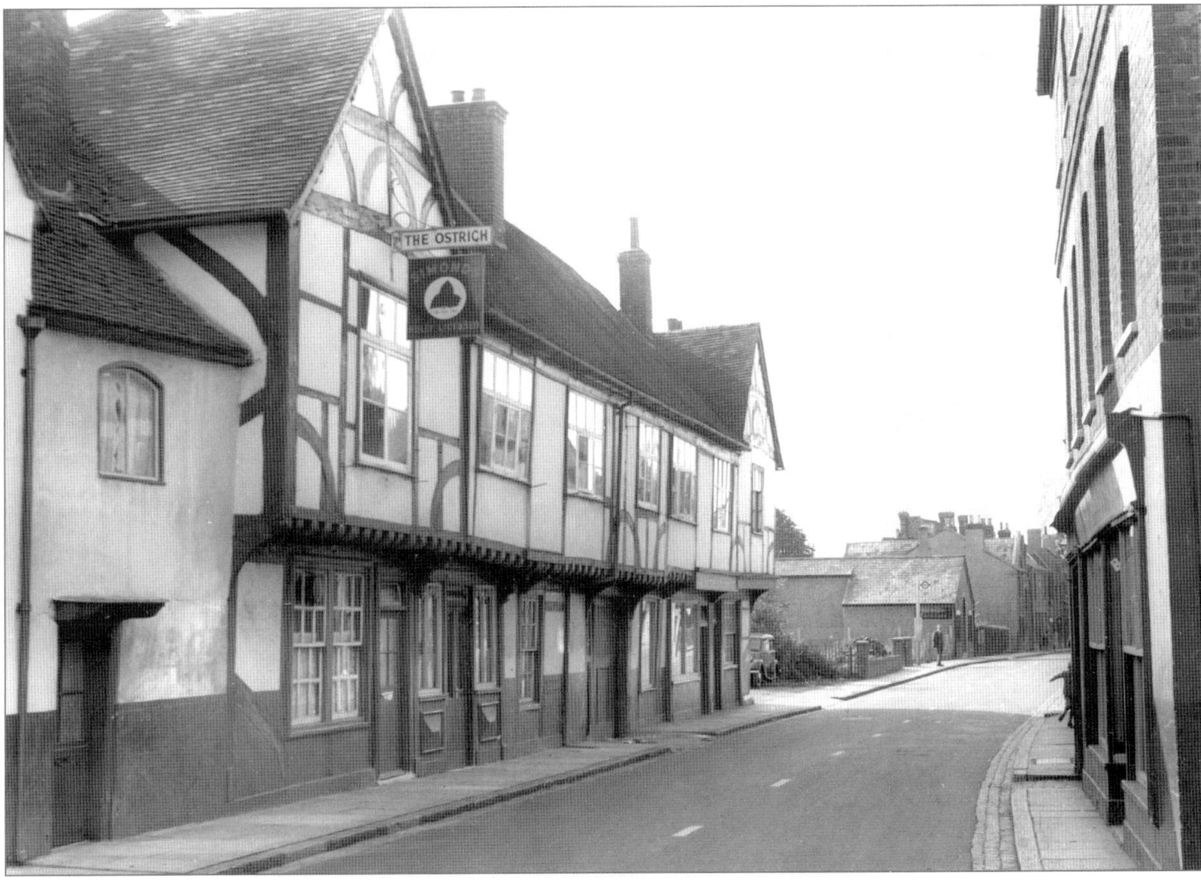

COLNBROOK, *The Ostrich c1955* C494004

The final view in this chapter is in Colnbrook, on the far side of Slough. The river Colne was at one time the county boundary with Middlesex, and then with Surrey after 1974; now the whole of Colnbrook is in Berkshire, part of Slough Borough. In a village much damaged by 1950s road improvements, it is fortunate that the Ostrich survives, one of the best timber-framed buildings in the whole county. One of Colnbrook's several important coaching inns on the old Bath Road (now by-passed by the modern A4 and the M4), it is mainly 16th-century. The shops on the right were rebuilt further back (road improvement again).

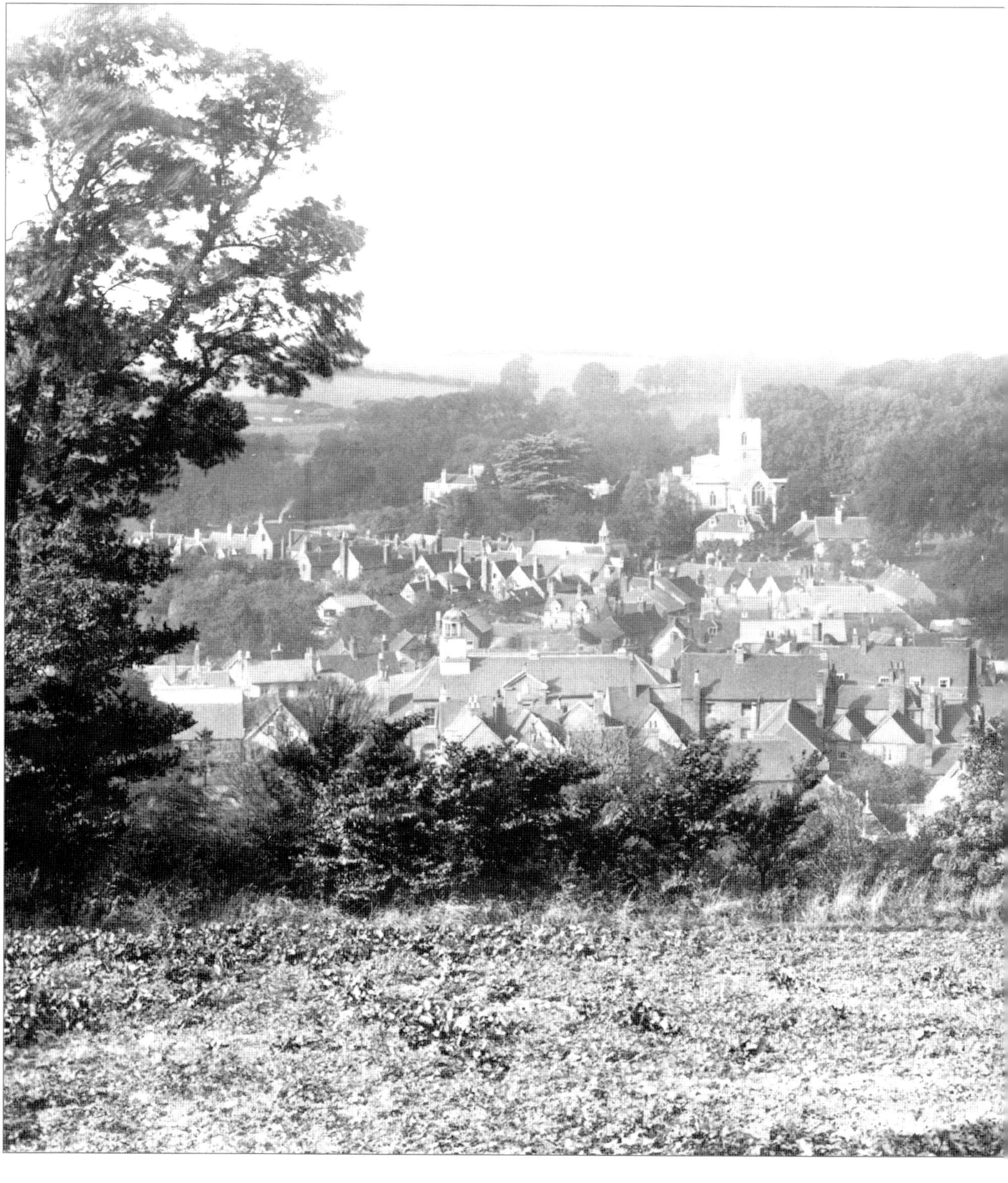

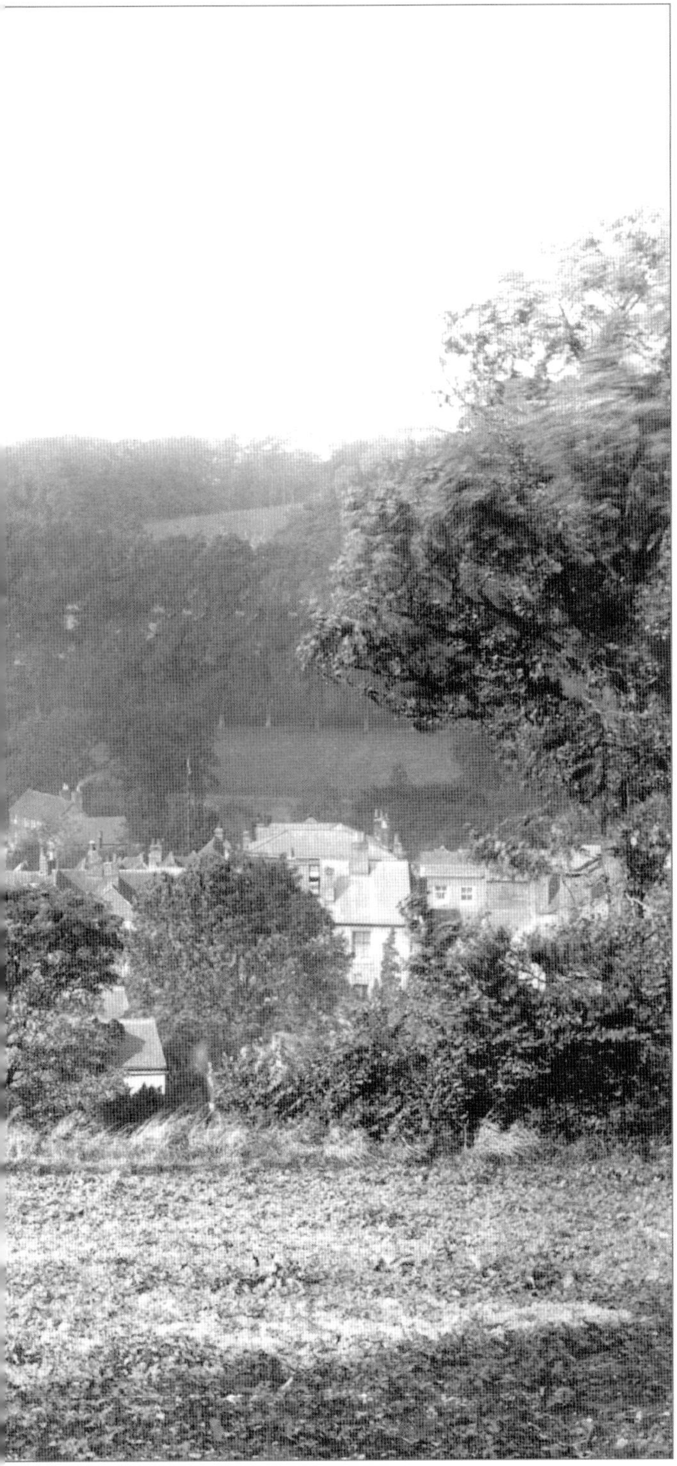

CHESHAM AND THE EASTERN CHILTERN HILLS

CHESHAM
General View from the East 1897
40531

The fifth chapter starts in Chesham, an attractive market town set in a deep and narrow section of the valley of the river Chess. Most of the town's post-1850 expansion took place to the north, away to the right of this view; it is remarkable that this view is little changed since 1897. We can still look across the waist of the town from this field towards the parish church with its 'Hertfordshire spike' spire and see the cedar tree and The Bury mansion to its left. The major change is the loss of the Market House, the building with the cupola in the centre.

► **CHESHAM,** *Town Bridge 1897* 40539

As we descend into the town, our tour starts at the southern end in Germain Street, south of the Market Square, where the young river Chess passes under the road. To the left are the water meadows, some of which survived the creation of the Water Meadow Car Park. This section of the stream was widened into a wagon splash, where carts had their wheels washed and the horses slaked their thirst. The wall and tree to the right belong to The Meades, a good house of about 1800 with an Ionic-columned porch; beyond, the sash-windowed cottages have been demolished.

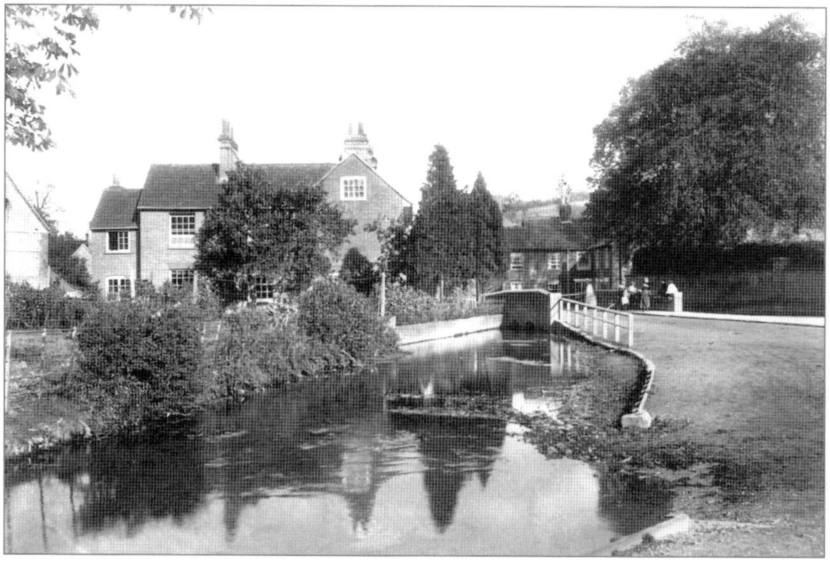

▼ **CHESHAM,** *Market Square 1897* 40536

The next two views, taken in the Market Square, show the old Market House or Town Hall. Chesham has a long history as a market town since at least 1257, when Hugh, Earl of Oxford, obtained a weekly market and an annual three-day fair charter from King Henry III. This Market House was built in the mid 18th century; it was extended and then virtually rebuilt in 1856 at the expense of Lord Chesham, who lived at nearby Latimer House.

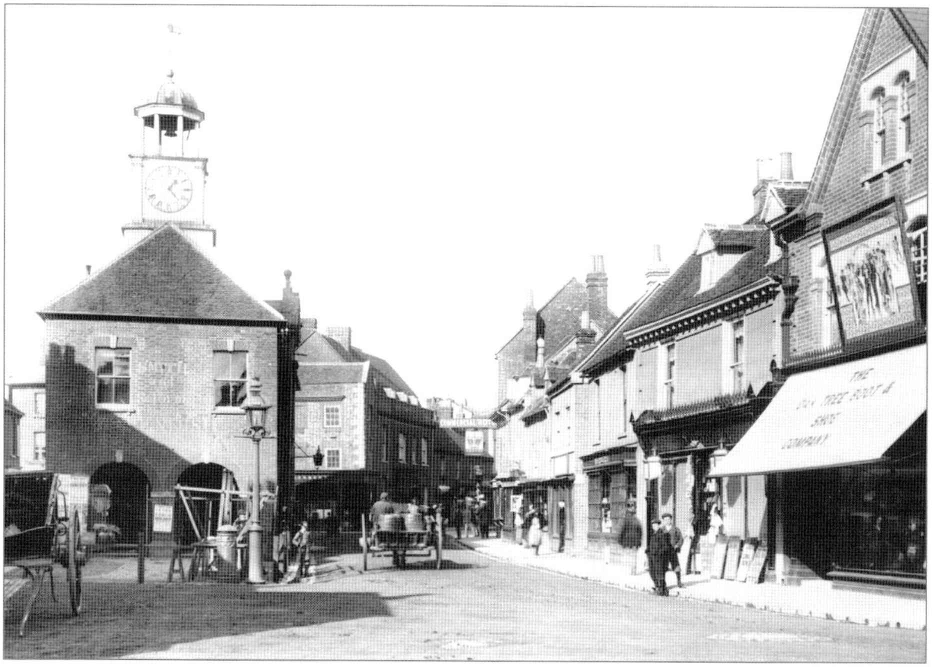

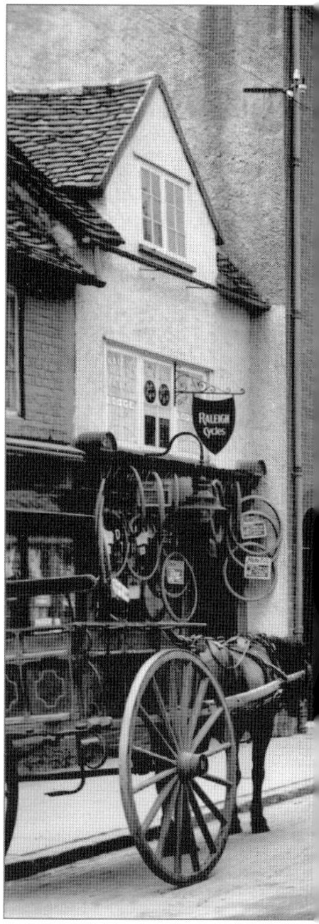

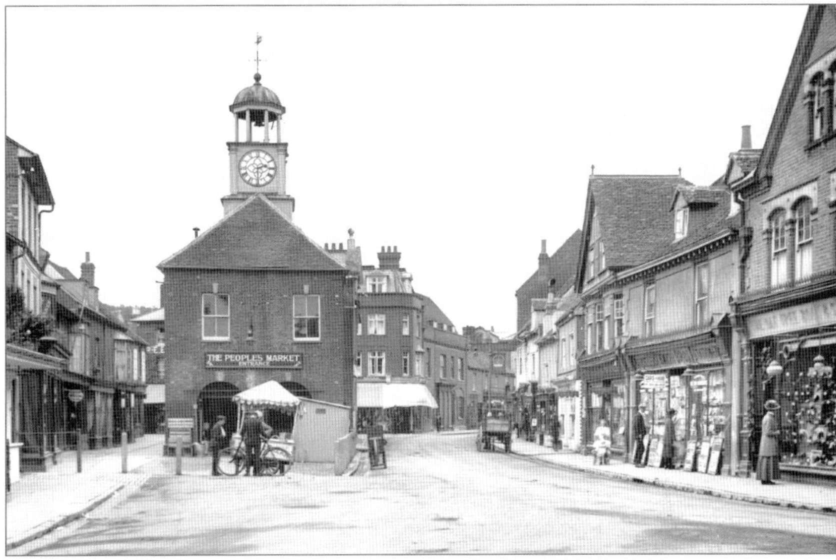

CHESHAM, *Market Square 1921* 70535

Soon after 1897, the Georgian building at the corner of the High Street behind the Market House was replaced, but the shop fronts of Smith Brothers, booksellers and stationers, and the Oak Tree Boot and Shoe Company on the right survive. Today Smith Brothers' premises are still a stationer's. In 1965 the Market House was demolished on highway grounds, and in the 1980s the foreground buildings were demolished to make way for the inner relief road. A clock tower was erected in 1992 on the site of the Market House as some compensation for its needless loss.

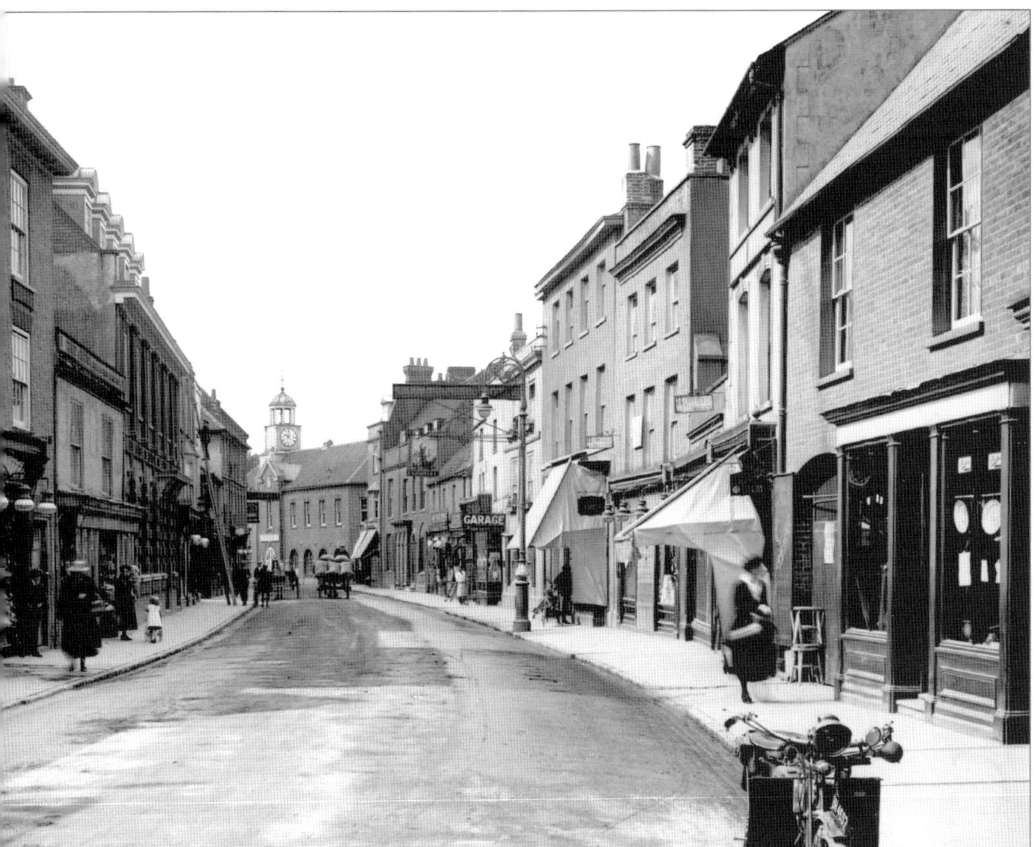

CHESHAM *High Street 1921* 70537

This view looks back down the High Street towards the Market Square, and shows how the Market House and its cupola closed the vista down the High Street in a most satisfactory way. The three-storey building on the left is still a shoe shop today, Stead and Simpson rather than Freeman Hardy & Willis. The lower building beyond it was demolished, and a brick and stone-fronted Moderne-style bank built in about 1930, a complete and aggressive contrast to the Georgian buildings all around.

CHESHAM
High Street
1897 40538

This view and No C81009 look north up the High Street towards the three-storey cliff of the former Chess Vale Temperance Hotel of about 1898. The rather good three-storey Georgian building on the right with the arched central windows, and the building to its left, were replaced by the Queen Anne-style National Provincial Bank in 1912, now the NatWest, built in fiery red and grey brick. Note the rather fine ornate gas lamp standard on the left.

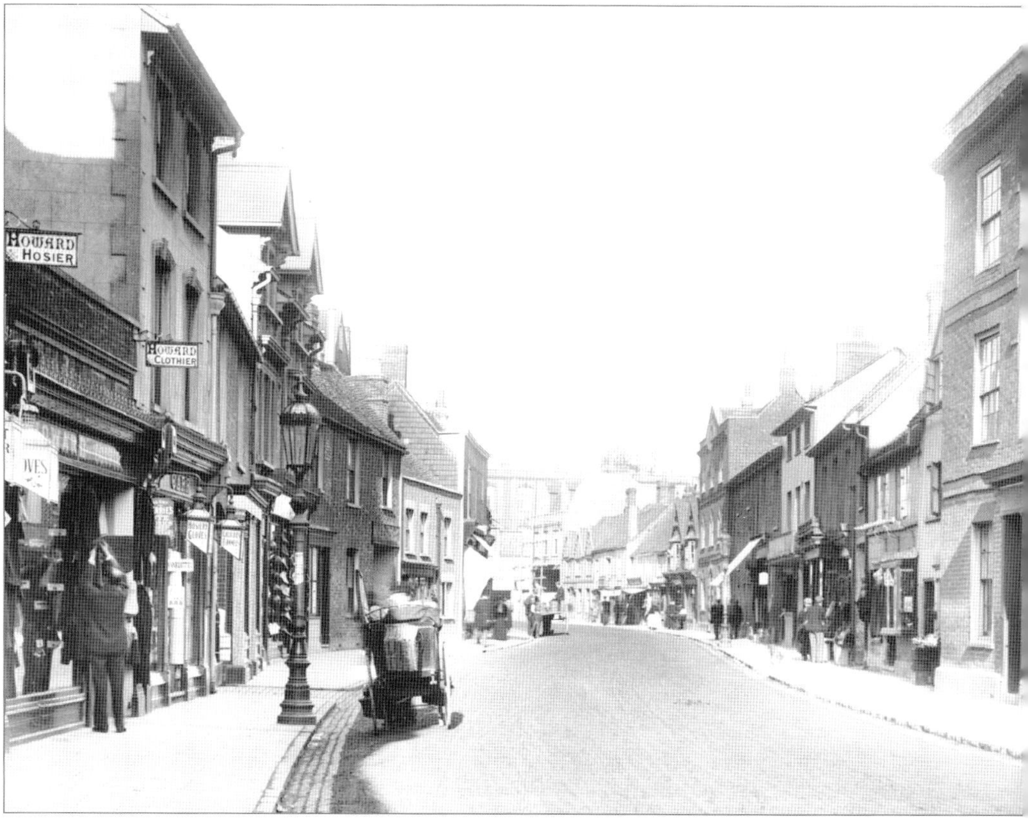

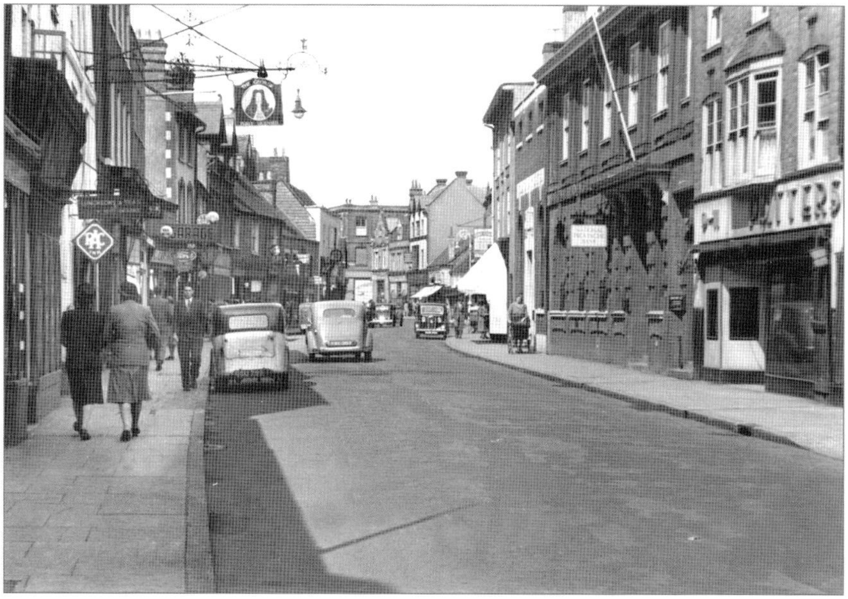

CHESHAM, *High Street*
c1955 C81009

Here we see the ornate National Provincial Bank of 1912 on the right, and immediately beyond it the 1930 Midland Bank. On the left, the white-painted brickwork belongs to the George (now the George and Dragon), whose early Georgian facade conceals a 17th-century timber-framed building. The garage beyond has gone. In its place is now Baines Walk, named after a leading local councillor, antiquarian and historian, Arnold Baines - it leads to the Town Council offices. The High Street is now traffic-calmed, paved with clay paviours, a one-way street and virtually traffic-free.

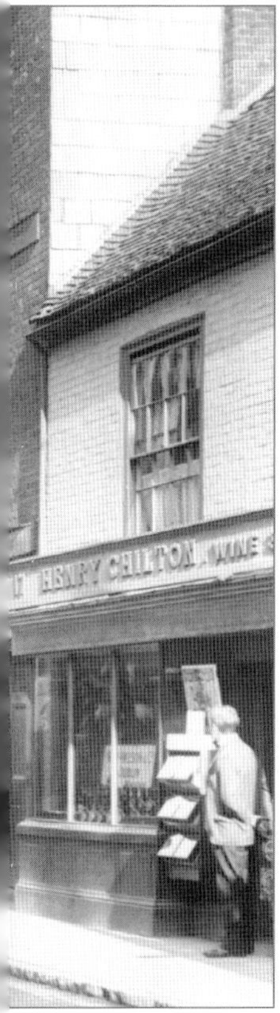

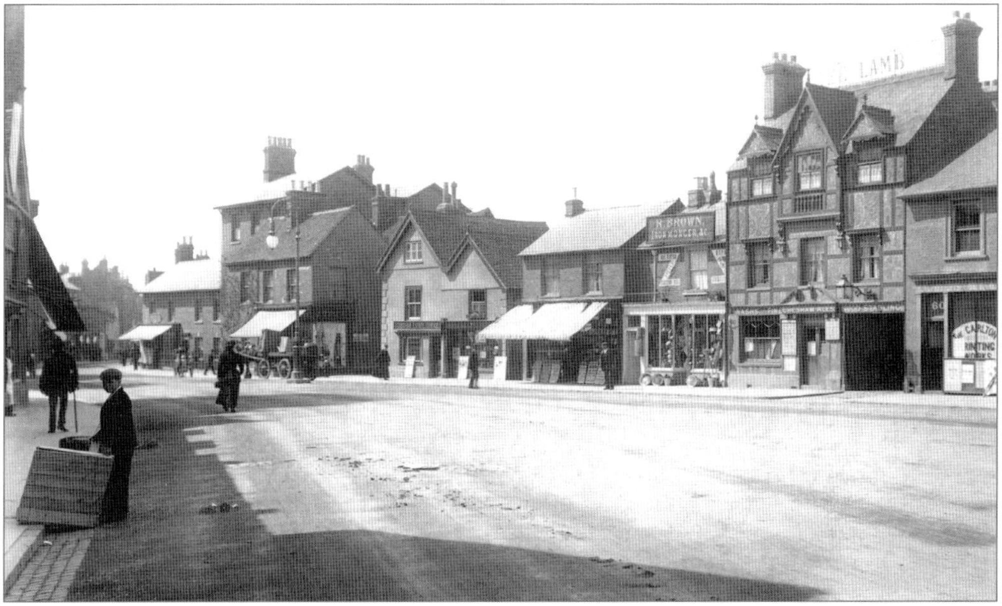

▲ **CHESHAM,** *The Broadway 1906* 53647

This area was once known as Pillory Green, but this name gradually fell into disfavour, and it has been known as The Broadway since the mid 19th century at least. Here the High Street widens where Blucher Street comes in from the west, before narrowing to continue north as far as White Hill. This view looks south-west into the High Street. Everything from the tall five-chimney stack at the left to The Carlton Printing Works was demolished in the 1960s and 1970s (the Lamb went in 1974) to be replaced by dire modern buildings.

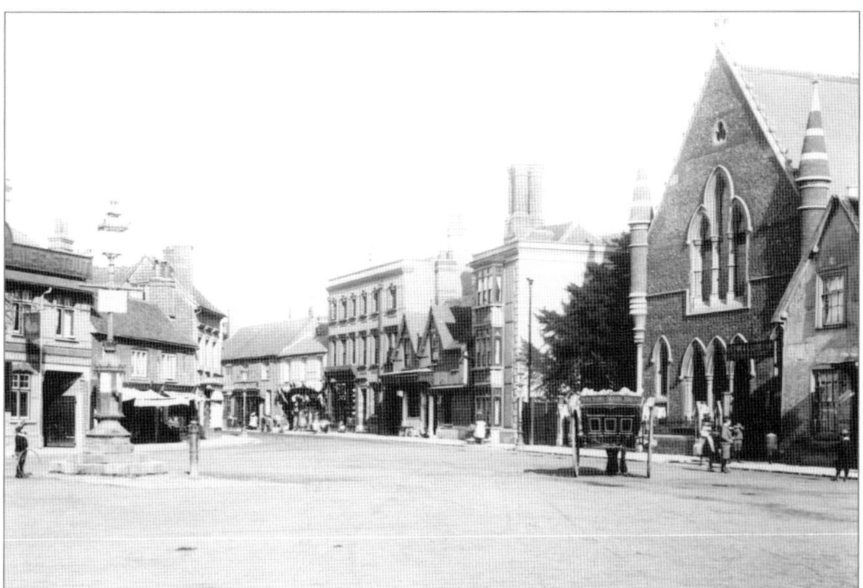

◄ **CHESHAM**
The Broadway 1897 40534

This view looks north into the continuation of the High Street, with the ornate street lamp and pump as the centrepiece being admired by a boy with a hoop. Beyond the baker's cart is the Congregational church of 1886, uncompromisingly Gothic in style, here just over ten years old and replacing a Georgian chapel of 1724. The Cock pub on the left was rebuilt in the 1890s, replacing a ramshackle timber-framed building. The building next to the church with the fine 17th-century four-shaft chimney stack was for years the post office.

▼ **CHESHAM,** *Town Square c1965* C81089

Many changes have taken place since 1897 (No 40534), the most obvious being the replacement of the ornate central street lamp by the World War I memorial in still pristine white Portland stone. Erected in 1921, like such memorials all over the country, it had further names added for the Second World War. Next to the Cock (centre left), the shops were replaced by a neo-Georgian Barclays Bank in the 1950s. This in its turn was replaced in the 1980s. It is sad that the good shop fronts in the distance that we saw in view 40534 have succumbed to 1960s modernisation and blandness.

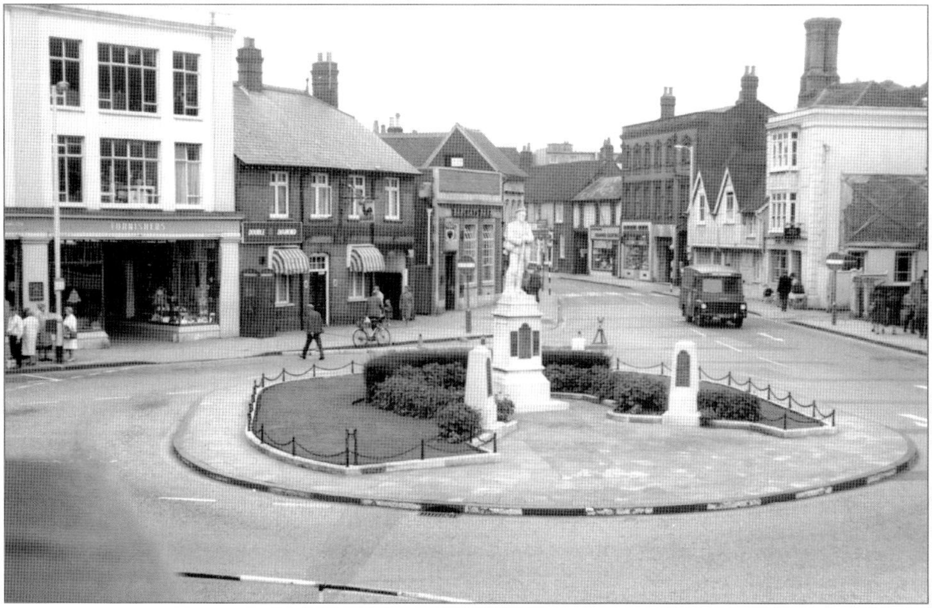

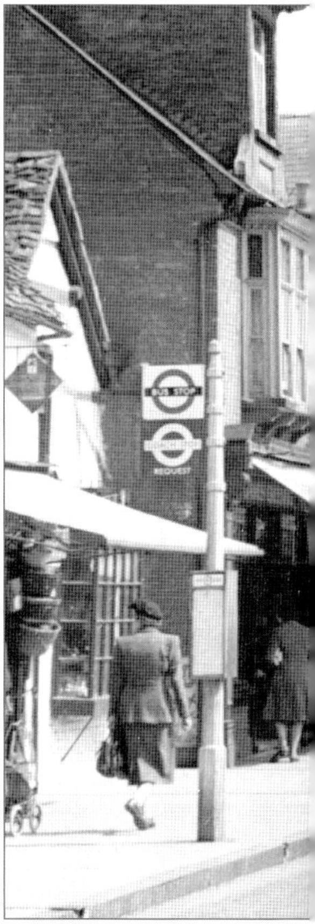

► **CHESHAM,** *The Bury 1897* 40544

To the west of the town centre, and accessed from Church Street (still the best street architecturally in the town), a drive leads between two neat lodges into the grounds of The Bury. This mansion, now used as offices, was built in 1712 for William Lowndes, Secretary to the Treasury. In 1700 Lowndes had already built himself Winslow Hall in Winslow, his native town. Here we see The Bury from across the lake, which was made by damming a chalk stream. The central five bays are Lowndes's; then in about 1800 the outer bays were added, and further additions were made to the left in the 1850s. Behind is the parish church tower.

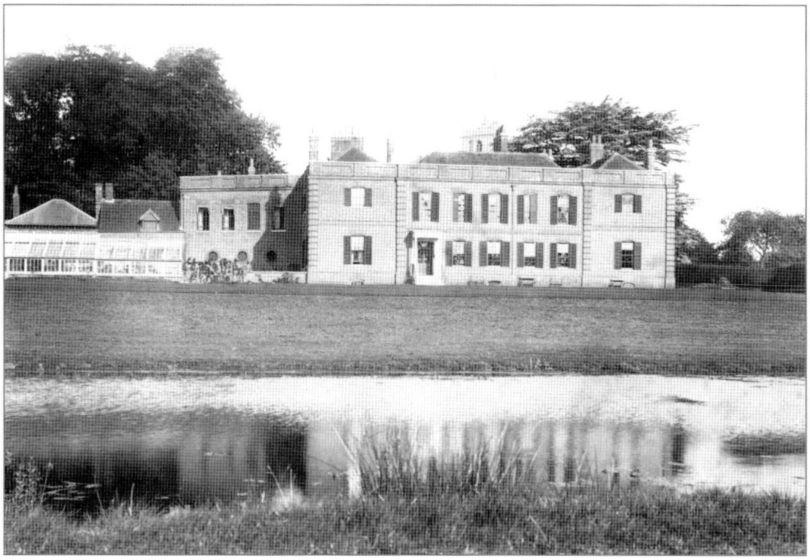

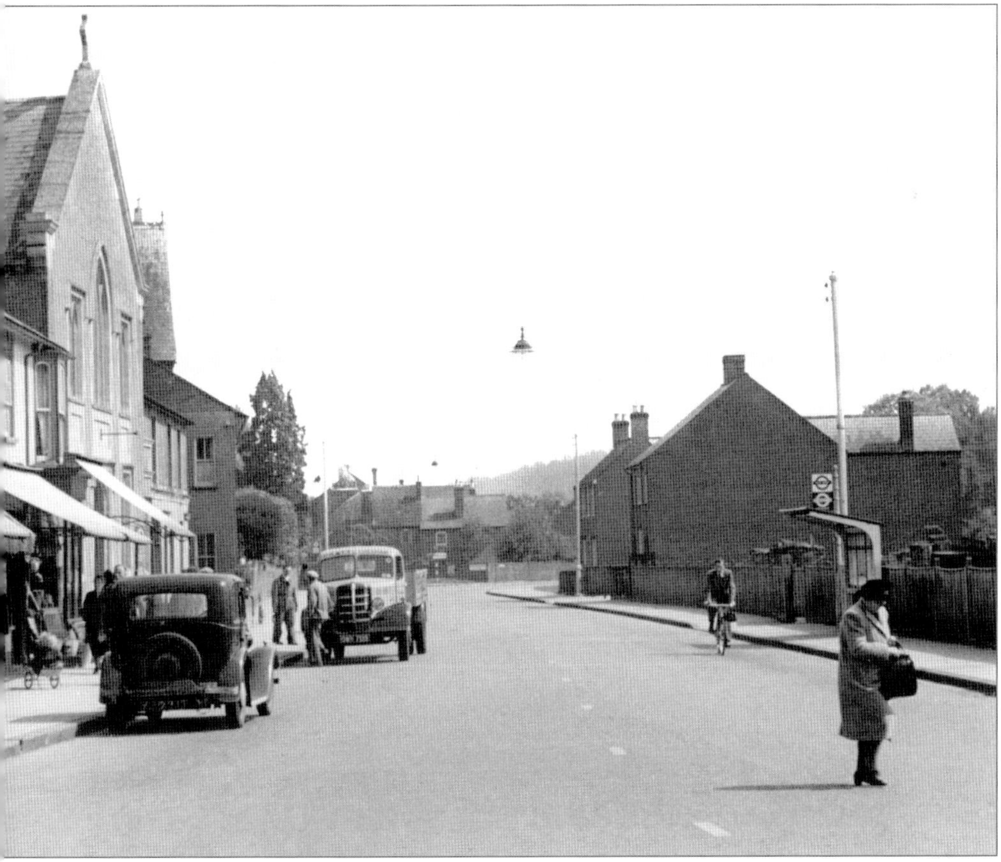

◄ **CHESHAM**
Red Lion Street c1950 C81001

We head back to the town centre, and our tour now heads for the Chess valley via Red Lion Street. The river runs alongside the trees at the far right. The original Red Lion at the corner of Germain Street had been demolished for 1930s road improvements and rebuilt further back. On the left, by the bus stop, is a 17th-century timber-framed building, and the gable fronted building beyond is the Zion Hall, formerly the Zion Baptist church of the 1880s, and beyond is the roof of the former Hinton Baptist Chapel of 1897. They merged in 1968.

► **CHESHAM,** *Waterside 1897*
40547

To the south-east of Chesham town centre the River Chess flows along a flat-bottomed valley, with water meadows to the south side and the settlement of Waterside along its north bank. It consisted mostly of 19th-century cottages for the workers in the workshops, small factories and water-powered and then steam-powered mills that lined the valley. The weatherboarded workshops on the left were replaced around 1900. This view also shows the now demolished church hall to the right of Christchurch, the church to the right of the cottages.

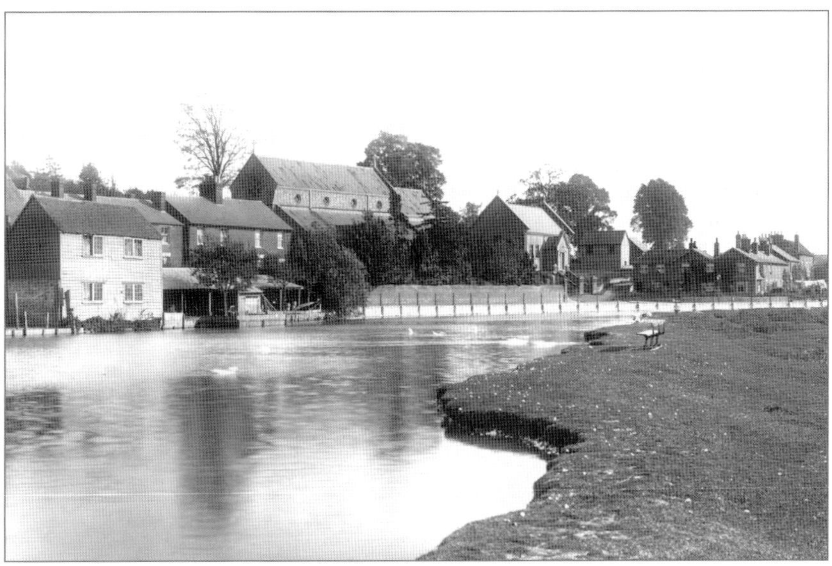

CHESHAM
Christchurch 1903
49242

Behind the idlers watching Frith's photographer and providing incidental local colour, Christchurch is a somewhat bleak and austere flint church with stone dressings built to serve the new industrial suburb of Chesham. Designed by the locally prolific Raphael Brandon, it was built in the early 1860s. There used to be a multi-chimneyed vicarage behind in a similar austere style, this time Tudor, which was demolished some years ago and replaced by dull terraced houses.

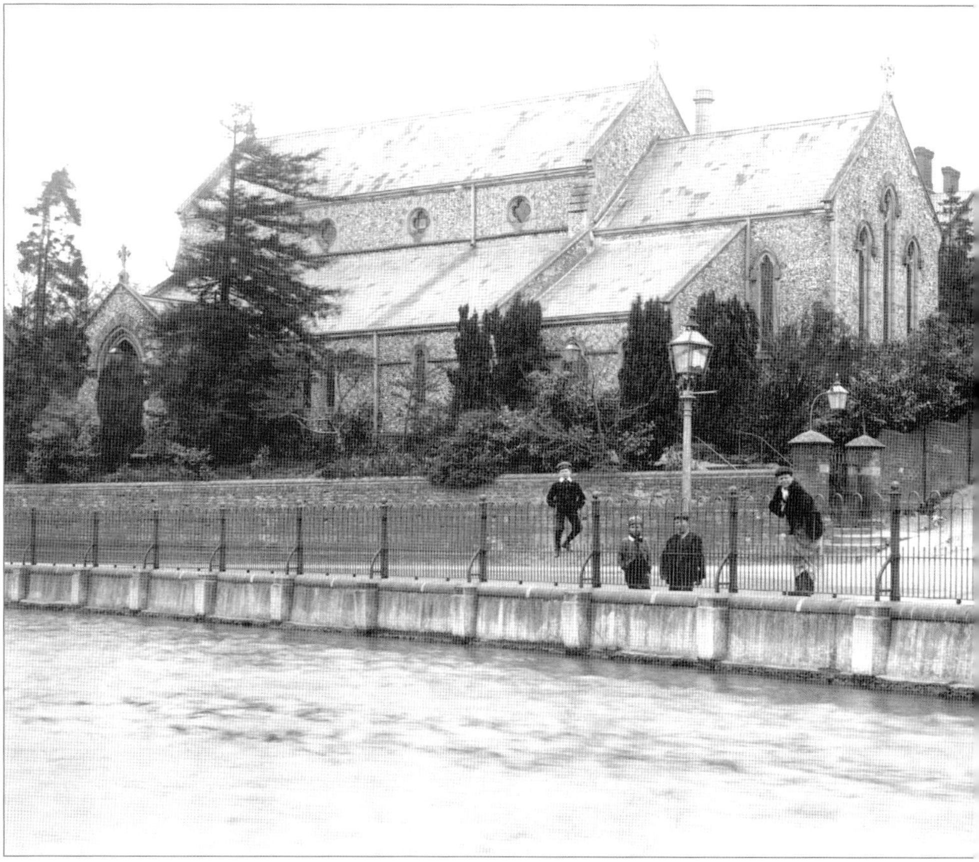

CHESHAM BOIS
The Church 1906 53657

We climb out of the Chess valley to the chalk ridge between Chesham and Amersham to Chesham Bois, whose key feature is the common. The parish church lies half a mile north of the common in a more rural location. The manor became an independent parish during the Middle Ages, and the church includes 14th-century elements. However, it was almost entirely rebuilt in 1881. In 1884 the tower was added, and in 1911, five years after this view was taken, the nave was extended two further bays to the left.

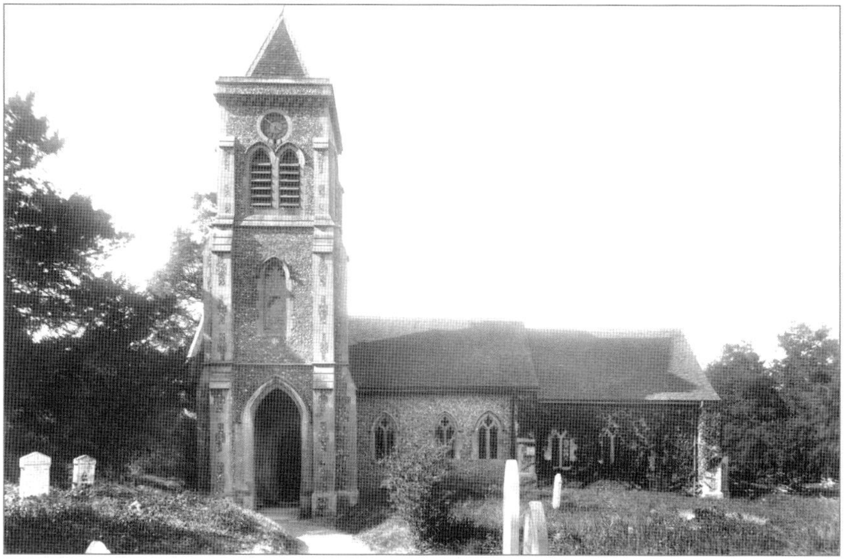

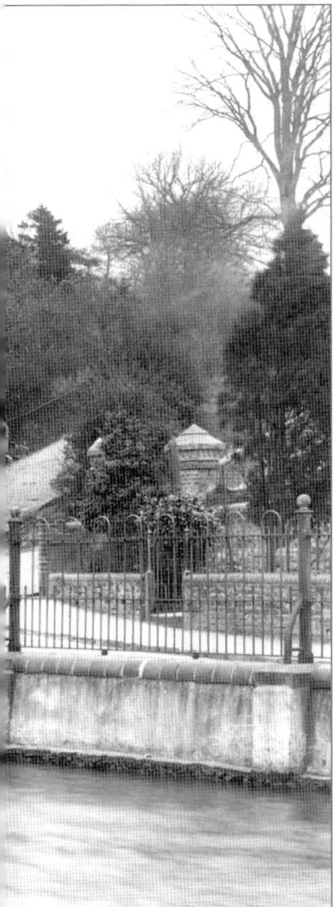

▼ **CHESHAM BOIS,** *Anne's Corner c1955* C693305

The name 'Bois' comes from one of the three manors of Chesham - this one was named after William de Bosco (Latin for woods) or de Boies (the French for woods). This view looks north along Bois Lane beside the east edge of the common; the mock-medieval Anne's Corner is complete with a timber-framed and jettied upper storey and a chequered stone and flint lower storey. To the left we can glimpse the lower part of the war memorial of 1921. On the right, the shop with the glazed veranda is the post office, which opened around 1897. In more recent years the post office moved to premises across the road, but it closed in 2003.

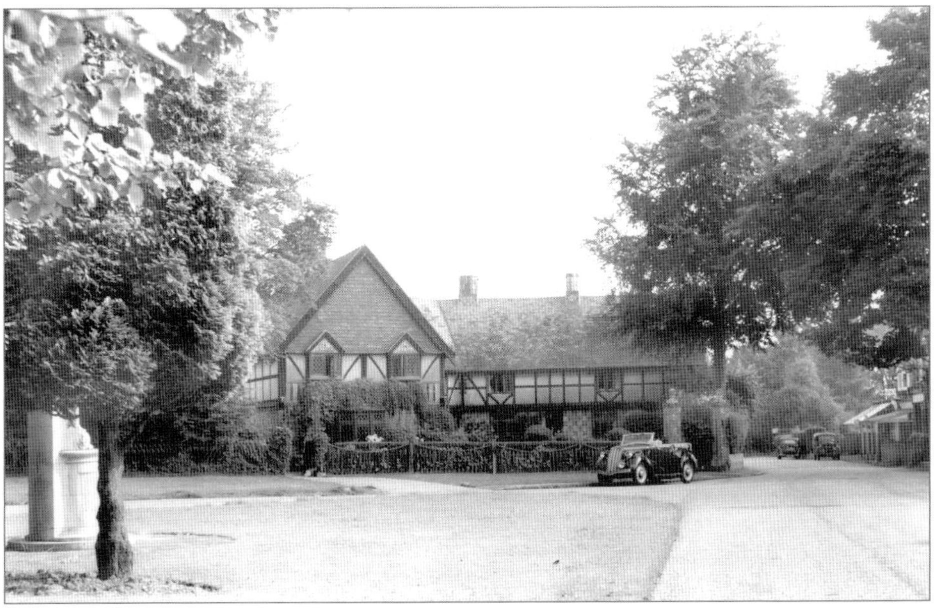

► **CHESHAM BOIS**
The Common 1906 53656

In 1906 there is of course no war memorial, which was erected to the left of the big tree. The foreground lane is North Road; the houses front Bois Lane, which runs along the east side of the common. These are late Victorian houses - the one to the right of the big tree, Sloe Cottage, is dated 1890. The common is now surrounded by Metroland housing, for the railway arrived down the hill in Chesham in 1889 and at Amersham on the Hill, with which Chesham Bois now merges, in 1892.

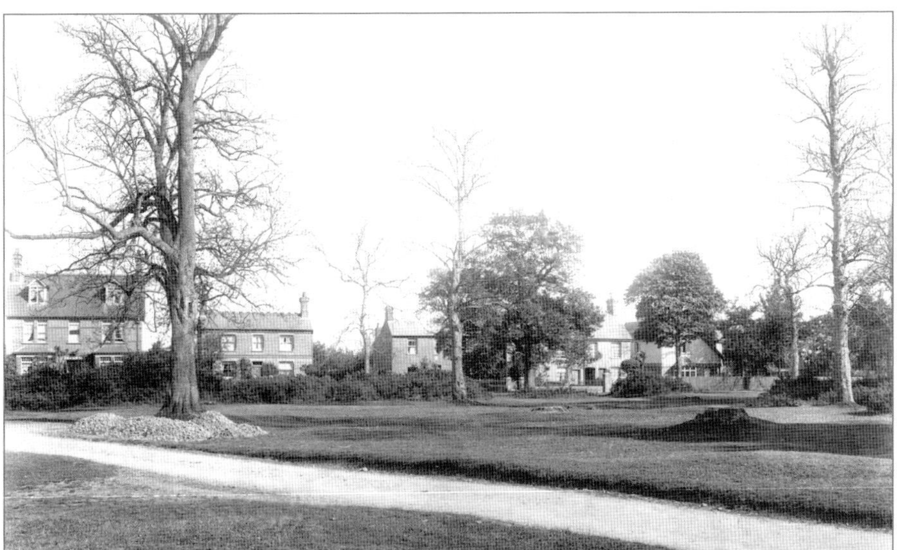

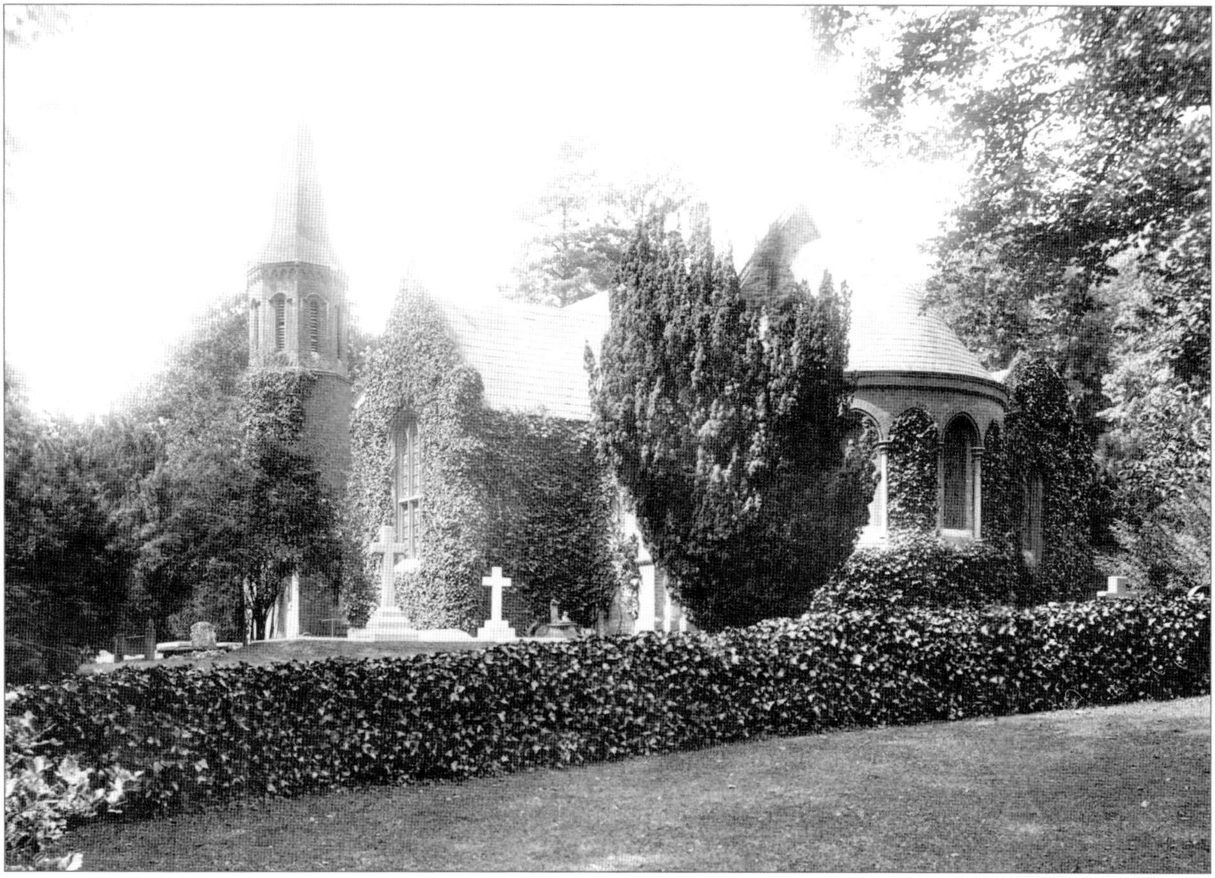

LATIMER, *The Church 1897* 39694

Descending back into the Chess valley, our tour reaches Latimer. Here Lord Chesham's mansion, Latimer House, lies to the west of the village and looks down on the valley – it is now the offices of an accountancy firm. Lord Chesham rebuilt the house in Gothic style in the 1830s, using the architect Edward Blore. At the edge of the grounds is the church Lord Chesham also had rebuilt by Blore in 1841. The great architect Sir George Gilbert Scott further enlarged the church in 1867, for Scott's uncle was the rector here.

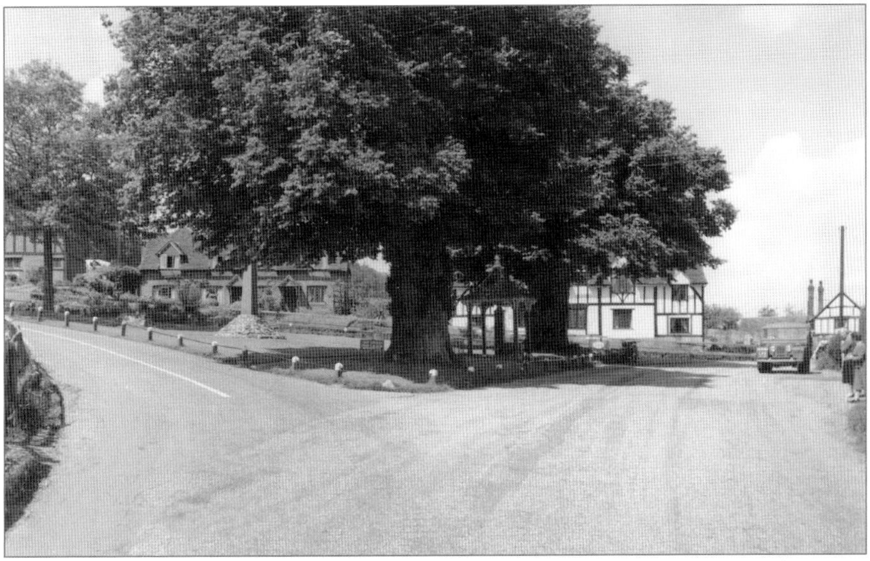

LATIMER, *The Village c1955* L504003

The village lies downhill in a deep valley, Finedon Bottom, that runs north from the river Chess. This delightful green is surrounded by timber-framed 17th-century cottages and 19th-century estate cottages. While the village pump protected by its tile-roofed structure survives, the two great trees have gone since this view was taken. The sign to the left of the tree points to the Joint Services Staff College, later the National Defence College, which until the 1980s was at Latimer House; its former buildings to the north are now a smart housing estate.

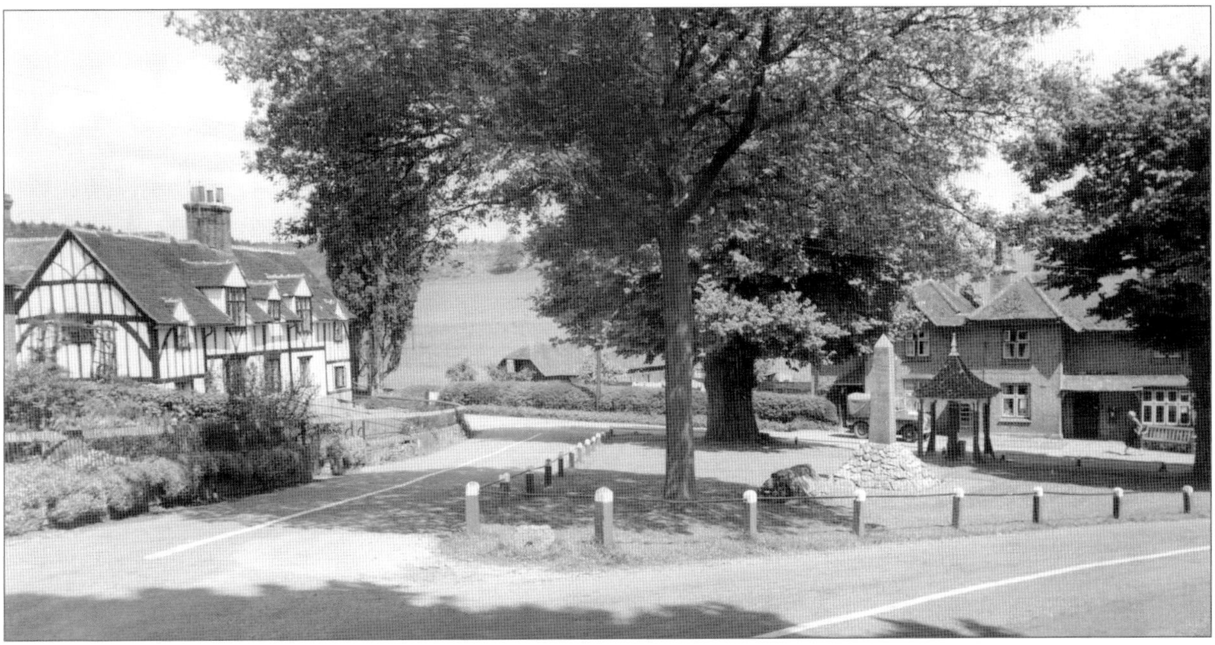

LATIMER, *The Village c1955* L504004

This view looks downhill towards the rather cluttered green. Here stands not only the village pump, but also a granite obelisk memorial to those who served in the Boer War in South Africa, many of them with Lord Chesham, who had commanded a company of the Bucks Hussars there. In front of the obelisk is the grave of a horse. When Lord Chesham was in South Africa, his life was saved during the Battle of Boshof by a French general, De Villebois Mareuil, who was killed and his horse wounded. Lord Chesham brought the horse back to Latimer, where it spent an honourable retirement before its burial here.

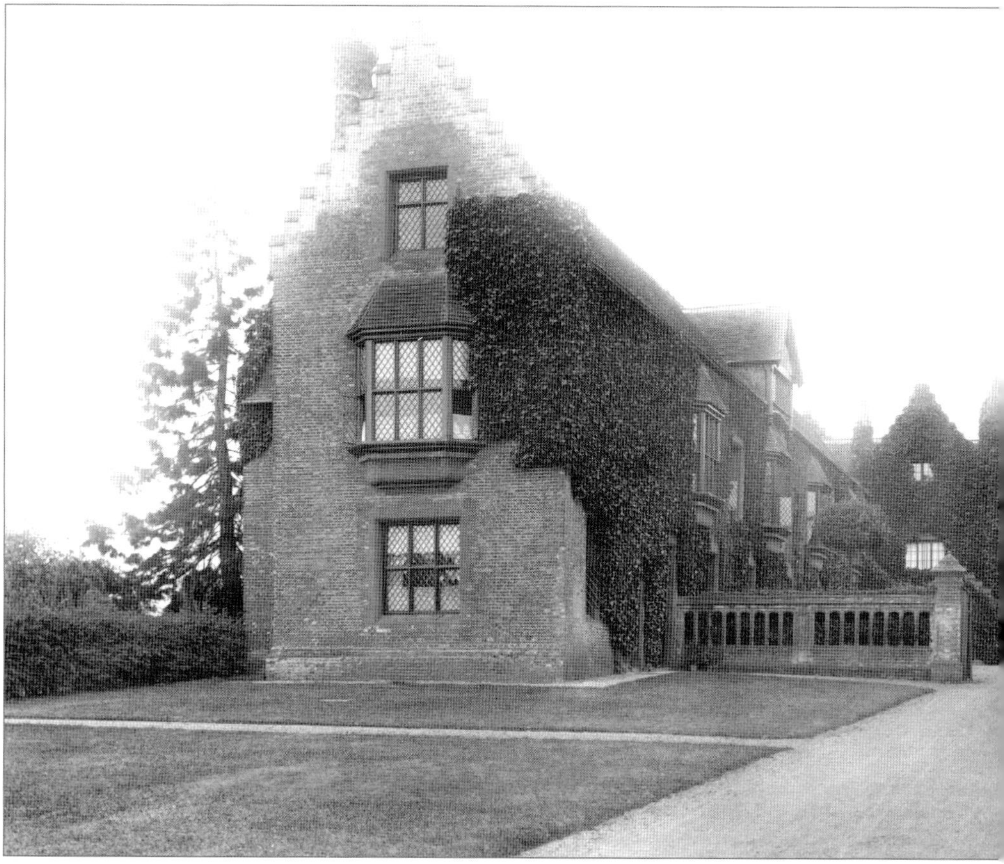

CHENIES
The Manor House 1897 39680

Chenies, a mile downstream along the River Chess from Latimer, takes its name from the Cheyne family. They held the manor from the 13th century until the 16th, when it passed through marriage to the Russells, later the Earls and Dukes of Bedford. The creeper-covered hall in the distance was built by the Cheynes in the late 15th century, while the left-hand range was added around 1530 by Sir John Russell, later Earl of Bedford, as a lodgings range for distinguished guests, who included Queen Elizabeth I.

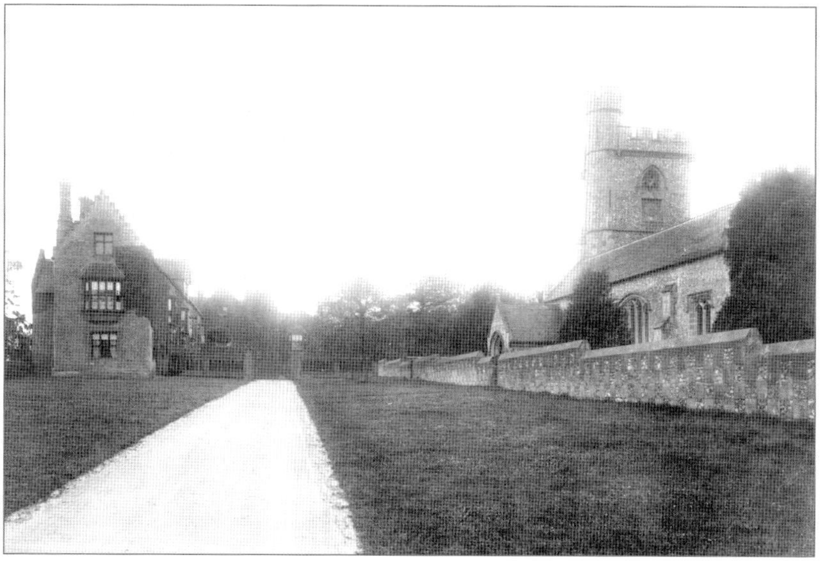

CHENIES, *The Manor House and the Church 1903* 49313

The manor house was built entirely in brick, and became a farmhouse after the Russells moved their seat to Woburn Abbey in Bedfordshire. Decaying dramatically, it was finally restored by Lord Wriothesley Russell in the 1830s. The medieval church, meanwhile, remains the Russell family mausoleum, for they added a private chapel in 1556, much rebuilt and enlarged since. In it repose a quite splendid collection of their effigies and monuments from the 16th century to the present day. The bleak atmosphere of this photograph is relieved by a number of trees nowadays.

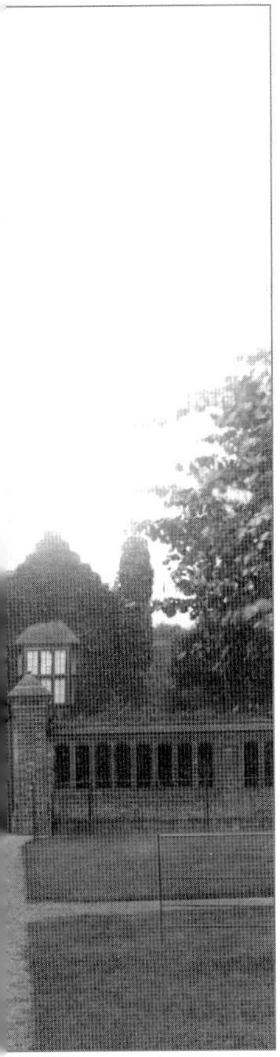

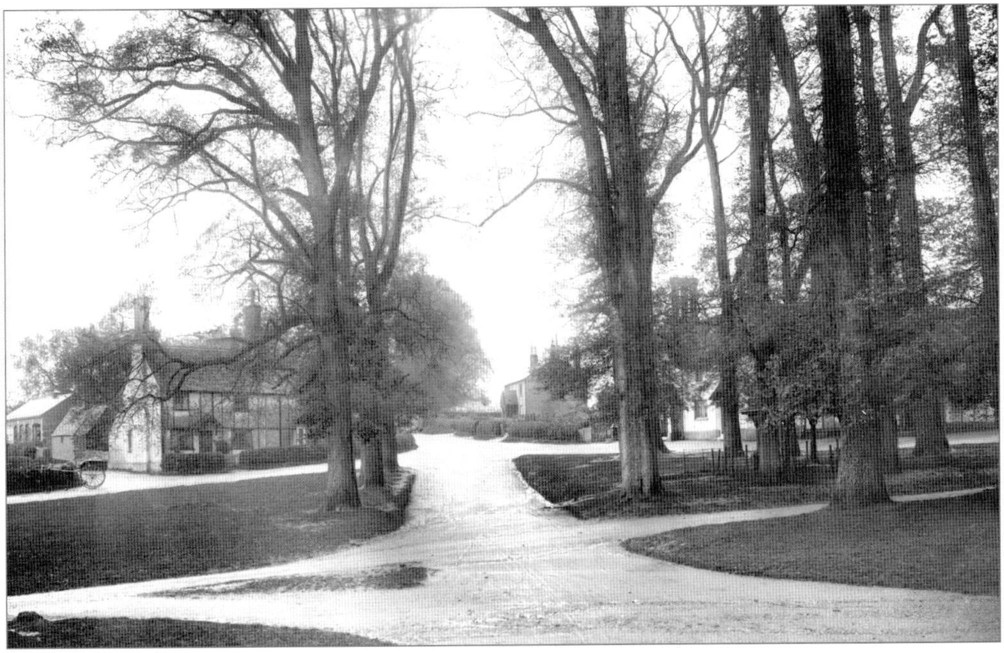

▲ **CHENIES,** *The Green 1897* 49314

Although there are a few older cottages, Chenies village is basically the creation of the Dukes of Bedford. The majority of the cottages date from the 1820s, 1840s and 1850s in their estate style: brick, simplified Tudor detail with lattice leaded windows. This view looks east from the manor house drive to the village green, all but engulfed in tall trees. The trees have long gone - there are more modest trees in their stead now, and the green is more open.

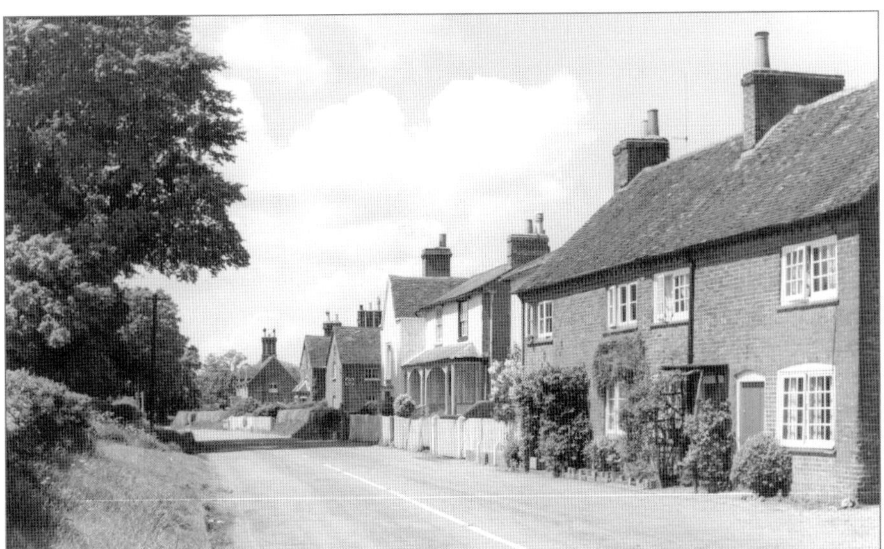

◄ **CHENIES**
The Village c1955
C609013

As we move down the lane from the green (a rather contrived piece of village-scape), we find a cluster of architecturally more diverse buildings around the Red Lion and the Baptist chapel. From left to right are estate cottages in picturesque Tudor mode, one dated 1845, then a Regency-style rendered cottage with a slate-roofed veranda, and nearer the camera a terrace of late 18th-century brick cottages.

▼ **CHENIES,** *The Post Office c1955* C609032

We now move further back towards the village centre, where we have a closer view of the estate cottages we saw in view C609013. The house on the left, Field Cottage, is in the slightly more elaborate Tudor style of the 1840s and 1850s, and is dated 1845. It has dormers, a gabled porch and leaded lattice windows, and the Bedford plaque on the gable. The main elaboration to the right-hand cottages is the multi-flued chimneystacks. The left-hand cottage was the village store, but is now a private house named The Old Village Shop.

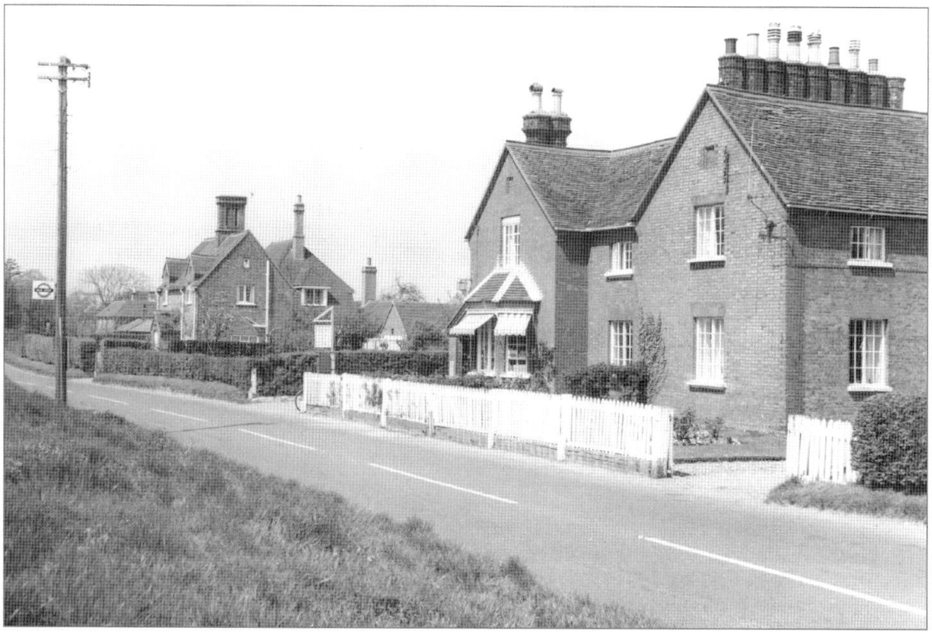

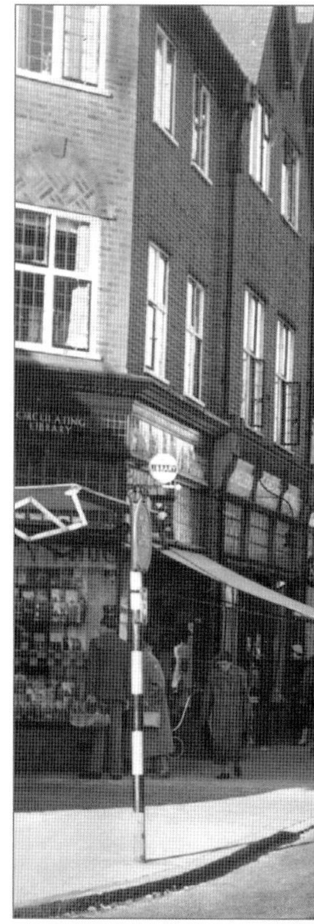

► **CHENIES,** *The Village c1955* C609016

Here Frith's photographer looks in the opposite direction towards the Red Lion, an early 19th-century pub with attractive bay windows. Beyond, the railings (which date from 1840) and notice-board belong to the Baptist chapel, built in the 1770s and enlarged in 1799. It is a delightful brick building, its hipped roof slate-tiled; inside it has galleries on three sides, lit by upper windows. The trees and hedges on the right have been removed since the 1950s and a wide grass verge created.

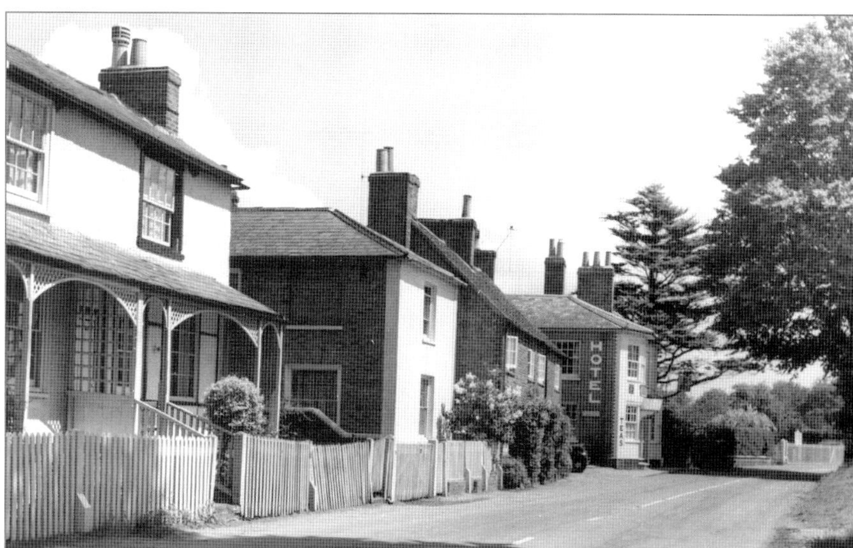

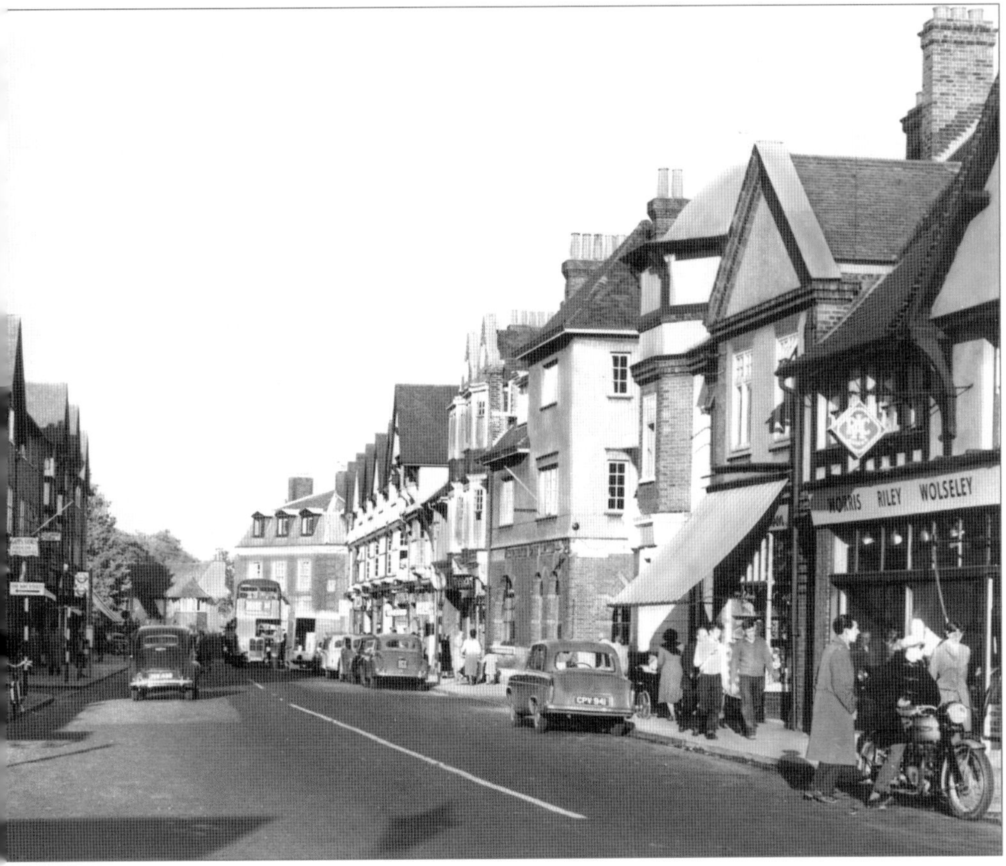

GERRARDS CROSS
The Highway or Packhorse Road 1957 G228014

The arrival of the Great Western-Great Central Joint Railway transformed Gerrards Cross into Metroland, with attractive roads of affluent commuter houses to the north and south of the old common. The station opened in 1909, and stands behind the photographer. This view shows the handsome shopping centre that was developed in the years before and after World War I. For example, the W H Smith building on the left is dated 1924, and the dormered Wren-style former bank behind the bus is of 1911.

GERRARDS CROSS
The Packhorse Inn c1965 G228026

This view shows the north end of the common, with Packhorse Road, the main shopping street on the right, which leads past the railway station. Behind the pub sign is the post office, built in the 1920s, and a tall mock timber-framed building, also of the 1920s, now Brown and Merry's. The pub was extensively altered and made more cottagey in the 1930s. Two of the lime trees survive - the third was sacrificed for a bus turning circle.

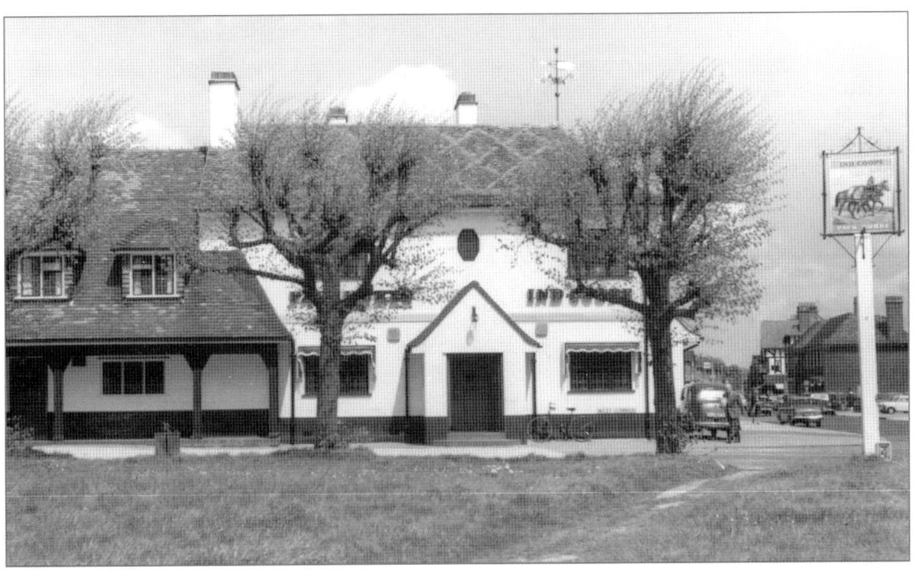

GERRARDS CROSS
The Pond c1960 G228015

The pond is at the west end of West Common. The early 19th-century rendered house at the right, Waterside, gives an idea of the type of earlier houses that were developed around the common before Metroland arrived. The other houses in this view are post-railway, and the gap between them and Waterside is now filled by a modern bungalow. On the south side of the common, the Bull Hotel is a former coaching inn and a reminder of the importance of an older form of transport.

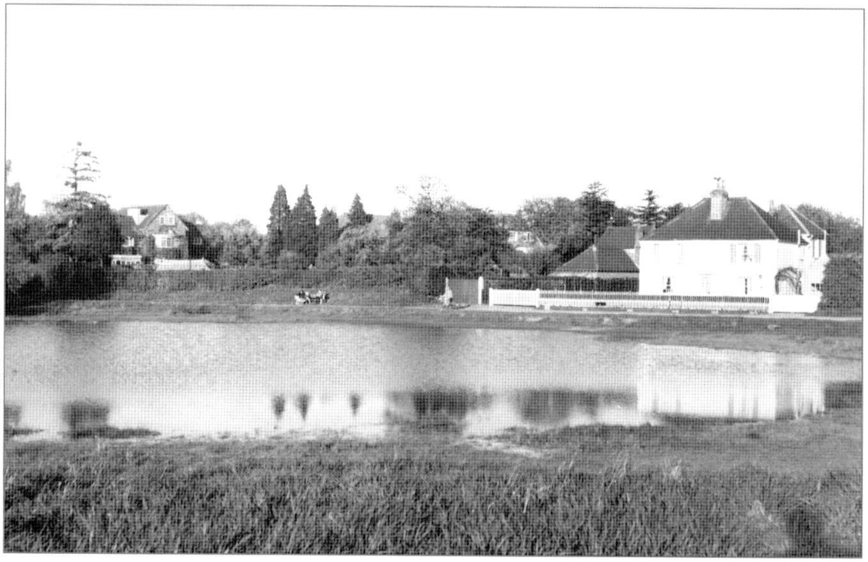

GERRARDS CROSS, *Chalfont Park c1965* G228031

North-east of the village centre, and separated from Gerrards Cross by the A413 Amersham Road, the country house of Chalfont Park stands in the Misbourne valley; at the time of this photograph, it was the offices of the aluminium company, British Alcan. They left in the 1990s, and the house has now been converted to apartments. The company's modern buildings have been demolished, and more flats and houses replace them. Designed in 1755 by John Chute for Horace Walpole's niece, the wife of General Charles Churchill, Chalfont Park is, as we might expect, in the Strawberry Hill Gothick style, but it seems to have been given a more ponderous feel by Salvin in the 1830s.

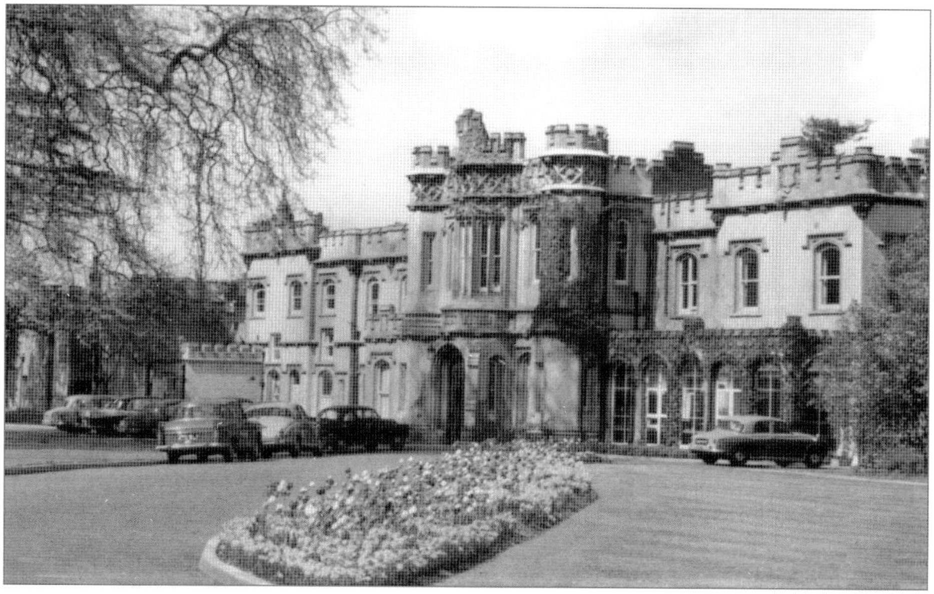

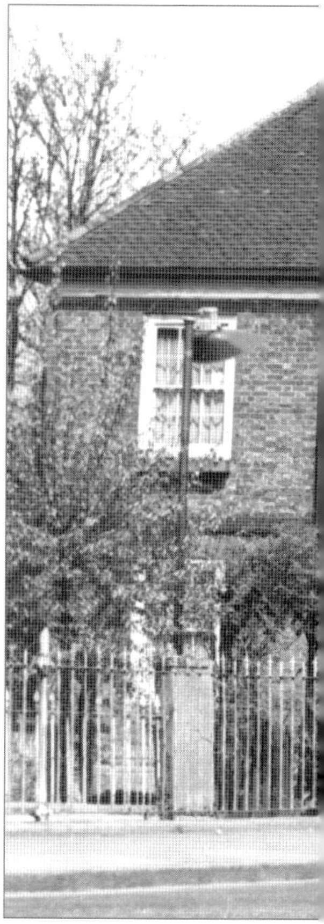

CHALFONT ST PETER
High Street c1950 C524007

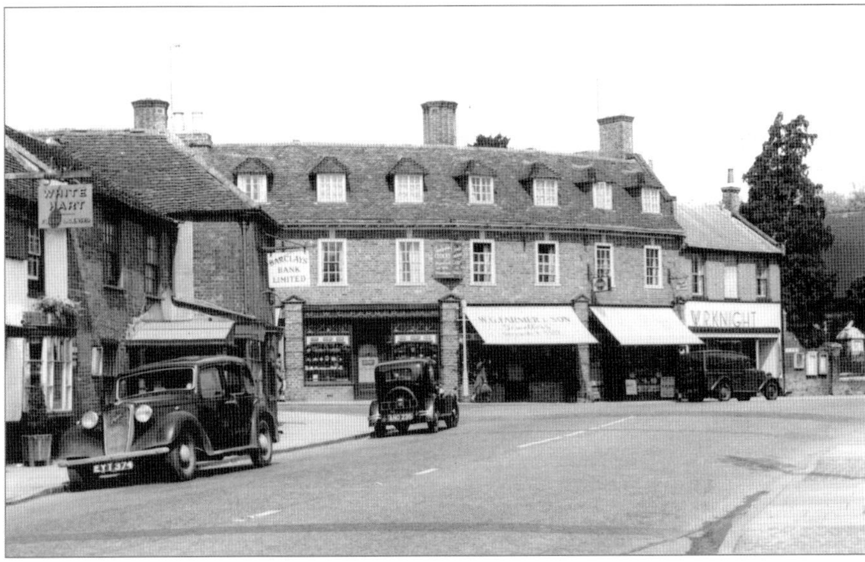

The old centre of Chalfont St Peter has suffered greatly. The A413 Amersham Road by-pass is too close, and the village is swamped by housing estates on either side of the Misbourne valley, merging with the more affluent housing of Gerrards Cross to the south. The White Hart on the left survives, but the 18th-century building housing Barclays Bank was removed and rebuilt in the 1950s to allow junction improvement. The 1930s shop terrace turns the corner blandly but effectively.

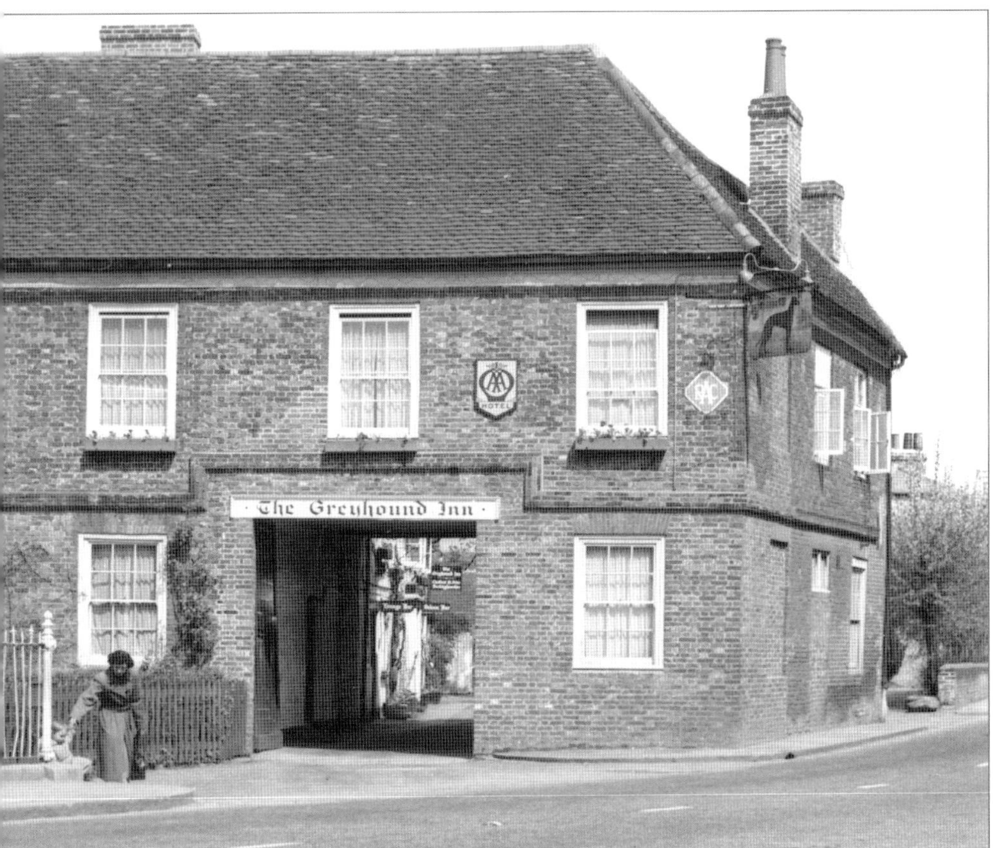

CHALFONT ST PETER
The Greyhound Inn c1950 C524004

Beyond the polychrome brickwork of St Peter's (in the 1850s, G E Street enlarged and altered a 1714 Georgian brick church), the Greyhound Inn survives, but all beyond was swept away in the 1960s for the dual carriageway and roundabout by-pass. The Greyhound consists of this early 18th-century brick block with a 16th-century timber-framed range beyond, visible through the carriageway; the carriageway is now glazed in, and the railings have been extended to the corner of the building. The foreground railings protect the Misbourne, which flows under the High Street here.

CHALFONT ST PETER
High Street c1950 C524002

This is a much changed scene today: all the buildings on the left were swept away, some for slum clearance, and were replaced by St Peter's Court, a very modern concrete-framed shopping parade around a car park with two storeys of flats over, built in 1966 and considered by many to be the kiss of death to the old village's character. On the right is the Misbourne, and beyond it St Peter's churchyard. In the distance is the old Barclays Bank at the junction with the Market Place.

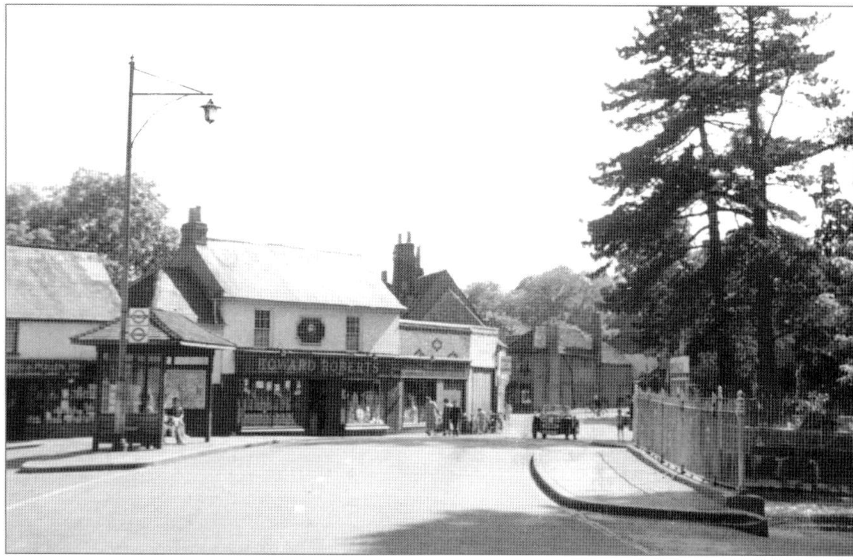

CHALFONT ST PETER
Market Place c1955 C524008

The Market Place leads uphill from the village centre to Gold Hill Common. The walled grounds of Holy Cross Convent School are on the right, and a mock-Tudor shopping parade with flats over of 1922 on the left. Note echoes of wartime in 'The Bombed Shop', left, now an Indian restaurant. A mix of gabled bays and dormers provide interest as the terraces step downhill towards the village centre. The buildings at the end were demolished for St Peter's Court of 1966.

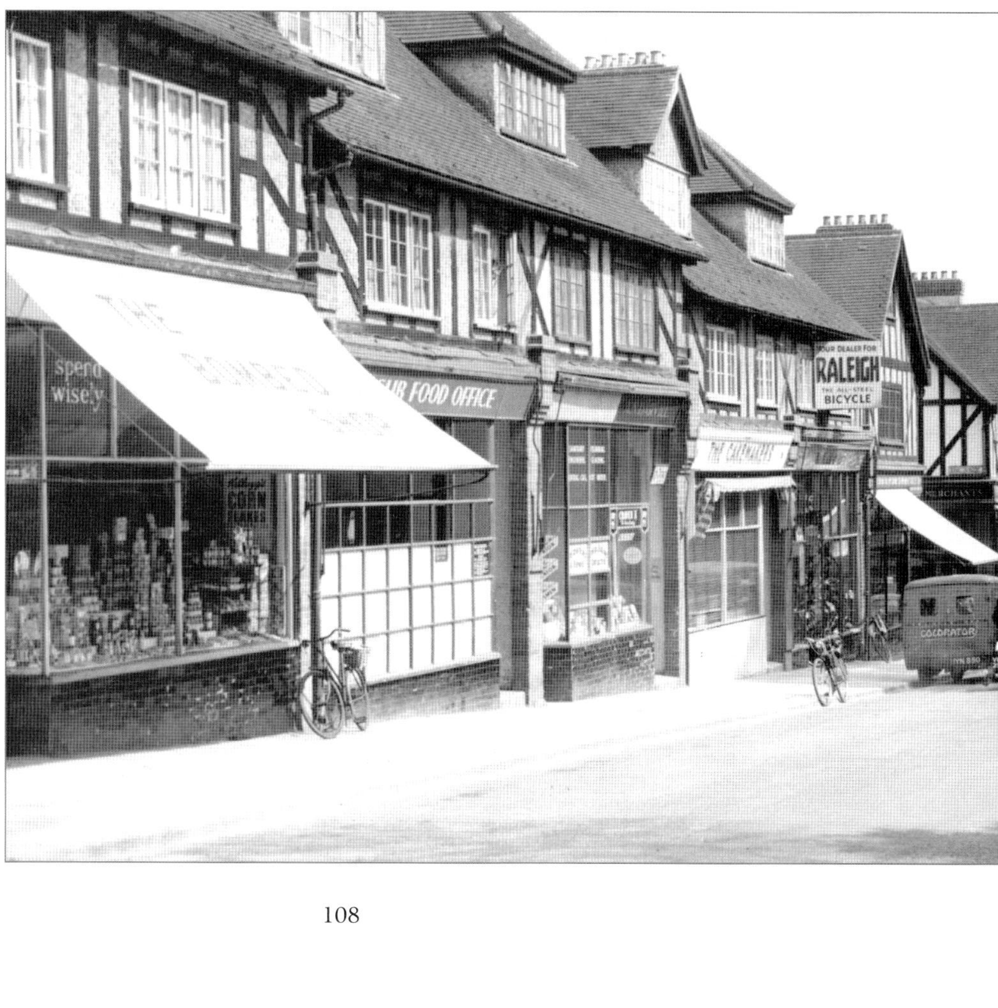

CHALFONT ST PETER, *The Village c1960* C524039

At the top of Market Place we enter Gold Hill Common. This view looks downhill towards the Tudor-style shopping parades we saw in view C524008. In the foreground is the clock installed by the village to commemorate the Coronation of Queen Elizabeth II in 1953. The yews have grown up to obscure the whole of the post upon which the clock sits.

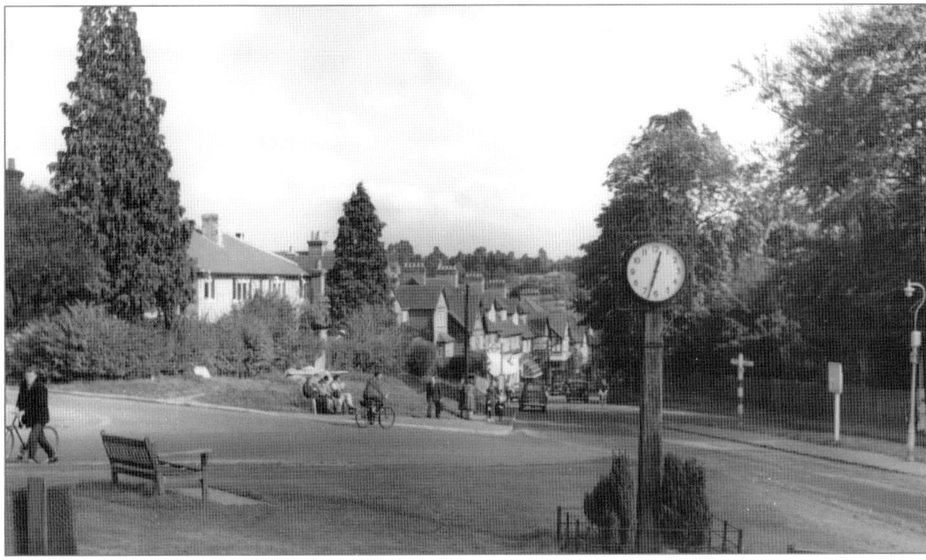

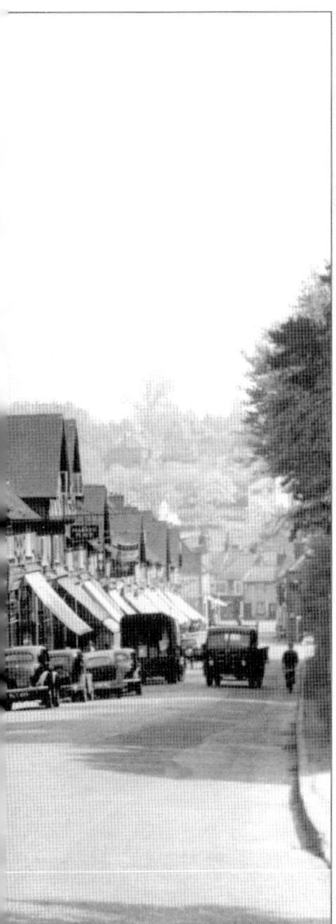

CHALFONT ST PETER, *Gold Hill Common c1960* C524049

Gold Hill Common lies on the ridge; it is a substantial triangular area, mostly grass but with some scrub and woodland, and some of it used for football pitches. It is a most attractive area, with suburban housing to the north, but earlier, mostly 19th-century, houses and cottages along the other two sides. This view looks into the south corner with the Baptist church dominating the scene – it was built in 1871, but the 1970s extensions at each end are of poor quality. On the right is the Jolly Farmer pub and some good 19th-century houses.

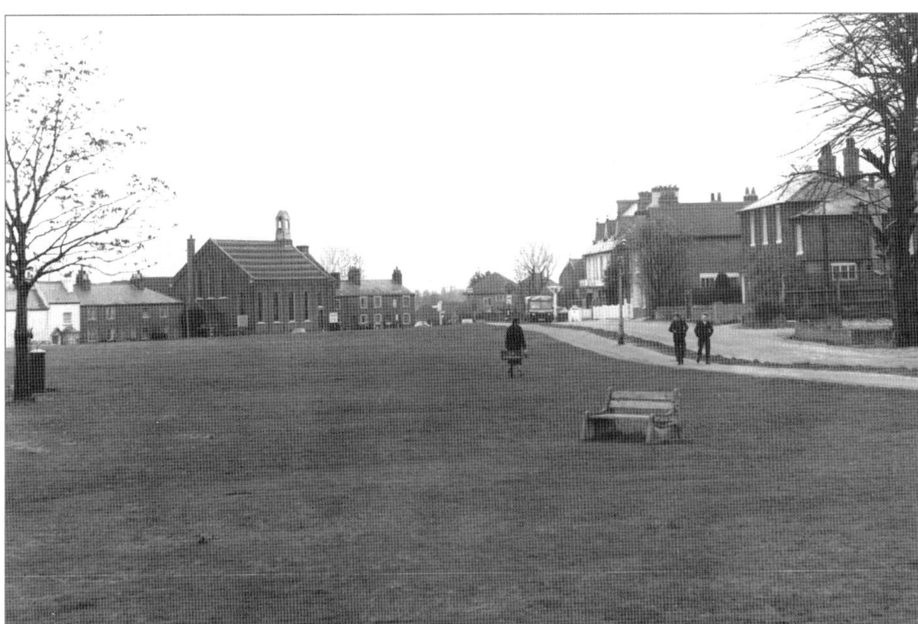

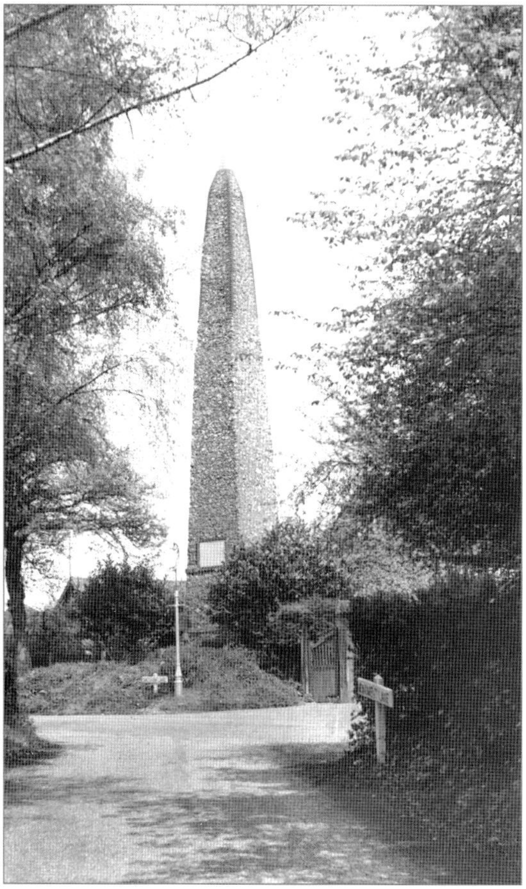

CHALFONT ST PETER
The Obelisk c1955
C524011

Climbing out of the Misbourne valley, to the east of Chalfont St Peter we reach Monument Lane and its junction with Chesham Lane. This flint obelisk was erected in 1785 by Sir H T Gott of Newlands Park, apparently to commemorate the killing of a stag in front of King George III. It serves as an overscaled milestone, and was restored in 1879. Today's visitor will be surprised to see that it survives as only two-thirds of its full height (in fact since 1964). Behind is the well known Chalfont Centre, run by the National Society for Epilepsy and founded in 1895 as a home and training centre.

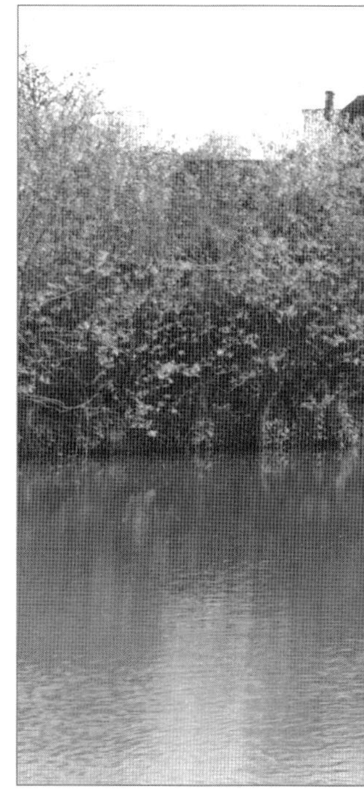

CHALFONT ST GILES
The Village c1950
C498015

We are looking west uphill along the High Street. The jettied timber-framed cottages on the left span an alley leading to the church and its rotating lychgate. On the right the hard red brick pub, the Crown, is dated 1890, while beyond is the Feathers, a good 17th-century timber-framed house refronted in the 19th century. Partly hidden by the lorry, the three-gabled building belongs to A J Axe, the former ironmonger's, whose 19th-century facade conceals another timber-framed building; remains of late 16th-century wall paintings were found here during 1980s repairs.

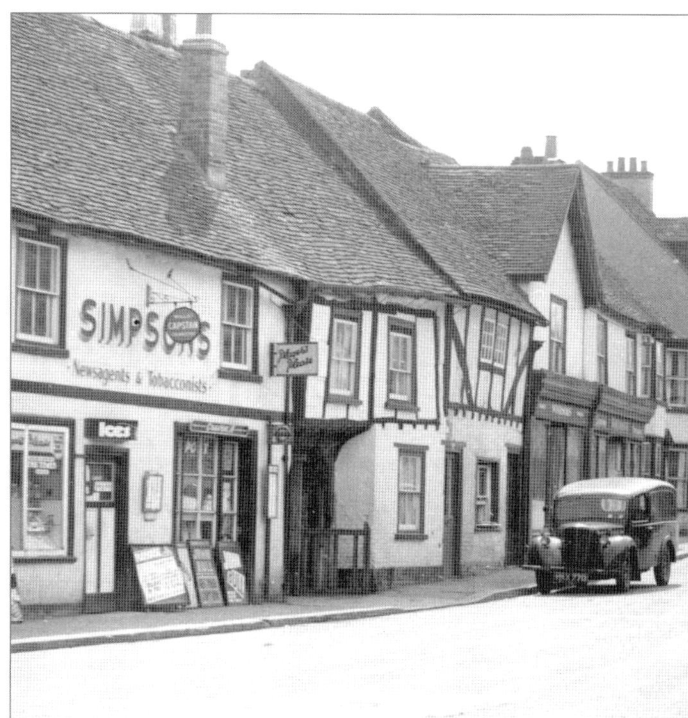

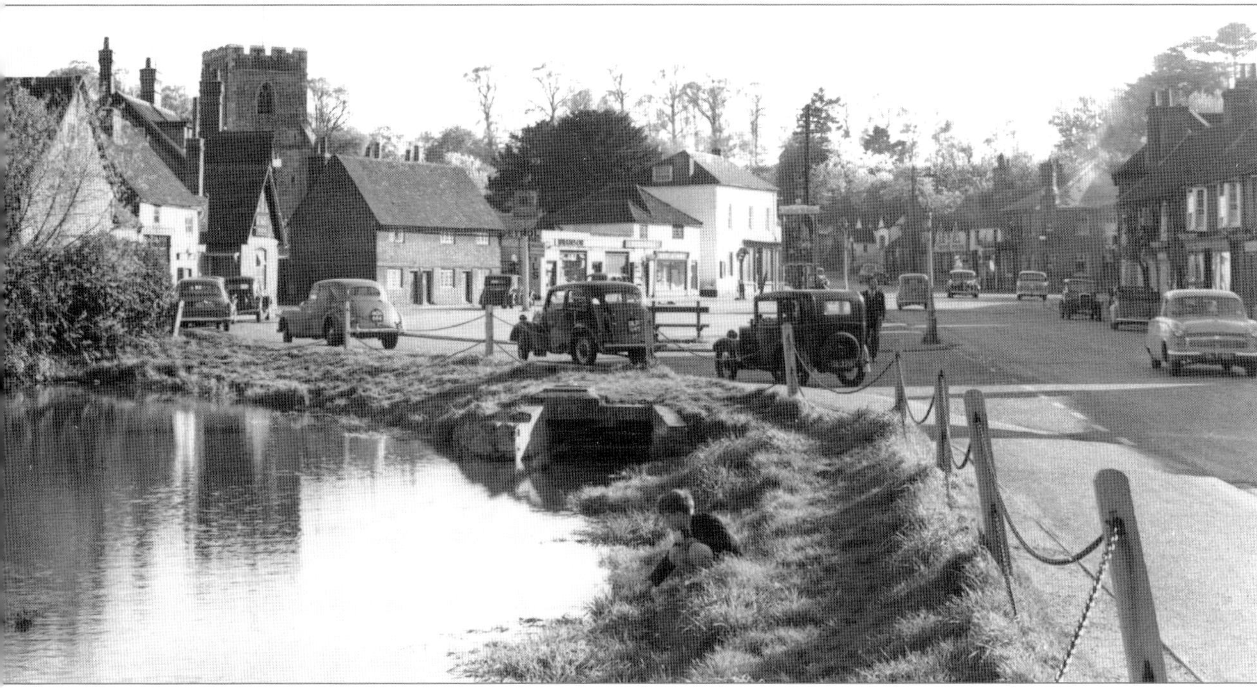

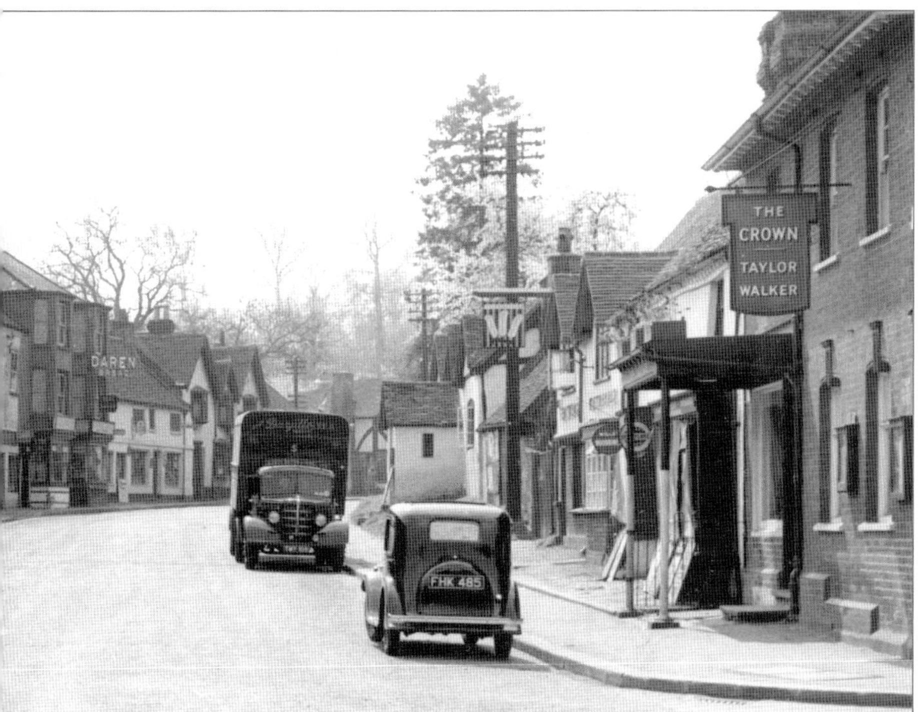

▲ **CHALFONT ST GILES**
The Pond c1955
C498022

Chalfont St Giles has fared much better in keeping its character than its neighbour Chalfont St Peter. It has a charming pond, then a small village green; its High Street is lined with good buildings, many of them 17th-century timber-framed ones, and the scale is near perfect. The medieval parish church tower completes the picture. The church has a Norman south aisle and sits in a pretty churchyard with the backs of timber-framed cottages on one side and the river Misbourne in its valley on the other. Modern expansion is largely to the west, so the older part of the village remains intact in its rural setting.

▼ **SEER GREEN,** *Chalfont Road c1960* S568009

South-west of Chalfont St Giles, up on the chalk plateau, lies the small village of Seer Green, enlarged on all sides in the 20th century. The smartest Metroland-style houses are in Long Grove, towards the railway station and the golf club house. Seer Green became a separate parish only in 1847, and the church was built in 1846 in anticipation of the new status by James Deason at a cost of £1700. We can see its bellcote and roofs behind the cottages, and the flint and stone of a window between them.

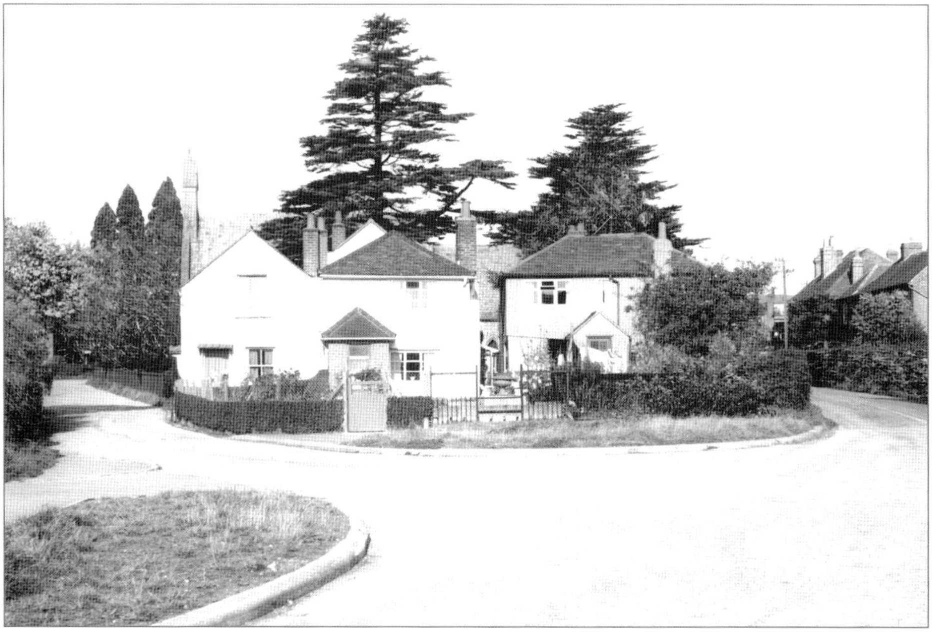

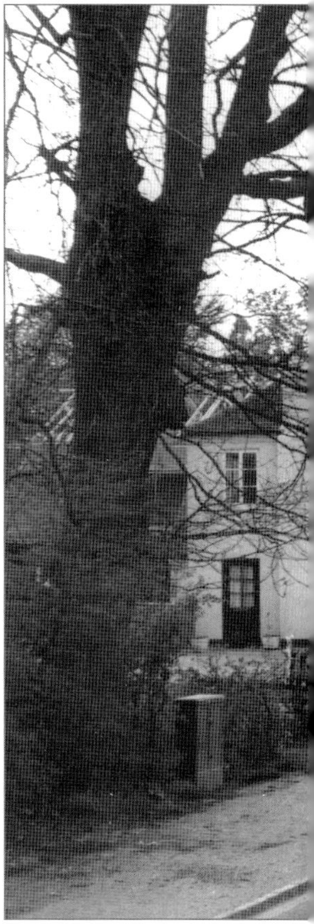

► **COLESHILL**
The Church c1955 C496008

Further north, a mile south of Amersham, we reach Coleshill, until 1844 an enclave of Hertfordshire, and noted for its many fine 16th- and 17th-century timber-framed farmhouses and cottages. The old chapel of ease was demolished around 1800, and the parish had to wait until 1860 for G E Street to design this rather ordinary and typical small Victorian Chiltern church. As an enclave outside Buckinghamshire, Coleshill had long been popular for gatherings of Dissenters, so the new church was an attempt to bring the village back into the Anglican fold. In 2000 the churchyard acquired a Millennium lychgate.

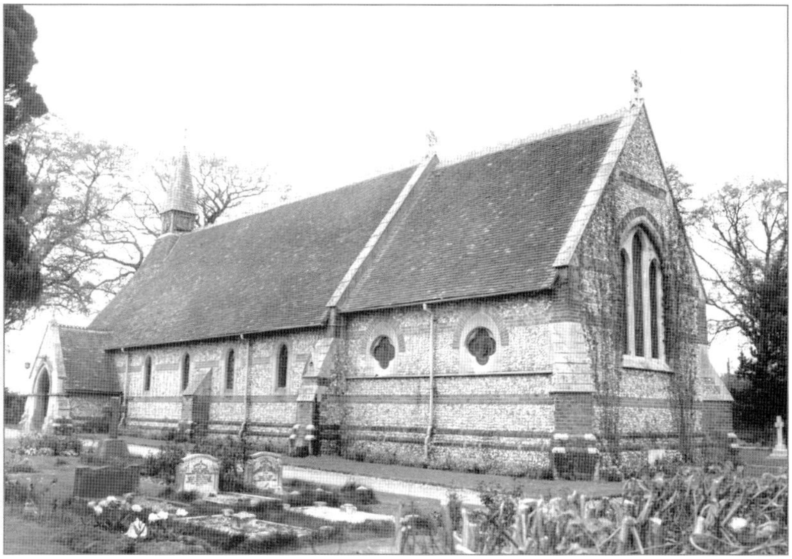

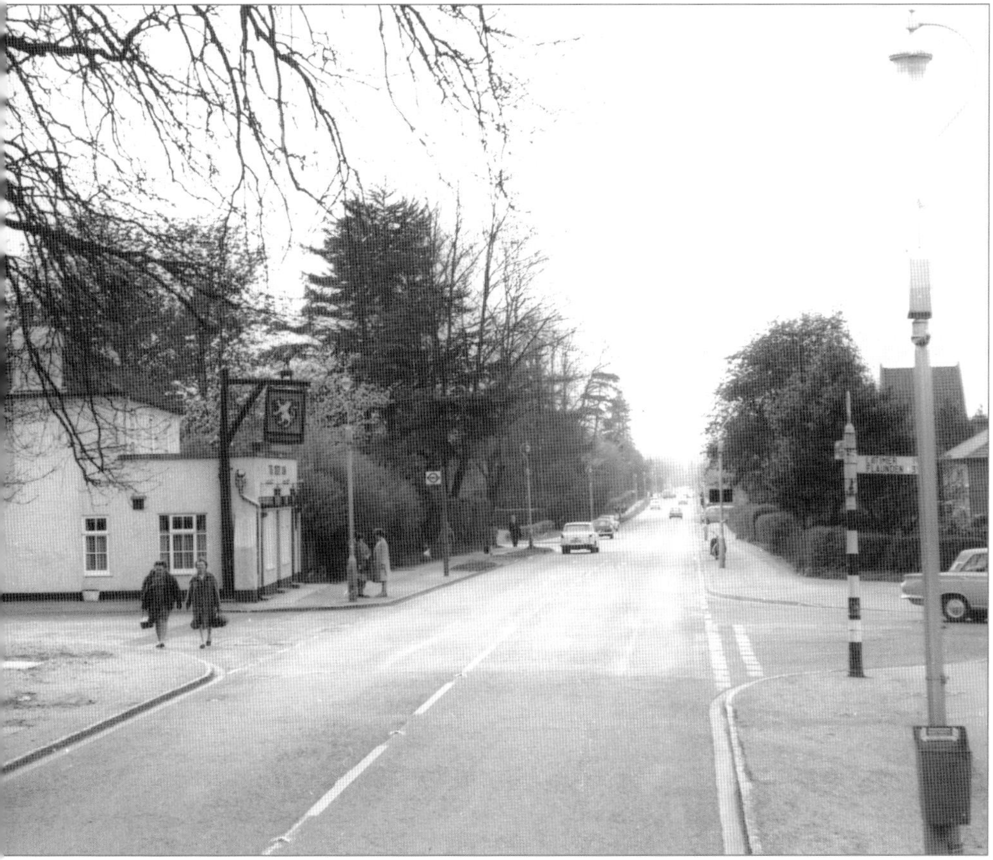

◄ **LITTLE CHALFONT,** *White Lion Road c1955*
L505019

From Amersham on the Hill the A404 passes along the ridge, heading through suburbia towards Chorleywood and Rickmansworth. The area around here developed from a few farms and houses in fields when the railway station at Chalfont and Latimer on the Metropolitan Railway opened in 1889 (the station was then known as Chalfont Road Station before changing its name in 1915). Here we look west past what are now the grounds of St Aidan's Roman Catholic church of 1964 past the White Lion pub, originally 19th century and much extended.

► **AMERSHAM ON THE HILL**
Sycamore Road c1950
A373027

The new town of Amersham on the Hill developed uphill from old Amersham from the 1890s onwards when the lords of the manor, the Drakes, finally allowed the railway age to reach their town. The station opened in September 1892, and development followed rapidly. Architecturally, however, the styles and scales were somewhat disparate, with mock-Tudor vying with neo-Georgian and one storey with three storeys. Oakfield Corner on the left dates from about 1910, and the buildings further away from the 1920s and 1930s.

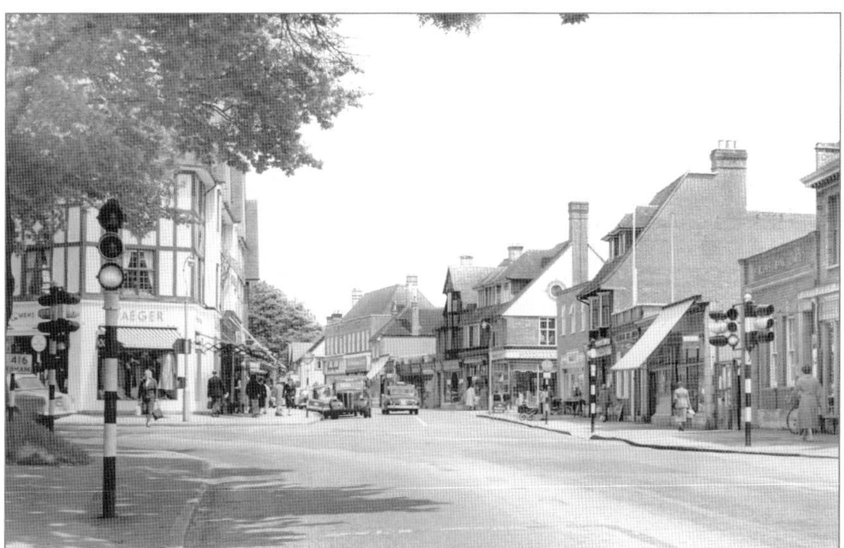

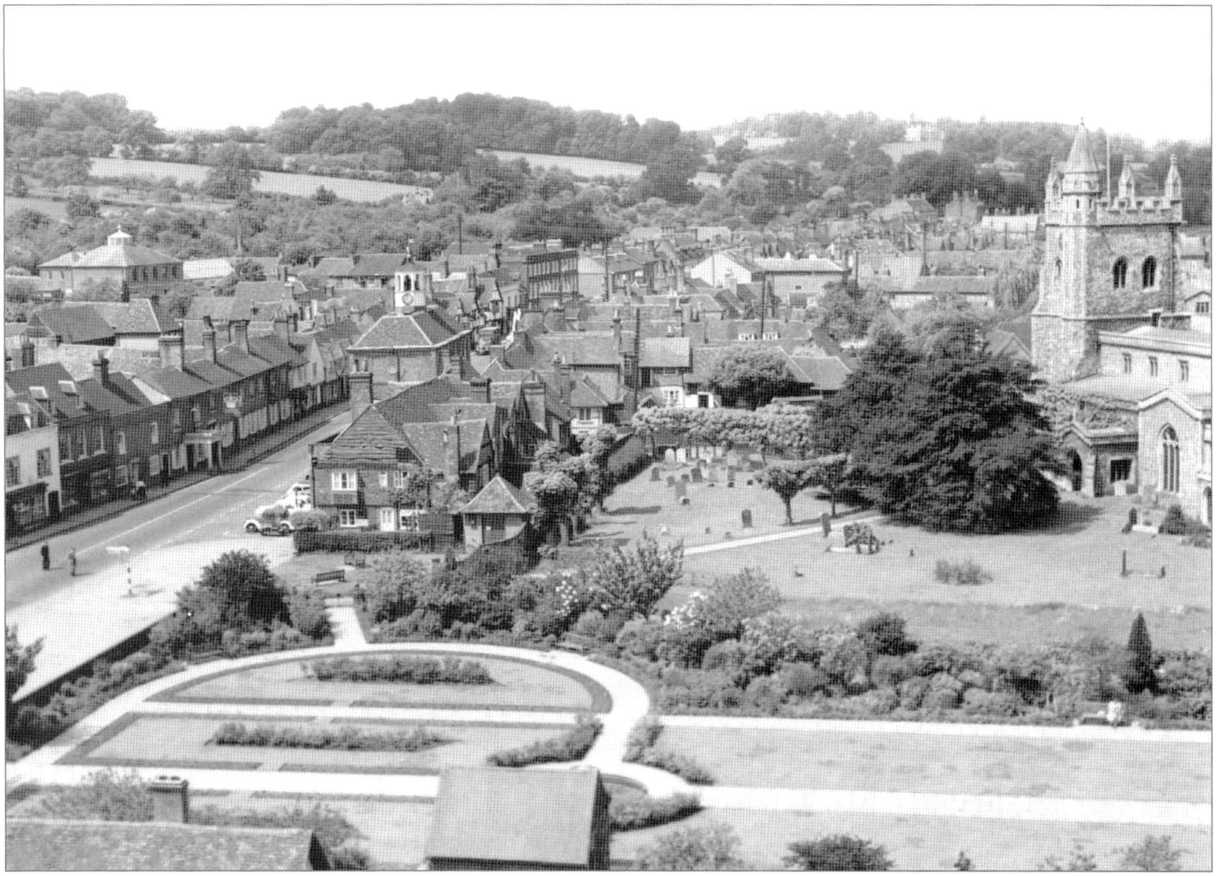

AMERSHAM, *General View looking West c1955* A148068

Our tour finishes, fittingly, in one of Buckinghamshire's finest and most complete historic market towns, nestling in the valley of the river Misbourne. This view, looking west across the Memorial Gardens, shows the High Street with the 1682 Market Hall and its cupola. To the right is the parish church, and to the left, behind the High Street frontages, rears the slate roofed Baptist Lower Meeting House of the 1780s. In the distance, the white house on the hill is Shardeloes, the Drake's 1760s mansion by Stiff Leadbetter and Robert Adam. From here they administered their town and preserved it from unwelcome change.

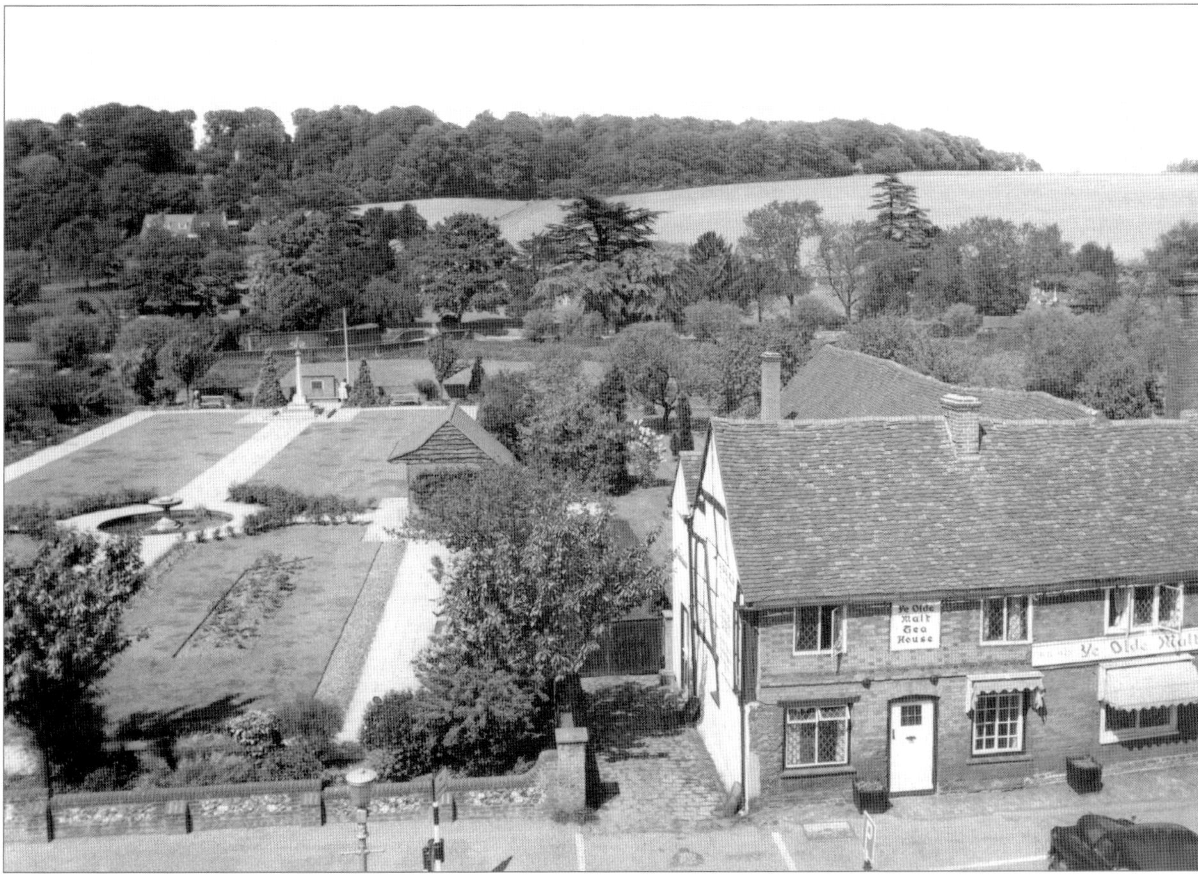

AMERSHAM, *The Garden of Remembrance 1958* A148061

The Garden of Remembrance was created in 1949 as a double war memorial. It lies partly on the site of rows of timber-framed cottages on Church Alley that had encroached on the market square - they were cleared in 1939. This view looks north from an upper window of the Griffin, a fine coaching inn and now an ASK restaurant. Behind the war memorial cross of 1921, which was relocated from the churchyard into the gardens, is now a stylish 1985 pyramidal-roofed rectory by Sir Basil Spence, the architect of Coventry Cathedral.

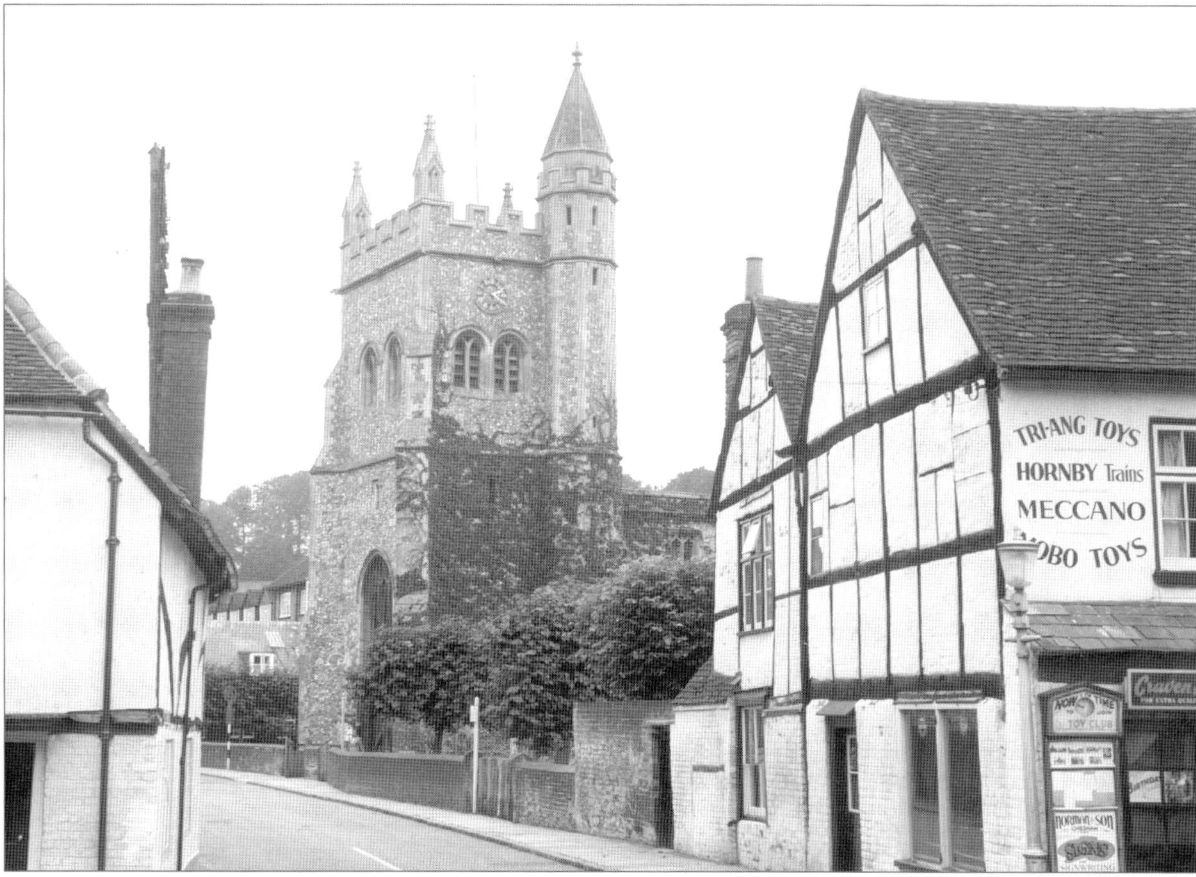

AMERSHAM, *St Mary's Church c1955* A148052

This view looks up Church Street with No 15 on the left, a medieval house with a good crown post roof. On the right, the shop has evocative makes of toy painted on its façade; it is now a chemist, its gable timber-framing entirely renewed. The church tower is 15th-century, but refaced in the 1880s. Beyond is the old Weller's Brewery, which closed in the 1930s; it became the Goya perfume factory from 1946, but in the 1980s it was converted into stylish apartments.

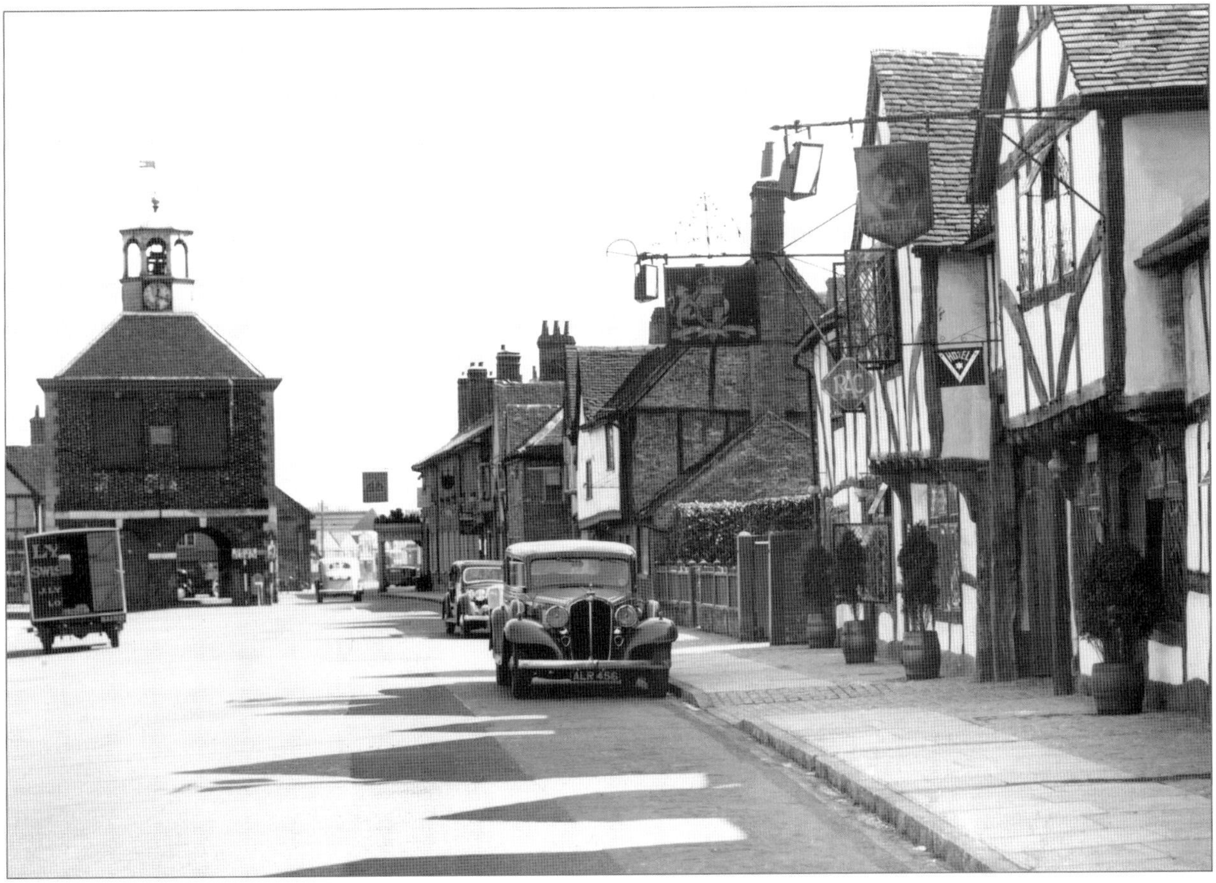

AMERSHAM, *High Street c1950* A148012

Here we look east along the High Street back towards Market Square. We have a good view of the end elevation of the Market Hall, crowned with its octagonal bellcote cupola, which was built for the town by Sir William Drake of Shardeloes in 1682. Opposite is the portico of the Crown Hotel, its 18th-century brick elevations hiding a 16th-century timber-framed interior. The portico was demolished, no doubt for highway safety reasons, and it is remarkable that unlike Chesham's, Amersham's Market Hall survived – it was a traffic bottleneck until the 1980s by-pass was constructed.

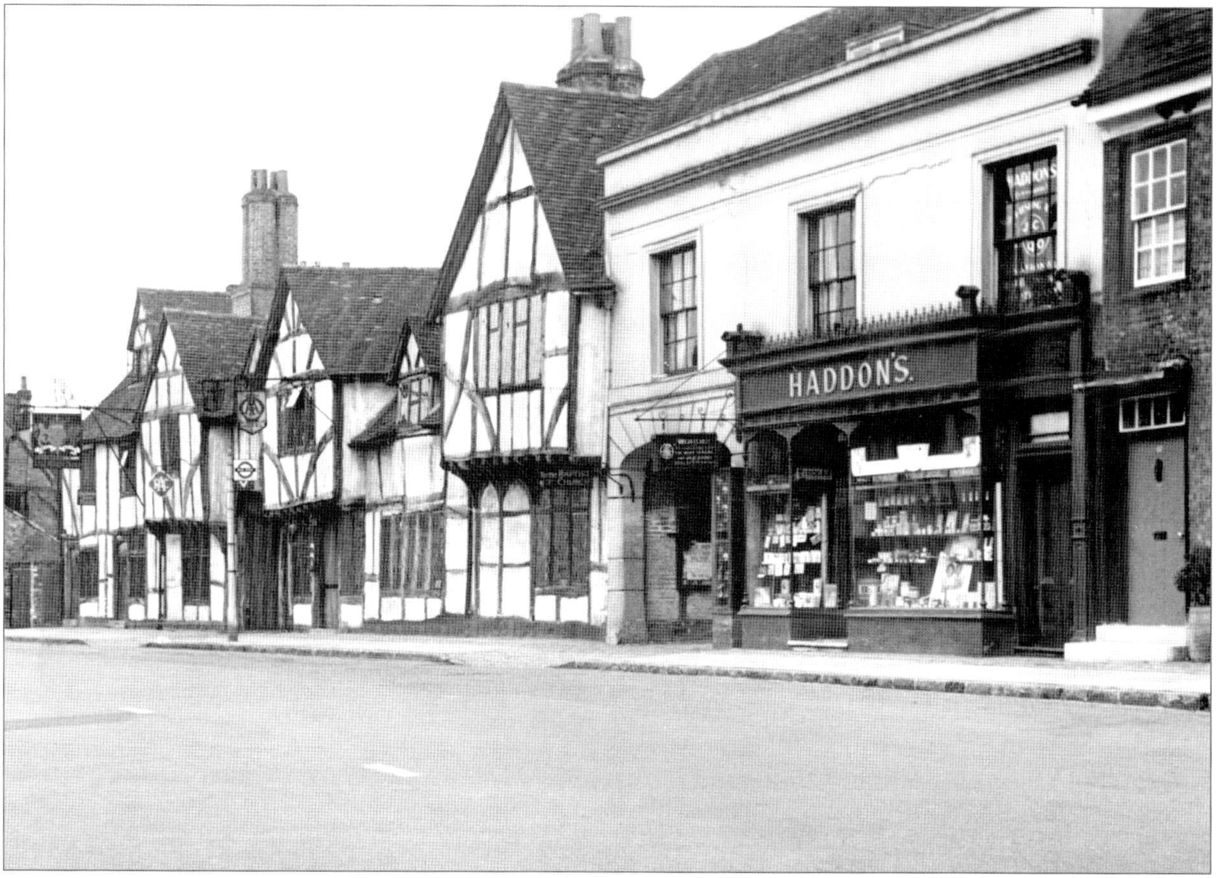

AMERSHAM, *The Kings Arms c1955* A148037

The final view is of the King's Arms, which is not all it seems: all the timber-framing beyond the RAC sign dates only from 1936, when a Georgian building was medievalised using old timbers. The other two gables are genuine, and belong to a 16th-century hall house with jettied cross wings. Haddon's fine shop front survives, but without the cresting – it is now Liz Quilter. The rusticated rendered archway leads through to the Baptist Lower Meeting House we saw in view A148068.

INDEX

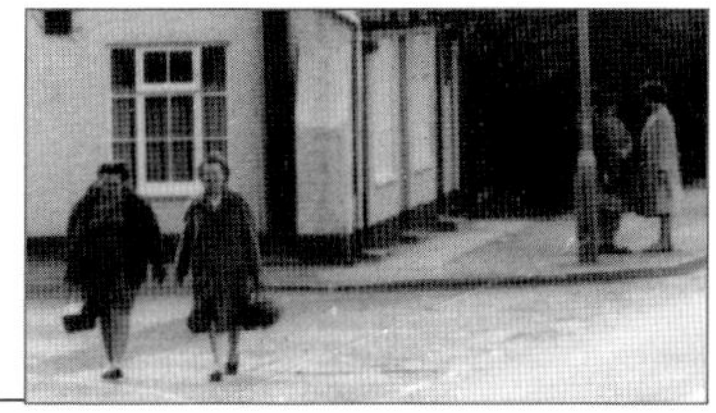

The Francis Frith Collection Titles

www.francisfrith.com

The Francis Frith Collection publishes over 100 new titles each year. A selection of those currently available is listed below. For latest catalogue please contact The Francis Frith Collection.
Town Books 96 pages, approximately 75 photos. ***County and Themed Books*** 128 pages, approximately 135 photos (unless specified). Pocket Albums are miniature editions of Frith local history books 128 pages, approximately 95 photos.

Accrington Old and New
Alderley Edge and Wilmslow
Amersham, Chesham and Rickmansworth
Andover
Around Abergavenny
Around Alton
Aylesbury
Barnstaple
Bedford
Bedfordshire
Berkshire Living Memories
Berkshire Pocket Album
Blackpool Pocket Album
Bognor Regis
Bournemouth
Bradford
Bridgend
Bridport
Brighton and Hove
Bristol
Buckinghamshire
Calne Living Memories
Camberley Pocket Album
Canterbury Cathedral
Cardiff Old and New
Chatham and the Medway Towns
Chelmsford
Chepstow Then and Now
Cheshire
Cheshire Living Memories
Chester
Chesterfield
Chigwell
Christchurch
Churches of East Cornwall
Clevedon
Clitheroe
Corby Living Memories
Cornish Coast
Cornwall Living Memories
Cotswold Living Memories
Cotswold Pocket Album
Coulsdon, Chipstead and Woodmanstern
County Durham
Cromer, Sheringham and Holt
Dartmoor Pocket Album
Derby
Derbyshire
Derbyshire Living Memories
Devon
Devon Churches
Dorchester
Dorset Coast Pocket Album
Dorset Living Memories
Dorset Villages
Down the Dart
Down the Severn
Down the Thames
Dunmow, Thaxted and Finchingfield
Durham
East Anglia Pocket Album
East Devon
East Grinstead
Edinburgh
Ely and The Fens
Essex Pocket Album
Essex Second Selection
Essex: The London Boroughs
Exeter
Exmoor
Falmouth
Farnborough, Fleet and Aldershot
Folkestone
Frome
Furness and Cartmel Peninsulas
Glamorgan
Glasgow
Glastonbury
Gloucester
Gloucestershire
Greater Manchester
Guildford
Hailsham
Hampshire
Harrogate
Hastings and Bexhill
Haywards Heath Living Memories
Heads of the Valleys
Heart of Lancashire Pocket Album
Helston
Herefordshire
Horsham
Humberside Pocket Album
Huntingdon, St Neots and St Ives
Hythe, Romney Marsh and Ashford
Ilfracombe
Ipswich Pocket Album
Isle of Wight
Isle of Wight Living Memories
King's Lynn
Kingston upon Thames
Lake District Pocket Album
Lancashire Living Memories
Lancashire Villages

Available from your local bookshop or from the publisher

The Francis Frith Collection Titles (continued)

Lancaster, Morecambe and Heysham Pocket Album
Leeds Pocket Album
Leicester
Leicestershire
Lincolnshire Living Memoires
Lincolnshire Pocket Album
Liverpool and Merseyside
London Pocket Album
Ludlow
Maidenhead
Maidstone
Malmesbury
Manchester Pocket Album
Marlborough
Matlock
Merseyside Living Memories
Nantwich and Crewe
New Forest
Newbury Living Memories
Newquay to St Ives
North Devon Living Memories
North London
North Wales
North Yorkshire
Northamptonshire
Northumberland
Northwich
Nottingham
Nottinghamshire Pocket Album
Oakham
Odiham Then and Now
Oxford Pocket Album
Oxfordshire
Padstow
Pembrokeshire
Penzance
Petersfield Then and Now
Plymouth
Poole and Sandbanks
Preston Pocket Album
Ramsgate Old and New
Reading Pocket Album
Redditch Living Memories
Redhill to Reigate
Richmond
Ringwood
Rochdale
Romford Pocket Album
Salisbury Pocket Album
Scotland
Scottish Castles
Sevenoaks and Tonbridge
Sheffield and South Yorkshire Pocket Album
Shropshire
Somerset
South Devon Coast
South Devon Living Memories
South East London
Southampton Pocket Album
Southend Pocket Album
Southport
Southwold to Aldeburgh
Stourbridge Living Memories
Stratford upon Avon
Stroud
Suffolk
Suffolk Pocket Album
Surrey Living Memories
Sussex
Sutton
Swanage and Purbeck
Swansea Pocket Album
Swindon Living Memories
Taunton
Teignmouth
Tenby and Saundersfoot
Tiverton
Torbay
Truro
Uppingham
Villages of Kent
Villages of Surrey
Villages of Sussex Pocket Album
Wakefield and the Five Towns Living Memories
Warrington
Warwick
Warwickshire Pocket Album
Wellingborough Living Memories
Wells
Welsh Castles
West Midlands Pocket Album
West Wiltshire Towns
West Yorkshire
Weston-super-Mare
Weymouth
Widnes and Runcorn
Wiltshire Churches
Wiltshire Living Memories
Wiltshire Pocket Album
Wimborne
Winchester Pocket Album
Windermere
Windsor
Wirral
Wokingham and Bracknell
Woodbridge
Worcester
Worcestershire
Worcestershire Living Memories
Wyre Forest
York Pocket Album
Yorkshire
Yorkshire Coastal Memories
Yorkshire Dales
Yorkshire Revisited

See Frith books on the internet at www.francisfrith.com

FRITH PRODUCTS & SERVICES

Francis Frith would doubtless be pleased to know that the pioneering publishing venture he started in 1860 still continues today. Over a hundred and forty years later, The Francis Frith Collection continues in the same innovative tradition and is now one of the foremost publishers of vintage photographs in the world. Some of the current activities include:

INTERIOR DECORATION

Today Frith's photographs can be seen framed and as giant wall murals in thousands of pubs, restaurants, hotels, banks, retail stores and other public buildings throughout the country. In every case they enhance the unique local atmosphere of the places they depict and provide reminders of gentler days in an increasingly busy and frenetic world.

PRODUCT PROMOTIONS

Frith products are used by many major companies to promote the sales of their own products or to reinforce their own history and heritage. Frith promotions have been used by Hovis bread, Courage beers, Scots Porage Oats, Colman's mustard, Cadbury's foods, Mellow Birds coffee, Dunhill pipe tobacco, Guinness, and Bulmer's Cider.

GENEALOGY AND FAMILY HISTORY

As the interest in family history and roots grows world-wide, more and more people are turning to Frith's photographs of Great Britain for images of the towns, villages and streets where their ancestors lived; and, of course, photographs of the churches and chapels where their ancestors were christened, married and buried are an essential part of every genealogy tree and family album.

FRITH PRODUCTS

All Frith photographs are available Framed or just as Mounted Prints and Posters (size 23 x 16 inches). These may be ordered from the address below. Other products available are- Address Books, Calendars, Jigsaws, Canvas Prints, Notelets and local and prestige books.

THE INTERNET

Already ninety thousand Frith photographs can be viewed and purchased on the internet through the Frith websites and a myriad of partner sites.

For more detailed information on Frith companies and products, look at this site:
www.francisfrith.com

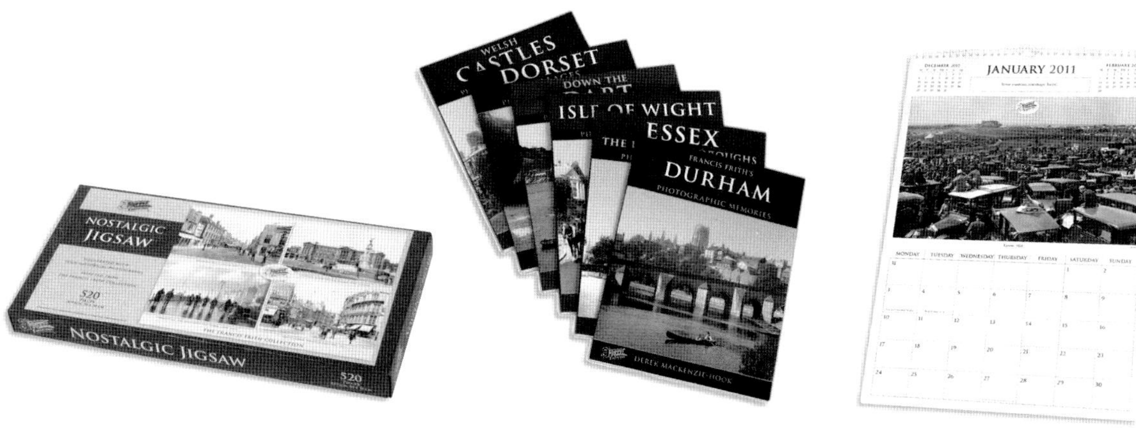

See the complete list of Frith Books at: www.francisfrith.com
This web site is regularly updated with the latest list of publications from The Francis Frith Collection. If you wish to buy books relating to another part of the country that your local bookshop does not stock, you may purchase on-line.

For further information, trade, or author enquiries please contact us at the address below:
The Francis Frith Collection, Unit 6, Oakley Business Park, Wylye Road, Dinton, Wiltshire SP3 5EU.
Tel: +44 (0)1722 716 376 Fax: +44 (0)1722 716 881 Email: sales@francisfrith.co.uk

See Frith products on the internet at www.francisfrith.com

FREE PRINT OF YOUR CHOICE

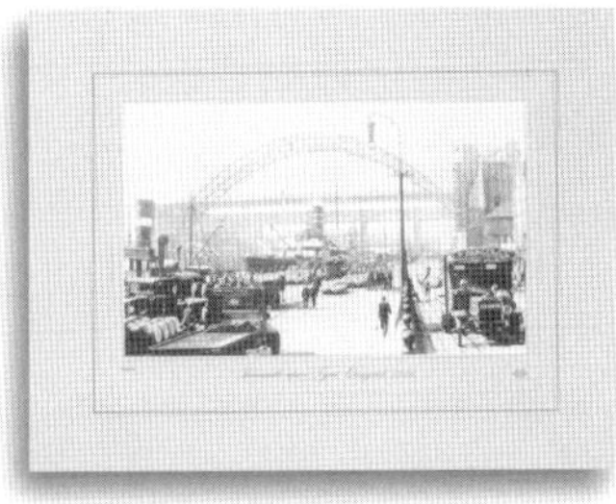

Mounted Print
Overall size 14 x 11 inches (355 x 280mm)

Choose any Frith photograph in this book.
Simply complete the Voucher opposite and return it with your remittance for £3.50 (to cover postage and handling) and we will print the photograph of your choice in SEPIA (size 11 x 8 inches) and supply it in a cream mount with a burgundy rule line (overall size 14 x 11 inches).
Please note: aerial photographs and photographs with a reference number starting with a "Z" are not Frith photographs and cannot be supplied under this offer. Offer valid for delivery to one UK address only.

***PLUS:* Order additional Mounted Prints at HALF PRICE - £9.50 each** (normally £19.00)
If you would like to order more Frith prints from this book, possibly as gifts for friends and family, you can buy them at half price (with no additional postage and handling costs).

***PLUS:* Have your Mounted Prints framed**
For an extra £18.00 per print you can have your mounted print(s) framed in an elegant polished wood and gilt moulding, overall size 16 x 13 inches (no additional postage and handling required).

IMPORTANT!

These special prices are only available if you use this form to order. You must use the ORIGINAL VOUCHER on this page (no copies permitted). We can only despatch to one UK address. This offer cannot be combined with any other offer.

Send completed Voucher form to:
The Francis Frith Collection, Unit 6, Oakley Business Park, Wylye Road, Dinton, Wiltshire SP3 5EU

CHOOSE A PHOTOGRAPH FROM THIS BOOK

Voucher *for **FREE** and Reduced Price Frith Prints*

Please do not photocopy this voucher. Only the original is valid, so please fill it in, cut it out and return it to us with your order.

Picture ref no	Page no	Qty	Mounted @ £9.50	Framed + £18.00	Total Cost £
		1	Free of charge*	£	£
			£9.50	£	£
			£9.50	£	£
			£9.50	£	£
			£9.50	£	£
			£9.50	£	£
			* Post & handling		£3.50
			Total Order Cost		£

Please allow 28 days for delivery. Offer available to one UK address only

Title of this book ....

I enclose a cheque/postal order for £ ....

made payable to 'The Francis Frith Collection'

OR please debit my Mastercard / Visa / Maestro card, details below

Card Number:

Issue No (Maestro only): Valid from (Maestro):

Card Security Number: Expires:

Signature:

Name Mr/Mrs/Ms ....

Address ....

....

....

.... Postcode ....

Daytime Tel No ....

Email ....

978-1-84589-561-7 Valid to 31/12/12

Free Print - see overleaf

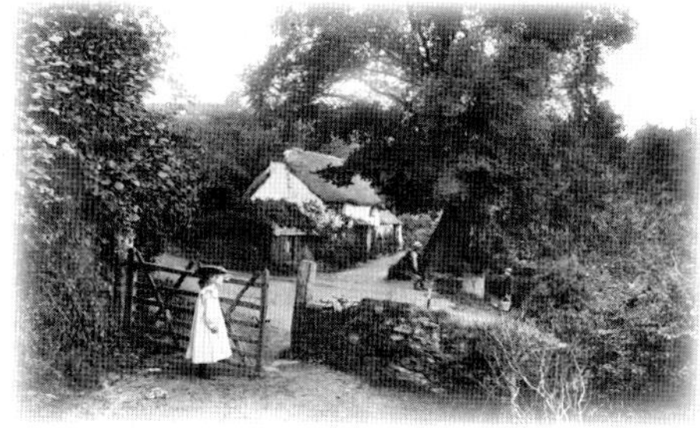

Can you help us with information about any of the Frith photographs in this book?

We are gradually compiling an historical record for each of the photographs in the Frith archive. It is always fascinating to find out the names of the people shown in the pictures, as well as insights into the shops, buildings and other features depicted.

If you recognize anyone in the photographs in this book, or if you have information not already included in the author's caption, do let us know. We would love to hear from you, and will try to publish it in future books or articles.

An Invitation from The Francis Frith Collection to Share Your Memories

The 'Share Your Memories' feature of our website allows members of the public to add personal memories relating to the places featured in our photographs, or comment on others already added. Seeing a place from your past can rekindle forgotten or long held memories. Why not visit the website, find photographs of places you know well and add YOUR story for others to read and enjoy? We would love to hear from you!

www.francisfrith.com/memories

Our production team

Frith books are produced by a small dedicated team at offices near Salisbury. Most have worked with the Frith Collection for many years. All have in common one quality: they have a passion for the Frith Collection.

Frith Books and Gifts

We have a wide range of books and gifts available on our website utilising our photographic archive, many of which can be individually personalised.

www.francisfrith.com